JUST PLAIN DICK

JUST PLAIN DICK

Richard Nixon's Checkers Speech and the "Rocking, Socking" Election of 1952

KEVIN MATTSON

B L O O M S B U R Y
New York   London   New Delhi   Sydney

Published by Bloomsbury USA, New York

All papers used by Bloomsbury USA are natural, recyclable products made from wood grown in well-managed forests. The manufacturing processes conform to the environmental regulations of the country of origin.

LIBRARY OF CONGRESS CATALOGING-IN-PUBLICATION DATA HAS BEEN APPLIED FOR.

ISBN: 978-1-60819-812-2 (hardcover)

First U.S. edition published by Bloomsbury USA in 2012
This paperback edition published in 2013

Paperback ISBN: 978-1-62040-068-5

1 3 5 7 9 10 8 6 4 2

Typeset by Westchester Book Group
Printed and bound in the U.S.A. by Thomson-Shore Inc., Dexter, Michigan

For Vicky, once more and with more

The Fifties were not the Eisenhower years but the Nixon years. That was the decade when the American lower middle class in the person of this man moved to engrave into the history of the United States, as the voice of America, its own faltering spirit, its self-pity and its envy . . . its whole peevish, resentful whine. The Nixon years belonged to . . . the graduates of those courses in how to influence people since it was no longer of value to win friends . . . clerks who call themselves junior executives, young men ashamed of their origins and of themselves.

—MURRAY KEMPTON, "*TIME* AND NIXON,"
NOVEMBER 13, 1962

The presidential candidate ought to think of himself as similar to the manager of a crew of house-to-house salesmen. His function is to give them confidence in their product.

—JAMES L. WICK, *HOW NOT TO RUN
FOR PRESIDENT*, 1952

Every Presidential election really is a self-portrait of America.

—SAMUEL LUBELL, *THE FUTURE OF
AMERICAN POLITICS*, 1952

CONTENTS

INTRODUCTION

PORTRAIT OF THE YOUNG POLITICAL ARTIST AS MADMAN (FROM THE INNER CRANIUM TO HISTORY)

I.

If the brain waves of Richard Nixon had been read between September 18 and 22, 1952, they might have gone like this:

Goddamn bastards want me out. They want to sack my political career. They don't have much on me, but they'll use what they have. That's how they play, those sluggers and smear boys in the liberal press. Here I am slumping in a chair on my train, just rattling along, heading out of California—my fair state—towards the soggy center of Oregon. And all I'm hearing from that fat little man who bubbles with fine political advice and fumes about my enemies is that the press boys are going wild with this thing. I could feel my eyes glancing back at that headline in the left-wing smear-sheet, the New York Post*:* SECRET RICH MEN'S TRUST FUND KEEPS NIXON IN STYLE FAR BEYOND HIS SALARY. *That was one bastard of a headline.*[1]

What have they got on me? Not much. A crummy $18,235—a "fund"—given to me by businessmen in real estate, ranching, oil, and banking. Well, not directly to me. They gave it to Dana Smith, a fine tax lawyer and a friend *of mine. And as Smith was talking to the press the other day, he paid me the biggest compliment I could imagine. He called me the "best salesman against socialization." That sounded like a fine job description to me, a nice addition to having been a congressperson, senator, and now vice-presidential candidate. I am a salesman of ideas, that's right. I'm not getting rich off the fund, but what better honor than to stick my neck out for the small business guy against big government. Good old Dana would deposit the checks, report out payments, and keep it aboveboard. And things were going pretty well until those liberal press boys pounced on the story and ran with it.[2]*

And I'm hearing about it now. Every time I head for the back of the train to give a stump speech I know I'm going to get an ear and an eyeful of the crap they've been smearing me with. I go out there and first hear the good people cheering but then scan the crowds and what's that? Some wisecracking college kid waving a sign: NO MINK COATS FOR NIXON—JUST COLD CASH. *Damn straight, I'm thinking, no mink coats like the one given to some secretary in Harry Truman's White House as a lousy bribe. I feel the words come right out of my mouth: "That's absolutely right. There are no mink coats for the Nixons. I am proud to say my wife, Pat, wears a good Republican cloth coat." Oh, the crowds on my side loved that one. They start yelling to tear down the sign and calling the young man waving it a "Dirty Communist." Looks like a fight is breaking out.*

Then later that day this sort of thing gets worse. I get out of my train with Pat, and there are more bastards waving signs about "Poor Nixon" and throwing pennies and nickels at my head. They've dressed up like blind beggars, which really wasn't that funny except to them. Some even came up and shoved me. I'm in a small-scale war.[3]

I remember just a few days ago, winding down a speech, I watched these guys break from a car, looking like hoodlums, and run towards my rally screaming out, "Tell us about the sixteen thousand dollars!" They didn't even have their numbers right, it was more like eighteen thousand. But I didn't care about that. Damn train had started to pull out, and I turned around, gripping the rail to keep steady, and screamed, "Hold the train! Hold the train!" It lurched to a stop a football field's length from the station. And I'll tell you, there's nothing like watching a crowd of people, friend and foe, running straight at you. I looked out at the faces and found that man who had been doing the yelling. And boy, did I let him have it. I pointed right at the bastard and explained the situation: "You folks know the work that I did investigating Communists in the United States." The crowds cheered at that. "Ever since I have done that work, the Communists and the left-wingers have been fighting me with every possible smear. When I received the nomination for the vice presidency I was warned that if I continued to attack the Communists in this government, they would continue to smear me." And there you have it, there they were—the smearers right in my midst. And they weren't just smearers, like I was trying to explain, they were doing the work—whether they knew it or not—of the Communists. I had taken down one big kingpin Communist named Alger Hiss back in my days in Congress, and now these men running from cars and waving signs were looking for revenge. It was a new front in the Cold War.[4]

What a man needs at a time like this is a strong boss who bolsters you, tells you things will be fine. Like a good football coach who is stern but gives you a pep talk at halftime to get through the rest of the game. But what do I have? General Dwight D. Eisenhower, once Supreme Commander of the Allied Forces during the Second World War. I still remember the first time I saw him in a celebration parade when the war wound down. He was waving his hands and looking into the crowds with his piercing blue eyes and giving them that warm grin he had. And I remember just getting a shiver up my back. He looked strong but also kind. But now he had grown aloof on me. Here I am wondering if I'm going to remain the vice-presidential candidate, and here's Ike halfway across the country sending out all these mixed messages to the media. He was sounding like some bank manager with stiff arms who couldn't make up his mind about a loan. When he heard about the fund crisis, he said, "I intend to talk with" Dick "at the earliest time we can reach each other by telephone." But then he didn't call me for days, just kept me hanging, saying he wanted to see where things headed, kept pushing all of this onto my table,

*making it seem that he was too damn busy to take the time to talk it out
with me.*

*I bet he's talking to other people. That's what I thought. There's that damn
circle of men, some of them his golfing buddies and fishing partners, sitting on
the train, I can just imagine, unloading all this crap about me. There was
campaign manager Sherman Adams, blue-blood Eastern Establishment type
from New Hampshire, cold and chiseled face full of defenses. Sherm just
clammed up, like he was hiding something from you, even though he knew full
well there was talk about getting a replacement for me on the ticket at the time.
Then there was the worst: Bill Robinson, publisher of the* New York Herald
Tribune *and an old golfing buddy of the general's, who was getting his boys
at the newspaper to call for my goddamn resignation, right there in the op-ed
section. And I bet Ike's brother, Milt, who went everywhere with the general,
it seemed, was nodding his head at Robinson. Then there was "Mr. Chapman" of "New York," code name for Tom Dewey, the failed presidential candidate and governor of New York and the man who originally recruited me onto
Ike's team back in spring. He liked me once, smiling at me with that little
mustache of his that would stretch his face out and show the space between his
teeth. But now Dewey was getting cold feet about the situation. Man could
turn hard fast; sometimes he seemed like a real phony. He'd call me up at odd
hours and tell me I should quit and get off the ticket. Kill my political career.*[5]

*What I can't get through to these guys is that I have a gift. Like I said to
Tom Dewey on the phone: "I know something about politics!" What I didn't
say is what I was thinking: I'm not sure Ike understands politics. It's his first
time running for office, and he lacks "experience in political warfare." Sure, the
general could fight the big chess games over in Europe, moving huge battalions
of men across maps of great expanse, but he sure as hell couldn't fight the
trench operations of an American election. That's why he needs me right now.
The nice old general had to have a "running mate who was willing to engage
in all-out combat." God damn, I'm thinking, why won't he call me so I can
tell him this?*[6]

Then I got lucky, and the phone rang late one evening. Ike was on the line, just after he had been to dinner with friends who wanted me off the ticket. I had been having a massage for the damn neck pains I was getting. He sounded distant coming over the wires, almost faint, the way most voices at midnight would sound. He was telling me that he thought I should go on television and talk about the fund and come clean. He was asking me to bare my soul and look out through a camera at millions of faceless Americans in their living rooms and tell them my story, to set the record straight. And to let them decide my fate so that he didn't have to. I had been having the same idea—and the fat little man with the good advice, Murray Chotiner, had been, too. So I said yes, that sounded good. But then I said, well, General, once the show's off the air, will you announce that this mess is over with, that I'm your running mate and we can get on with this campaign? And then he went back to his hemming and hawing. Something inside me burst. Maybe the distance between us—the two-thousand-plus miles—and the voice that had no face connected to it made me snap. I said, "There comes a time in matters like this when you've either got to shit or get off the pot." I knew right away I shouldn't have said that, so I softened it a bit: "The great trouble here is the indecision." And the general just wished me good luck, told me to keep my "chin up," like I was some sort of grade school kid going to the playground, when I was a full-grown man about to face millions of Americans on television who would decide my fate.[7]

And all I wanted right then was to get back to my damn massage, because my neck hurt so bad. And then I thought about my mother taking care of the kids back in D.C. while I'm out here putting myself into these near riots at the campaign stops. Tears welled in my eyes when I learned my mother had said a prayer for me. I feel like a goddamn madman right now.[8]

II.

Richard Nixon was angry, depressed, and balled up inside. His boss, Dwight Eisenhower, had just handed him the reins of his political destiny by telling him to go on national television to explain the

political fund set up by Dana Smith that was drawing so much criticism. Or perhaps the general had handed him the rope to hang himself with. Nixon wanted to move fast toward the speech. His career
was on the line. He was only thirty-nine years old at the time (Ike
thought him older when he was placed on the ticket). "Young man on
the rise" and "in a hurry" went the mantra about him in the political
magazines. Dick had loved few things except playing poker (a skill he
honed while serving in the Navy) and the high-stakes politics that
vaulted him up the echelons.

He began as a '46er, coming into national office during an off election in a wave of Republican victories across the country that made
President Harry Truman's job a headache. He had defeated an old
New Deal Democrat named Jerry Voorhis. Once in office, he had
helped put the communist spy Alger Hiss behind bars—bringing himself "national prominence"—and then clipped the wings of the starlet
Helen Gahagan Douglas by orchestrating a "fighting, rocking, socking campaign" against her for the U.S. Senate in 1950. He won that
election big-time. The rungs on his ladder got closer together. Now he
was running to become the Senate vote tiebreaker and the man a
heartbeat away from the presidency. That was the story of Nixon's life:
high stakes and quick leaps. Now all that might come to an end.[9]

He had already faced a potential career killer. It came when he
was investigating Alger Hiss—a time his wife Pat remembered as
when "everybody and everything . . . seemed against" him. He was
the one member of the House Un-American Activities Committee
(HUAC) who kept pushing on the case when others—some of them
suckered by Hiss's smoothness and prestige—had their doubts. Nixon
wanted to go all the way to take Hiss down by cooperating with a
former Communist spy, Whittaker Chambers, who had confessed
his own sins and assured the congressional inquisitors that he knew
Hiss, who was, at the time, working at the State Department. Cham-

bers was a bit fishy and dumpy-looking, but Nixon trusted him. There came a rather weird moment in the case when Chambers revealed that he had tucked some incriminating evidence into hollowed-out pumpkins on his farm, microfilm that showed Alger Hiss had pecked out State Department secrets on his own typewriter and given them to Chambers. At a make-or-break moment in the case, an investigation of the date of the film suggested Chambers had lied. The perpetually disheveled Chambers cried out: "It cannot be true, but I can't explain it. God must be against me." When Nixon was informed about the matter, he shouted to a friend, "Oh, my God, this is the end of my political career. My whole career is ruined!" Ultimately, after further investigation, he and Chambers learned the microfilm was legit, and the two men came out stronger for battle, ready to slay their enemy. Hiss went down in the end and was put behind bars. Remembering this moment of crisis and redemption now fortified Nixon for his upcoming battle.[10]

His inner circle stood beside him, knowing he was battle-ready. Murray Chotiner, his chief political adviser and the man who had masterminded his 1950 Senate win, kept telling Nixon that he should go on national television and talk directly to the American people, that the press was killing him but the people would accept him if he could face them in their living rooms. Nixon liked the idea. He would talk about it late at night with his other confidante, his wife, Pat, while they traveled on the *Nixon Special* through California into Oregon. Nixon went wobbly about the whole thing, suggesting he might quit the ticket and throw in the towel as the vice-presidential candidate. Pat knew just the right thing to play upon: his manliness. "You can't think of resigning," she told him. "If you, in the face of attack, do not fight back but simply crawl away, you will destroy yourself. Your life will be marred forever and the same will be true of your family." She had recently been bragging, in a national publication, about what a tough and steely guy her husband was, that he loved competition and sports and the rough road of politics. This was no time for him to cower.[11]

It was easy to find the code of manliness that Pat appealed to in 1952. It played out in the hard-boiled men who populated the pages of the pulps and the screens of Hollywood and that newfangled thing called television. The world of popular culture—a world the Checkers speech both inhabited and helped nurture—defined the macho qualities Nixon hungered for as much as the world of politics did. They could be envisaged in the sweaty but unmoved face of Gary Cooper—a real man, no sissy—in *High Noon*, a film released just a couple of months before the Checkers speech. There was Coop, abandoned by his wimpy townsmen, as he walked the streets of Hadleyville ready for a showdown with an evil posse coming to kill him, drawing upon some inner reserve to fight it out as a gunslinger. Or you could see it in John Wayne—the macho actor who usually played in war films or westerns and who happened to be Richard Nixon's favorite— bare-knuckling Communists to their knees in the film *Big Jim McLain*, out a month after *High Noon*. Or you could crack open one of the bestselling pulp paperbacks (always with some saucy woman in a seductive pose on the cover—America was not as prudish during the 1950s as some assume) slammed out by Mickey Spillane. Take 1952's *Kiss Me Deadly*, in which Spillane's hero, Mike Hammer, a tough private detective, takes out the mob and tries to rescue his helpmate and broad, Velda. Hammer explained that he "wasn't the cops" or "the feds" but just "one guy by himself" who left a "trail of dead men" in his personally sanctioned pursuit of justice. Even better than Hammer, because he was far more upstanding, was Joe Friday—the hero of TV's *Dragnet*, a show that catapulted up the ratings throughout 1952 (with the help of a Chesterfield cigarette sponsorship). Friday, played by Jack Webb, who bore some resemblance to Nixon with his dark hair, five o'clock shadow, and darting eyes, worked the mean streets of Los Angeles. Friday hunted the "facts" about criminals and managed his way through a cumbersome urban police bureaucracy. He'd chase the bad men down, thriving on the suspense of under-cover work and accompanied by the trademark music played at each show's opening: *Dumm, de-dum-dum. Dumm, de-dum-dum . . . dummm.*[12]

That could be Richard Nixon's theme music. He had the suspense set for his own drama. The nation was trying to figure out, along with him, his political fate. The election might hinge on this—if he quit the ticket (or was forced off), it would make Ike's original choice and therefore his judgment look bad. If he stayed on without address-ing the matter, it would look like a whitewash. The messages from Ike were ambivalent at best, but Nixon remembered the cheers (along with the heckling) on his whistle-stop tour. For sure, the press aligned against him, but he could get away from the scrutinizing eyes and commentaries of the op-ed writers and gumshoe journalists if he went directly to the people on television. He could pull off one of history's greatest feats of telepopulism.

Television. That was to be Dick's format. His speech would sym-bolize just how much politics and television had merged by 1952. This was the first year both political parties' conventions, in their entirety, would appear on screens in Americans' homes, and the first year of "spots" (thirty-second television advertisements) that required candidates to pony up millions of dollars. This was a time when some thought seeing was believing—that a politician could project his au-thentic self onto the screen, no longer able to hide body language or facial expressions as could be done on the radio. Richard Nixon would engage in an existential act of self-definition by going in front of cameras and baring his soul. He would plead his case and make the audience see him as an ordinary guy. His speech would be com-pared to the soap operas that played on radio and were moving onto

television at the time, the shows that played to heartstrings and emotions. Nixon had to connect—to become sincere and authentic for
the "lonely crowd" watching his image in living rooms.

Summoning his courage to go in front of the cameras, Nixon
would move from despair and frustration into a manic sense of political rebirth. Maybe this crisis could work for him. Perhaps the lone-
liness and anxiety, the knotted stomach, the tense muscles, the "tingle"
in his nerves would help him reach people who were like him. Maybe
he could speak to the millions of Americans who would understand
the struggle of a young man on the rise in postwar America. There
were all those midlevel managers waiting for a raise that didn't come,
for a promotion they deserved but that never materialized, for an
invitation to go golfing with the boss who constantly snubbed them.
Nixon could speak to those people, and *for* them, in explaining his
own personal crisis. Thinking of Eisenhower at this moment made
Nixon understand the universal humiliation of working for a boss;
he was, after all, not really a self-made man but a creature of bureaucracy, an "organization man" and "other-directed character," a man
validated by his higher-ups and the impression he made on them. He
knew personal humiliation and described feeling like a "little boy
caught with jam on his face" during the fund crisis. That feeling could
work for him right now and could resonate throughout the country
with the working man trying to get a leg up.[13]

Nixon was an everyman versus Ike, who was a great man. Nixon
had been a junior officer in the Navy during World War II, not a
five-star general barking out orders. Nixon had been in the South
Pacific "when the bombs were falling," as he stated passively during
the Checkers speech. He was more a midlevel bureaucrat, a paper
shuffler who saw little or no combat, like some of those portrayed in
James Jones's *From Here to Eternity* (1951). "It is hard to be adventurous
about the uniform when you have to polish your own boots," Jones
wrote. "And this explains why [those] above such menial tasks, are

capable of such exciting memoirs of war." They could stand high and mighty above the fray. Nixon wouldn't say this sort of thing about Ike, for sure, since a tone of resentment would disrespect the boss. But he knew full well that he was like those midlevel guys who didn't perch on top of the military hierarchy. And now he was like the postwar strivers and strugglers that those midlevel men had become, looking to buy a house in the suburbs and to own a car, radio, and television set and to get on with life. They were not the great men. They belched and cussed. Their wives didn't lie in bed all day, the way Mamie Eisenhower did. Instead, they scrubbed the floors and sewed their own drapes and put food out for the dog, the way Pat Nixon did.[14]

And the 1952 election should be theirs. For there were many more of them than there were five-star generals. As Dick would say during the Checkers speech, quoting a line attributed inaccurately to Abraham Lincoln: "God must have loved the common people, he made so many of them." His speech would identify the sentiments rising from these common people. He would connect and play to their hearts. Sure, their opponent in the race, Adlai Stevenson, the Democratic candidate for president, wanted the election to be about high-minded ideas, debates, and sensible discussion. That's what *every* egghead who had gone to prep school and the Ivy Leagues wanted. But what Nixon wanted was a rocking and socking campaign, a political gunfight, expressed not with the bullets of the day's westerns but with tough talk mixed with authenticity and sincerity, sentiment over intellect. The Checkers speech accomplished this, and it garnered the largest television audience to date in history.[15]

To tell the story of a speech watched by millions requires a broader narrative about Nixon's capturing the national spotlight. The place to start is the spring of 1952, when Nixon caught the eye of Tom Dewey and started working his way onto the Eisenhower team. It was an anxiety-ridden period in American history that sets the stage for an anxiety-ridden story. What follows will zero in on Richard Nixon himself but also draw a panorama of other political figures, the movies of Hollywood, the culture of television, the buzzing of op-ed writers in the press, and the world of "eggheads" and ideas. In painting a picture of Richard Nixon during the 1952 election cycle, this portrait offers a view not just of a political salesman but of the country as a whole. For in its essence, this is the story of an everyman.

CHAPTER ONE

ANXIETIES . . . OF A COLD WAR SPRING AND AN "INSIDE DOPESTER"

*Within the next decades will be decided whether all mankind is to
become Communist, whether the whole world is to become free, or
whether in the struggle, civilization, as we know it, is to be
destroyed. It is our fate to live upon that turning point in history.*

—WHITTAKER CHAMBERS, *READER'S DIGEST*, MAY 1952

May 1952: Young men in the trenches of Korea felt dirty and
miserable, "wondering when they would hear the whistle of that
homebound transport," as General Matthew Ridgway explained.
The number of casualties continued growing, and morale among
the troops sank lower and lower. The mission to defend the southern
portion of the country against totalitarian Communism to the north
now appeared an "indecisive stalemate." The political cartoonist Bill
Mauldin called Korea a "slow, grinding, lonely bitched up war."
Thinking about the American dead in mud-filled trenches prompted
Richard Nixon to conjure a line for a future political speech: "Dead
Americans are live issues!" That was the only good or productive
thing Nixon could imagine creating from this mess.[1]

Heading into its third year, the war had accomplished little. President Harry S. Truman and his beleaguered secretary of state, Dean Acheson, had tried diplomatic talks, but they dragged on without much result. Truman had been trying to resolve the crucial issue of what to do with North Korean and Chinese prisoners of war by pressing for "voluntary repatriation," giving captured men some say in their fate, not just pushing them back to their Communist homeland. This may have sounded just, but the North Korean and Chinese governments were balking. As the cruel spring month of May dawned, the news reported that POWs were rioting against miserable conditions.

The American public was getting sick of it all. The war—or what Truman called a "police action," orchestrated by the United Nations as much as by the United States—had started two years ago with a whopping 75 percent approval. But that melted away as the war dragged on. A year in, only 30 to 35 percent of Americans "looked with favor" on further action in Korea. The numbers continued to dip as casualties mounted. Some Americans wondered why Truman didn't use atomic weapons (the idea was considered), but this, too, just added to the anxiety that the Korean War might escalate into World War III.[2]

The war by now had made its domestic mark, disrupting the lives of citizens on the economic home front. Truman wanted to put industrial manufacturing on a war footing (the way the country had during World War II), ensuring that labor conflicts would not damage the steady production of goods needed for the fight in Korea. Eyeing a potentially huge conflict in the steel industry—with unions poised to strike against recalcitrant company owners whose profits were going up—Truman decided in April to seize steel industry plants, ensuring the economic stability he thought necessary as commander in chief and president. But his takeover failed to stop union agitation. By May 1, 1952, the *Washington Post* reported that 650,000 steelworkers were on strike. Americans disapproved of Truman's seizure of private property as much as they disapproved of the war (in June the Supreme Court would concur and overrule Truman). Among his conservative critics, it felt like apocalypse: "If government can take over the steel companies, why not the grocery stores, the churches and everything else—even the farms or the homes as the government has done in Russia?" War, as usual, strengthened the executive branch, and now the man atop that branch seemed berserk with power, willing to gobble up free enterprise in his wake.[3]

No wonder Truman's poll numbers tanked. He was down to 32 percent approval. And he had already announced he wouldn't seek the presidency in 1952. There was at least one other person just as hated as Truman—Dean Acheson, the man sworn in as secretary of state three years ago, just as China fell to Communism. Critics found Acheson an insufferable elitist. He wore striped pants and had a gigantic mustache that looked preposterous. He had been to Groton, Yale, and Harvard Law School and then worked on Wall Street. Some thought he feigned a British accent. When he heard about conservatives attacking his policies he called them "the primitives." Richard Nixon, for one, really hated the guy. He could never forgive the secretary of state for defending his own archnemesis, Alger Hiss, back in 1950. Acheson had called Hiss a friend and said he did not intend to turn his back on him. He even cited the Bible (Matthew 25:36) and talked about an ethic of forgiveness. How much worse could you get, wondered Nixon; sure, Dick appreciated loyalty, but not if your friend was shown to be a Commie spy and had been convicted. Now, by the spring of 1952, Acheson, perceived as the architect of American action in Korea, had gotten the country involved in a war that it wasn't winning.[4]

It was logical, facing competition like Truman and Acheson, that Richard Nixon and his fellow Republicans could smell a White House victory in their near future. But the whiff of approaching triumph also prompted unease and anxiety for Republicans. After all, they had felt the same way four years ago and had lost. They now conjured one of the scariest images in a Republican's memory: the photograph of a beaming Harry Truman holding up a copy of the *Chicago Tribune* emblazoned with the words DEWEY DEFEATS TRUMAN. Of course, the reverse had been true, Truman had beaten Dewey, and that defeat haunted Republicans in 1952, along with the prior four Democratic wins of the presidency. Richard Nixon pondered the upcoming election and called it "the last chance for power for the Republican Party."[5]

On May 4, 1952, the Catholic Institute of the Press was staging its equivalent of the National Book Awards or Academy Awards, doling out prizes for cultural works (literature, journalism, and movies) that exemplified "Christian, Catholic principles." On the podium stood the movie director Leo McCarey, slightly bronzed, his black hair greased back in perfect fashion, smiling and looking proud.[6]

His film *My Son John* had been out less than a month and hadn't even opened yet in the nation's capital, where the movie's star, Helen Hayes, a friend of Dwight Eisenhower, had been born. But it was causing a stir already. The film answered a perilous question Richard Nixon had asked of Hollywood back in 1947 when the House Un-American Activities Committee inquisitioned Tinseltown. It wasn't enough for the Hollywood execs to ferret out the commies in their ranks, though that was a good start. Dick wanted more and had inquired of Jack Warner, a hotshot producer, and Eric Johnston, the chief of the Motion Picture Association of America, if they were "making at the present time any pictures pointing out the methods and the evils of totalitarian communism"? Leo McCarey had been a friendly witness during those HUAC hearings, talking about how he had put God into his movies (*Going My Way* and *The Bells of St. Mary's*, with Bing Crosby playing a Catholic priest), and now he had a film that had not only God but an anticommunist message that would have pleased Dick Nixon.[7]

The movie glistened from its opening scenes. Church bells rang out over tree-lined suburban streets. And there appeared two chipper and identical-looking young men, Ben and Chuck Jefferson, playing catch football with their father. These good Catholic boys are about to embark to the killing fields of Korea. Their father and mother love them very much. We learn they have a brother, John, a government official stuck in D.C. His presence is missed that evening at the dinner table. The cranky father pours wine and toasts the sons, and then the audience's eyes settle on an empty seat.[8]

When John arrives home after his brothers have left, the audience recoils. Here is a man to hate: He is a snob, dissing the homespun "bromides" his father offers and sucking up to the doctor who is checking up on his mother (John loves "science" and "reason," he explains). The family then goes to church, and John insults the priest. After John flees to see his professor from his "old alma mater," preferring the company of intellectuals to that of Mom and Dad, he returns home to laugh at his father's membership in the American Legion and belief that the Bible is "literal." John's father explains that he's writing a speech for the Legion. McCarey, who had directed Laurel and Hardy years ago (in addition to the Marx Brothers), has father and son break into a screwball "who's on first" routine about what's ailing America. Then the father, played by Dean Jagger in a way that seems self-lampooning, busts out with song:

> *If you don't like your Uncle Sammy*
> *Then go back to your home o'er the sea*
> *To the land from where you came,*
> *Whatever be its name,*
> *But don't be ungrateful to me!*

If you don't like the stars in Old Glory,
If you don't like the red, white, and blue,
Then don't act like the cur in the story,
Don't bite the hand that's feeding you!

John's response, as described by the film reviewer Robert War-show, becomes "icy-delicate feline mockery." Robert Walker, who played John (and a year before, a psychopath in Alfred Hitchcock's *Strangers on a Train*), had perfected the ability to rub his eyebrows, blow little puffs of cigarette smoke through his nostrils, and preen in such a way as to project an effeminate and sickly contrast to his bumbling macho father.[9]

The mother, played by Helen Hayes, is worried about John, growing more suspicious by the minute. She fears that the "highbrow professors" have gotten to him. She reminds him that her two great sources of learning are the Bible and the cookbook. And then John commits the most venal of sins: He tries to play the mother against the father. "Father is muddled, he thinks in the past," John tells his mother. He plays upon her own religious faith, saying that he loves "the downtrodden," which she still takes to be an expression of good Christian faith. Still upset, the mother gets John to swear on the Bible he's not a Communist, and though he does, the audience knows he's faking (John's phoniness matters as much as his suspected Communism). The father follows up the mother's sermonizing by beating John over the head with the Bible, a method he considers more appropriate to handle the problem. The family is in tumult now, still a comic, Hollywood kind of tumult in which the father can fall down the staircase drunk on beer and bourbon but not until after condemning the "Commie specialty" of "breaking up homes."

A Federal Bureau of Investigation officer visits John's mother and suggests her son's a Communist, which prompts her to go to D.C. to spy on him. She follows John around and sightsees in the nation's capital. She learns about a "Red spy ring" and a woman John had been communicating with on the phone in fervid, quiet conversations while at home. She learns that John even has a key to the spy queen's apartment. She returns home from D.C. distraught, but John is hiding there and appears from around a corner looking like a gangster. Mother and son have it out. "There will be no more fancy lies!" she shrieks. His retort is to play on her dumbness (she's overwhelmed at one point by the fact that her son has "more degrees than a thermometer"), explaining "there are issues that transcend a mother and son." Both John and his mother scream about "millions" on their side of the battle. The FBI agent enters the home and prompts John's mother to make an operatic speech around the metaphor of football: "You've got to get into this game and you've got to carry the ball yourself. John, take the ball." Meaning, become like your normal brothers— the "two halfbacks"—who served their country without question. She transforms herself into a cheerleader, chanting: "My son John! My son John!" But John just glares. How could a young man like John play football? In a fit of desperation, the mother tells the FBI agent to "take [her son] away." Communism has won, the family has lost.

Up to this point in the script, McCarey's filming had plodded along nicely. But then tragedy struck: His leading man died. Robert Walker had been having nervous breakdowns, and his doctor shot him full of a sedative without checking beforehand about the alcohol he had downed or possible allergies. The shot killed him. McCarey was a scrapper, and he borrowed some footage from *Strangers on a Train* (thankfully shot in D.C.), had John killed in a car chase, and then culminated the movie in a postmortem tape-recorded speech John gives to his alma mater. John has had an unwitnessed conversion experience back to old-time religion, and his speech wraps up the movie's themes. A light shines down on an empty podium while John's disembodied voice plays to rows of bored-looking students. The voice explains that he rejoiced when he was "immediately recognized as an intellect. I was invited to homes where only superior minds communed. It excited my freshman fancy." An effeminate intellectual easily turned from "stimulants to narcotics," threw away God, and then made "an enemy of my country." College became a gateway to national betrayal (Senator Joseph McCarthy would soon express concern that "parents throughout the country complain that their sons and daughters were sent to college as good Americans and returned four years later as wild-eyed radicals"). Leaving behind the cookbook and the Bible for the world of intellect led John to Communism and death.[10]

The movie's message was as blunt as its plotting was flawed, especially the parts glued together after Walker had died. Most film critics panned it. Robert Warshow, who wrote for the liberal and highbrow *Commentary*, argued the film showed a "wrong way, a dangerous way, to be anti-Communist." Bosley Crowther, sitting on his perch at the *New York Times*, wearing his tweed and puffing a pipe, found the film unreal, since the connections between the son and Communism were flimsy. It had a "hot emotional nature" that mixed "militance and dogmatism" for our "present and confused national climate." No shock here, seeing as Crowther was a man who preferred European films or serious American "social problem" films, like *Intruder in the Dust* (1949), about Southern racism, the sort of film that most Hollywood producers shied away from in the contemporary political climate. The Catholic magazine *America* concluded that *My Son John* created what André Gide called the sort of "fine sentiments that go to make bad literature." The film suffered from "slipshod . . . construction" and offered only "sentimental hokum."[11]

To which it was easy to imagine Leo McCarey responding: *Exactly.* His movie wasn't intended for the "highbrow professors" or liberal critics. This was a film for the guy who identified with the roughneck father. Like those who joined the American Legion, an organization that promoted the movie every chance it got. During one of the film's conversations, the mother explains to the father that he has "got more wisdom than all of us; you listen to your heart." It was easy to imagine McCarey saying: *That is what this movie offers—the insight of sentiment and a rebellion against the limits of intellect.* Sentimentalism fit the anxiety-ridden age, suggesting to viewers: *Think with your gut and your maudlin heart.*[12]

Richard Nixon looked sharp in his dinner jacket and bow tie, freshly shaven and bright as a bulb. He wanted to impress his audience, although the majority wouldn't see him; they'd be listening to their radios at home. It was the evening of May 8, and the speech would take place at the Waldorf-Astoria, a swank hotel smack-dab in the middle of Manhattan, the perfect setting for an East Coast Republican fundraiser. And there was Richard Nixon, golden boy from the West, stepping up to speak. Truth be told, he was nervous as hell. These weren't his people.[13]

The main man of the event, Tom Dewey, then governor of New York and twice-defeated Republican candidate for the presidency, smiled, stretching out his thin mustache over his pursing lips. He glowed less for Nixon's words, more for his flourish. He liked how young and sharp he looked. After crunching out his cigarette and applauding Nixon's talk about potential Republican victory in 1952, Dewey clasped the golden boy's arm and said, "That was a terrific speech. Make me a promise; don't get fat, don't lose your zeal, and you can be president someday." Dewey proceeded to introduce him around to others, suggesting *Here's a man you ought to know,* including a warm handshake with Herbert Brownell, Dewey's old campaign manager. Then Dewey invited Nixon to his room so they could chat about the young man's political future.[14]

The invitation might have made Richard Nixon uncomfortable. After all, Dewey reeked of defeat. Few blamed him for losing to FDR in 1944; that was like losing to God more than to a politician. But most Republicans blamed him one hundred percent for losing to that accidental president, that failed haberdasher from the sticks, Harry Truman, in 1948. That year, the Democrats had split into warring parties: the Dixiecrats to the right, the Progressive Party to the left. Instead of taking advantage of this dissolution, Dewey played it high-handed, preferring to speak in arch tones, becoming known as "the Boy Orator of the Platitude" (a derisive play on William Jennings Bryan's epithet "the Boy Orator of the Platte.") He refused to attack Truman, even though the president attacked him with vigor and populist gusto during his whistle-stop tour. One critic chided the Republican candidate, saying his speeches could be "boiled down to these historic four sentences: Agriculture is important. Our rivers are full of fish. You cannot have freedom without liberty. The future lies ahead." Dewey even refused those who came to his rescue, including a proposition from the leading advertising firm on Madison Avenue, Batten, Barton, Durstine and Osborn, to do radio "spots" in certain areas that might boost his approval. He thought such gimmicks below him. He lost any sharpness in contrast with Truman, obsessed with playing to the middle or what his critics labeled "me-tooism." Alice Roosevelt Longworth compared him to the "little man on top of the wedding cake," wanting to please the guests rather than engage in political combat.[15]

Dewey knew that many in his party hated him. But he hated them back. Just a year after his loss to Truman, he described the Republican Party as "split wide open." There was his own eastern contingent, who accepted welfare state provisions and American responsibility toward Europe in the Cold War ("Establishment" Republicans) versus a midwestern group who hated the New Deal and Europe and wanted to focus American foreign policy on liberating China and Southeast Asia from Communism. The latter included Dewey's archenemies— Robert Taft, Everett Dirksen, Douglas MacArthur, and Joseph

McCarthy. In his own state of New York, Dewey faced the rabble in the form of the Committee for the Preservation of the Integrity of the Republican Party. His foes always thought of themselves as real—him, a phony. Like Acheson, Dewey worried about "primitives" like Joseph McCarthy, the he-man senator who rolled up his sleeves and "burped in public." Dewey was well mannered and dapper in dress. He pined for sharp lookers, like Nixon that evening, and believed the golden boy from California was "a Senator who knew the world was round."[16]

Once in his suite, Dewey admitted to Nixon that he had already chosen his man for the 1952 presidential election: Dwight Eisenhower. So that quip about becoming president, well, that was just banter about the longer-range future. But what about the vice presidency? You're my kind of man, Dewey suggested. Nixon, after all, had supported the Marshall Plan, the classic foreign aid package that helped Europe recover from the ravages of war and created markets for American goods at the same time. That symbolized Eastern Bloc internationalism with its embrace of world responsibility. Dewey might not have known or recognized the passionate speech Nixon gave on behalf of General MacArthur, back in 1951, when Truman deposed the general after he had demanded that a war of liberation be extended from Korea up into China. "The happiest group in the country over General MacArthur's removal will be the Communists and their stooges," Nixon had said. "They have been doing a hatchet job on him the past ten years and now the President has given them what they wanted—MacArthur's scalp." Plus a weak-kneed policy in Korea, Nixon would add. That sounded like Joseph McCarthy—who simply labeled the president a "son of a bitch" for firing MacArthur and then called for his impeachment. There was not that much distance between Nixon and McCarthy, certainly not as much as Dewey hoped.[17]

The sharpest line of division between Dewey and Nixon was their vision of political campaigning. When Nixon spoke about the upcoming 1952 election, he called for a "fighting, rocking, socking campaign"—a term he had been using since 1946—in which Republicans made clear they stood "for something." By June 1951, Nixon had already developed his speech, "The Challenge of 1952," much of which he had used at the Waldorf, where he set out his hard-line view of campaigning. He would begin by nailing the Truman administration's "whining, whimpering, groveling attitude" in diplomacy and its emphasis on "America's weaknesses and of America's fears rather than . . . America's strength and . . . courage." He highlighted how the Communists had "infiltrated the very highest councils of this administration," which refused to "take effective action to clean subversives out of the administrative branch of our government." Blame the administration for the ongoing war, he counseled, for "the failures in policy which led to 100,000 casualties in Korea." Point out that America had lost "six hundred million people" to Communism since Truman came to office. Be aggressive not just in campaigning but in crafting foreign policy: "Our foreign policy has suffered from the fact that we have constantly been on the defensive. . . . What is needed above all else is aggressive, new, dynamic planning and leadership in our State Department." That kind of rhetoric got him recognized in 1951 as a "future"-looking man. It was also the sort of rhetoric that Dewey had rejected during his losing battle against Truman as too confrontational and sharp around the edges.[18]

If Nixon were to review his own list of victories for Dewey, he couldn't avoid noticing the contrast between his own style of political campaigning and that of the governor of New York. Starting with 1950, when he ran against the New Deal liberal Helen Gahagan Douglas, Nixon attacked her left-wing politics, showing that she voted in line with a Communist sympathizer like Vito Marcantonio and was therefore "pink down to her underwear." Simultaneously, Nixon played up his own ordinariness in contrast to Douglas, who was a wealthy actress and a California celebrity as much as a congressperson. She spent a great deal of time away from her husband (also an actor) and children, being on the road so much, a mark against the 1950s ideal of domesticated womanhood. She was a real glamorpuss, while Dick came from "the very grassroots of the nation" with a nice house, a wife who sewed curtains, and two little girls. Or so a newspaper article presented Dick, an article the campaign quickly poached for its own promotional materials. Nixon was quick to personalize his populist campaign, to chastise wealth—at least of a certain celebrity sort—and to talk about what Dewey likely considered private matters best left alone.[19]

One of Nixon's craftiest moves was cultivating an under-the-table friendship with Senator Joseph McCarthy, that primitive who made Dewey uncomfortable. Nixon had forged relations with Joe back in 1950 by sharing HUAC materials so that the senator from Wisconsin might back up his accusations about hundreds of Communists in the State Department made in his famous February 9, 1950, Wheeling speech (a speech Nixon thought irresponsible because it got too specific on numbers). During the 1950 campaign, Nixon let McCarthy loose in his state to speak, without owning him. That was the fun of campaigning, letting people like that on board and blowing on the embers they left behind. It was just a show, after all. McCarthy struck perfect pitch while stumping for Dick: "The chips are down between the American people and the administration Commicrat Party of Betrayal." When he said this, Joe's head would peck the air like a mechanical drill against a wall, puncturing the listener's consciousness with *every . . . word . . . pronounced.* The word "Commicrat" would have its double *c*'s pounded into a listener's cranium. Nixon's supporters loved it, and it showed that Dick appreciated that primitives could put on a good show, whereas Dewey would shudder at the prospect. Such was the price of winning the "biggest plurality achieved by any Republican" in 1950, Nixon might have pointed out.[20]

Nixon's memory would then move from 1950 back to 1946, the year of his earliest campaign, remembered like a first love. That year, he beat Jerry Voorhis, another New Deal Democrat, who had been in office for a decade. Voorhis had been a Democratic Socialist once, and Nixon kept insinuating something fishy about the man, his campaign literature talking up a shady radical past. He portrayed Voorhis as a stooge for the CIO-PAC, the left wing of the labor union movement, and then did something he thought Dewey should have done two years later: played up the idea that Communists were insinuating themselves into the government. He told the American Legion—what better audience?—that Communists and fellow travelers were fast "gaining positions of importance in virtually every federal department and bureau" in the government. He warned that the feds could be "shot through with extreme left-wingers . . . boring from within" who would bring on the "socialization of America's basic institutions." He would boot out Voorhis as part of his overall plan to redeem government from Communist takeover.[21]

Only sharp political strategizing and polarizing could accomplish this. He used populist language updated for the times, speaking up for that "new forgotten man walking the streets," the "white-collar worker who has not had a raise" for some time. Hand those people their metaphorical pitchforks, and they could oust the socialist New Dealers. Nixon spoke for the automobile dealers, insurance brokers, ranchers, and bankers who helped recruit him to run in 1946. They loved his sharp rhetoric about a forked road ahead—one path "advocated the New Deal" based on "government control in regulating our lives," the other envisioned "individual freedom and all that initiative can produce." He could rally those faceless white-collar employees around anger and frustration. His campaign literature asked:

"Are you satisfied with present conditions? Can you buy meat, a new car, a refrigerator, clothes you need? . . . Where are all those new houses you were promised?" This played along with the Republican slogan of 1946, "Had Enough?"—the brainchild of an advertising executive named Karl Frost. Translated, it meant: Sick of regulations, public housing, rent control, bureaucratic government in general? Want more *stuff*? Vote Republican and get it. Nixon was a white-collar populist who united people around their "fierce desire . . . to regain control of their own lives."[22]

If Dewey had scrutinized a bit more carefully Richard Nixon's words the evening of May 8, he might have second-guessed himself (as he eventually would). But Dick Nixon could hide his MacArthur support, wild-eyed populism, and love of a "rocking, socking" campaign better than most. For he was also a good white-collar "organization man" who knew what it meant to be "other-directed," a term coined by a group of sociologists in 1950. Nixon could take cues from his higher-ups and peers; his eyes would dart around a room checking out the impressions his words made. He had an early propensity for mouthwash and became a perpetual club joiner and backslapper when he first entered politics, even if he was profoundly uncomfortable in social settings. He knew enough not to talk like a firebrand on the evening of May 8, recognizing that he was working his way into Dewey's and thereby Eisenhower's world. He could play a room and glad-hand, as he had been doing downstairs just a few moments before coming to Dewey's fancy suite.[23]

So Tom Dewey, whether he knew it or not, had discovered a complete package. Nixon offered sharpness, but he could also be what people wanted him to be. He could synthesize the discordant, serving as a Western golden boy palling around with the Eastern establishment. He could talk a populist anti–New Deal line and gung-ho Cold Warrior rhetoric. At the same time, he could walk that stuff back if it caused discomfort for those present. Most important of all, Dick Nixon could be what he, Tom Dewey, was not: a fighter ready for a tough campaign.

Richard Nixon had a young career, and many of the allies who helped build the career kept popping back into the public's consciousness. He had built associations with others—with Tom Dewey and Joseph McCarthy, for instance—who reminded him of questions about his own self-definition. May 24, 1952, became one of those days when a figure from his recent past walked back into his life. There was his name, Richard Nixon, splashed alongside the name of Whittaker Chambers, a man who, four years ago, had helped save his career by testifying to the guilt of Alger Hiss. Both names appeared in the pages of the *Saturday Review*, a high- to middlebrow magazine that had recently dropped *"of Literature"* from its cover page and was edited by a liberal internationalist named Norman Cousins. It was an odd meeting ground for the two men. But it allowed both to rekindle a friendship—or the closest thing to a friendship either man could have—that defined them both.

Three days before that issue of *Saturday Review* hit the stands, Whittaker Chambers had published his heartfelt, stunning memoir about being a spy for Soviet Russia and then becoming an informant for the United States who turned in Alger Hiss, the man Richard Nixon helped put behind bars. The book, *Witness*, became the literary sensation of the spring of 1952. Readers awaited with anticipation what the *Washington Post* labeled "this year's most sensational autobiography." *Witness* became a Book of the Month Club selection and then rocketed to number one on the bestseller list the next month.[24]

Witness rang with tones often as maudlin as *My Son John*. Chambers's, too, was a family story, a recollection of troubled relations with a father who had been a frustrated artist working for an advertising agency and who repressed his bisexual urges. Whittaker's family was sad and dark, holding secrets and tensions within, with the parents separating and his brother eventually committing suicide. Though his mother, who smothered and pampered him, didn't want him to attend an urban institution, Whittaker (effeminately named Jay Vivian by his parents) embarked for Columbia University during the 1920s where he read Russian literature, especially the high masters of tragedy, Dostoyevsky and Tolstoy. He himself had wanted to be a poet. Strangely, he was also a political conservative—a Calvin Coolidge fan in 1924, no less. But somehow, and there was always something a mystery about this, Chambers converted to Communism in 1925, a year of economic prosperity, not depression. He embraced Communism as a rejection of his family's bourgeois decadence and decline. Though it could not be explained fully, his conversion to Communist faith had something to do with the notion that absolute belief could get him out of despair and dissolution. He started off a writer for the *New Masses* but then plunged into the underground to become a spy.[25]

After disentangling himself from the Communist underworld in 1938, an act that required sleeping with a gun on his nightstand and a chronic fear that he was being followed on city streets, Chambers confessed his sins to Adolf Berle, the assistant secretary of state and an intelligence liaison to FDR. He also settled down in a good job at *Time* magazine. Here he wrote pieces about literature and honed his renewed conservative worldview in a friendship with *Time*'s publisher and media mogul, Henry Luce. He became an Episcopalian and then a Quaker (Nixon's religion). And then, one day, he was summoned by HUAC and testified that when a spy, he had known Alger Hiss, who was at the U.S. State Department. Chambers's testimony made him a celebrity despite his own wishes.[26]

Like Dostoyevsky's *Crime and Punishment*, *Witness* was less about a crime and more about the spiritual crisis of conscience and frame of mind buttressing it. In a climactic moment of the book reprinted in the May issue of *Reader's Digest*, Chambers recounted "the daughter of a former German consul general in Moscow" talking about her father who had become an arch-anticommunist. "'He was immensely pro-Soviet,' she said, 'and then—one night in Moscow—he heard screams. That's all. Simply one night he heard screams.'" Chambers heard screams, too, and he wanted his readers to hear screams, almost like an orchestral backdrop played on a phonograph record while turning the pages of his book. Those screams, of course, came from the victims of Communism in gulags. They helped create a spiritual crisis for Chambers, which he hammered onto the page. A fellow onetime Communist, John Strachey, wrote in the pages of the *Nation*: "His voice sometimes rises so high that the printed page itself seems to scream." This provided, in the words of another critic, the book's "intellectual melodrama." Arthur Schlesinger Jr., a Harvard historian and liberal who appeared alongside Chambers and Nixon in the *Saturday Review*, called the style "overwrought." The liberal journalist Murray Kempton quipped: "There was no one who could do the drumroll of alarm, of Western civilization come to the brink, like Chambers." Chambers would have taken much of this criticism as a compliment.[27]

The book offered a scary prognosis for America and the West more broadly. Chambers shot out barbs against the New Deal, which he termed "a genuine revolution, whose deepest purpose was not simply reform within existing traditions, but a basic change in the social, and, above all, the power relationships within the nation." Meaning that liberalism, not just Communism, was party to evil in the world. "Men who could not see that what they firmly believed was liberalism added up to socialism," Chambers warned ominously, "could scarcely be expected to see what added up to Communism." FDR or Harry Truman could never really fight Communism, following this line of reasoning. What was needed was a fervent faith—undoubtedly a Christian faith—to oppose the Communist worldview gobbling up the world. The West had to discover "in suffering and pain, a power of faith which will provide man's mind, at the same intensity, with the same two certainties" that Communism provided: "A reason to live and a reason to die. If it fails, this will be the century of the great social wars. If it succeeds, this will be the century of the great wars of faith." Such a project—a religious war that conjured images of the Crusades— could never be led by intellectuals, or what Chambers termed euphemistically "the most articulate section of mankind," since they had "ceased to believe in God" and had "deliberately rejected" faith. It was the "upper class" and the educated—Alger Hiss being the prime example—who had betrayed the country and pledged itself to Communism. Chambers recounted a conversation he had with a friend of Henry Luce's: "In the United States, the working class are Democrats. The middle class are Republicans. The upper class are Communists." The necessary solution to the crisis of America and the West would somehow have to come from below, from the ranks of believers.[28]

All of which gave a reader of *Witness* a sense of why its author could find a friend in Richard Nixon, whom Chambers's kids called "Nixie" (Nixon would also introduce Chambers to Senator Joseph McCarthy, forming a triadic friendship of sorts). There was much to bond over. Both Nixon and Chambers felt the repercussions of being unattractive, hard-to-love children, though they also had mothers who loved them intensely, often too much. They shared an enormous propensity for feeling like victims who had to go through life's trials unfairly. Chambers had an odd moment in *Witness* in which, even though it was clearly Hiss who was on trial, he described himself as "the defendant" in a case in which, "in a manner startlingly reminiscent of the mechanics of the great Soviet public trials, press, radio, public personages, organizations of all kinds and a section of the Government itself were mobilized against the chosen victim."

Both men had a propensity for gloominess and depression in the face of life crises. Chambers even attempted suicide, whereas Nixon never let his despair get him that down. They both knew dark nights of the soul and shared a faith, tinged with evangelical fervor, that allowed them to get out of the despair when fortunate enough.[29]

What Richard Nixon remembered most about first meeting Whittaker Chambers was how frumpy the man was. Chambers was "one of the most disheveled-looking persons I had ever seen," "wrinkled and unpressed," "short and pudgy." He had bad teeth. Chambers was like the loser kid in high school no one wanted to befriend, providing a sharp contrast to the man he was testifying against, Alger Hiss. Hiss was Mr. Popularity, "too suave, too smooth, and too self-confident" to be real, in Nixon's own words. *Slick and phony*, that is, able to skate on his good looks and prep school background. At one point during his testimony, Hiss reminded Nixon of Establishmentarian hierarchies: "I graduated from Harvard. I heard your school was Whittier" ("I had dreamed of going to college in the East," Nixon remembered with resentment). Nixon equated Chambers's dishevelment with honesty. He was more down-to-earth and sincere than the patrician Hiss. There had to be a sense of joy when the man from Whittier College and the lonely boy who read too many books as a kid avenged the snooty, silver-spooned Hiss. This was like a melodrama come true—those who first appeared losers living in darkness now vanquishing their enemies. Of course, Chambers would feel more tragic about the whole thing, Nixon more purely victorious. And their individual reactions pointed them to their respective professions: Nixon to be a politician and Chambers an intellectual who lived on a farm and wrote jeremiads for conservative magazines about the decline of the West.[30]

Now, in the spring of 1952, Nixon could repay the favor that Chambers had done for him by nailing Hiss and saving his career as a congressman. Nixon could now plug *Witness* as liberal intellectuals, like Arthur Schlesinger Jr., criticized the book's shortcomings. "I can hear now the epithets which will be directed" against the book, Nixon wrote about *Witness*, "in the drawing rooms, around the dinner tables and during the cocktail hours among the 'better people'— 'too emotional,' 'long and repetitious,' 'one of those anti-Communist things.'" The snobs would hate the damn thing, Nixon reasoned. They'd chitchat, in whispered and prurient tones, about that "fat repulsive little creature who said those terrible things about a 100 percent certified gentleman, Alger Hiss." But that was exactly why, Nixon reasoned, the book would sell well and be heralded as great. Because, just like the reactions in the highbrow press that *My Son John* garnered, the book's critical reception illustrated, in the words of *Life* magazine, the huge "gulf . . . between Chambers and his more sophisticated audience." Yes, Nixon would say, and which side of that gulf was preferable? The cocktail set would reject a man poorly dressed and rumpled as quickly as it would reject the heartfelt emotions and religious faith of those deemed unsophisticated. Nixon knew which side he was on.[31]

The Republican Party began to split open, the way Tom Dewey anticipated it might, from May 25 to 27 in the muggy town of Mineral Wells, Texas, during a statewide Republican Party convention. The event erupted into fistfights, caterwauls, sweaty panic, and the summoning of armed deputies. On one side of the split stood about two hundred fifty Texans, all of them chosen in precinct meetings to come to Mineral Wells, where they sweated and shouted about "a steal" and "Rob with Bob!" They walked out of the hall where they had gathered to listen to a Reverend Carrington grace their cause with a prayer: "We like Ike. God likes Ike. We will nominate and elect him." On the other side of the split were those who remained in the hall, disgusted by their enemies leaving behind a *real* Republican for a Deweyite phony named Eisenhower (some called him "Eisen-hewey"). They stood with their man, the senator from Ohio, Robert (Bob) Taft. They, too, had been chosen in precinct meetings, and some of them swung their fists at the Ike supporters, whom they con-sidered fake Republicans.[32]

Ever since his supporters placed his hat into the ring of the New Hampshire primary earlier in 1952—a primary he won with delight and surprise—Dwight Eisenhower had watched from abroad in Europe as the enmity of the Taftites in the Republican Party grew fiercer. Though Ike also showed very well in the Minnesota primary as a write-in candidate, losing to the state's native son Harold Stas-sen but beating Taft, most of the energy in other state primaries, in-cluding Joe McCarthy's state of Wisconsin, went to the senator from Ohio. A report from the Associated Press on May 18 showed Taft leading Ike, 374 to 337 in delegates. So now a state like Texas, which hadn't elected a Republican to the presidency since 1928, started to matter simply in terms of how many delegates were sent either Ike's or Taft's way. Not usually a state Republicans took seriously because of its heavy Democratic leanings, it became a hotbed of Republican Party quarrels in May.[33]

Taft had energized his side of the aisle for this battle over the heart and mind of the Republican Party. He was well defined, not all soft around the edges the way Ike appeared. He gave his supporters reasons to get up and fight. He'd been an old-school isolationist dur-ing World War II, opposing FDR's Lend-Lease package that provided early support to England against the Fascist powers before America officially entered the war. Taft even used the word "imperialism" to describe FDR's foreign policy. After the war, Taft criticized economic support for Europe, calling the Marshall Plan—the initiative Rich-ard Nixon endorsed, to the chagrin of his own supporters—a "vast give-away program" and "European TVA" (meaning the Tennessee Valley Authority, the New Deal agency that brought low-cost electricity to poor Appalachians and that conservative Republicans loved to hate). Taft became more schizoid as the Cold War proceeded, as did his party, voting against the North Atlantic Treaty Organization, a vote that prompted Ike to consider running against him in the first place, but eager to extend U.S. military aid to Formosa and seconding General MacArthur's call to expand American power in Korea and throughout Asia. Most explained this contradiction— zilch for Europe, full-on for Asia—as galloping along with the right wing of his own party. Taft felt the winds of change. When Joseph McCarthy moved into the limelight, the senator from Ohio panicked about his scattershot accusations about Communists lurking everywhere, but then he opened the floodgates by suggesting to Joe in March 1950: "Keep talking, and if one case doesn't work out, proceed with another." Which was just what McCarthy was doing and did. *Let your party take you where it takes you* appeared to be Taft's modus operandi. So long as it sharpened the difference with the other side of the aisle.[34]

Many perceived Taft as a rabid anti–New Dealer throughout the dark years of the 1930s. And although he picked and chose what he did and didn't like from FDR's smorgasbord of programs, he proffered fiery rhetoric when desired: "The New Dealers are proposing a totalitarian state which they have today in Russia." That sounded like the rhetoric Whittaker Chambers would offer, except the lines were uttered when the onetime spy was still shedding his red diapers. After the war, Taft opposed price controls and labor unions, crafting the Taft-Hartley Act, which started to repeal the power organized labor had accrued since the New Deal's Wagner Act of 1935. He single-mindedly led the charge against Truman and Fair Deal liberals to the point that in 1947 the *New Republic* referred to Congress as "the House, the Senate, and Bob Taft." He ran for the nomination in 1948, arguing he was more principled than Dewey (he had tried as early as 1940 for the nomination). Now, in 1952, Taft trumpeted his steadfastness to criticize reascendant Deweyism in his own party. Taft rejected the Republican Party's desire to appear more sympathetic to the center of the political aisle or to Democratic Party policies extending from the New Deal—slamming a "me-too" attitude on the part of some Republicans. He explained that he didn't "believe the New Deal wing of the Republican Party can guide the party to victory in the future any more than in the past." He argued that he'd serve as a true Republican, representing "a vast majority of the party who believe that victory can only be achieved by presenting our principles and program clearly to the people, without modifying those principles to secure the votes of New Dealers." Taft's fans believed that the senator from Ohio offered not just antigovernment sentiment but disdain for big business and Wall Street. Ike was too chummy with bankers and the CEOs of large businesses (for instance, he befriended the chairmen of U.S. Steel and Coca-Cola). The conservative magazine *Human Events* praised Taft's slogan— "Wall Street for Eisenhower, Main Street for Taft"—while also reminding its readers of the fact that Ike had voted for FDR in 1944. Taft was a man to scream and fight for, a *real* Republican.[35]

His devotees had to love his ideas and his steadfastness, because the man himself wasn't easy to love. He had the face of a frog. His jowls were bigger than Nixon's and his teeth stuck out in a strange way. Referring to his bald head, the British critic Alistair Cooke called him a "grapefruit with glasses on." Or rather a grapefruit balanced on top of a giant pear whose wide middle was hard to miss. He was shy and cold, no glad-hander. His speeches stank; he moved way too fast through them, 150 words a minute by some estimates. Where Dewey had East Coast charm, Taft had Midwestern plainness. He was no small-guy backslapper, like Nixon. He had been the son of a U.S. president (inheriting a sense of dynasty) and had grown up comfortable in an upper-class family from Cincinnati, Ohio, going to Yale and then Harvard Law School. He developed a sense of intellectual supremacy over the years. His political rigidity eschewed any spiritual sentimentalism. He spent, by many estimates, more time on the golf course on Sunday mornings than in church. And he brought his mechanical view of the world to the campaign he was now engaging. At the end of May, he told a reporter: "The campaign has gone just about as we programmed it." The reporter who recorded these words noticed a "tautness" in Taft's responses to critical questions from the press as the campaign proceeded.[36]

Texas, though, posed a problem to Taft's programming (he visited the state in March to try to sew up his support). Texas's Republican Party had grown provincial, ossified, and machinelike, and it was not normally paid much national attention, seeing as it was such a minority party. The state's party officials and leaders were almost all hard-core Taftites. But as the party started to hold precinct meetings to choose delegates on May 2, the leadership faced an onrush of pro-Eisenhower supporters. To try to stem this invasion of what they perceived as fake Republicans (sometimes called "one-day Republicans") choosing delegates, state officials constructed a "good faith" pledge that proclaimed a citizen voting for a delegate would also vote a straight Republican ticket in the general election. But Ike supporters refused to sign the pledge, and H. J. (Jack) Porter, a wealthy Houston oil industry man who was supporting Eisenhower, took out advertisements in newspapers across the state stating: "You can vote in both Democratic and Republican elections—do not be intimidated." So the precinct meetings became chaotic events, split very often between Taft supporters, who considered themselves real Republicans, and Ike supporters, who believed they had just as much a right to participate in choosing the next president of the United States. This set the stage for the statewide conflict about to occur in Mineral Wells.[37]

Henry (Harry) Zweifel was the leader of the Taftites and a National Committee Party leader from Fort Worth. He was chunky and mean-looking, with a propensity to sweat and get angry. And he really hated the fakers entering the ranks of the Republicans. He had a theory about what was going on in Texas. Ike's nomination, he'd tell reporters who cared to ask, was "backed by the Communist *Daily Worker*," and if that wasn't bad enough, "by the Political Action Committee of the Congress of Industrial Organizations." Zweifel's supporters sometimes suggested other explanations, blaming the "New Deal section of the Republican Party" for backing Ike. As the editors of the conservative magazine *Human Events* explained, Zweifel and his type were rejecting a "brazen attempt by Democrats to capture the Republican primary in Texas." Going into the convention, the question for them was: "Whether or not the GOP will become de facto an arm of a permanent Democratic Administration. The battle here is something like one of those European political imbroglios in which the Communists infiltrate and take over a local Democratic Party." Another Taft supporter told the journalist Joseph Alsop that there was a whole other "explanation" for the attempted Ike takeover, "but I can't give it you." It was that bad. What the Taftites could all agree upon, as Zweifel explained, was that they'd "rather lose with Bob Taft than win with Eisenhower." Remaining pure to principles was far better than winning elections. The man was juiced with the idea of booting out all the Ike supporters who came to Mineral Wells, and he held the gavel that would govern the convention.[38]

Zweifel refused to seat the Eisenhower delegates, churning up fights on the floor and then forcing Ike supporters out of the hall. That was just fine with Harry, who bellowed to those remaining behind: "It's wonderful to see you real, wonderful, outstanding, one hundred percent Americans out there before me." Still, Zweifel's iron fist and the fists flying on the floor hadn't settled anything. Ike supporters knew everything would be revisited at the national convention. The lockout had garnered national press attention. The political journalist and columnist Joseph Alsop went to Mineral Wells and instantly played up the idea of a "steal" orchestrated by the "Zweifel-Taft stooges." Soon after the Mineral Wells incident, governors across the country gathered in Houston and expressed concern: "We believe that if contested delegations are permitted to vote on the seating of other contested state delegations, the Republican Party will enter a vital and difficult campaign under a serious moral cloud." A photo spread in *Life* a little more than a week after the event showed the fisticuffs to its national readership. Though Zweifel was just doing what was in his authority (setting rules for his party), it was the Eisenhower side that sounded as though it occupied the high moral ground, based on its call for open participation in electoral processes. Whatever the case, the conclusion was obvious: *Settle it at the convention, boys.* Fisticuffs couldn't solve the presidential nomination of 1952. The stakes were too high. Still, the Taft fan club could take some joy from where things stood by the end of May. On May 26, the *Washington Post* counted 399 delegates for Taft, 359 for Ike. The Taftites looked to be slouching toward victory, after the fistfights broke up.[39]

Dwight Eisenhower would no longer have to wear a military uniform after June 1, 1952, but could now fit into a gray flannel suit. The commander of NATO troops would leave Europe that day and fly to the United States—abroad, a soldier, but back on American soil, a citizen and hero, someone called back to campaign for the presidency, having had others put his hat in the early race and having watched the conflicts with the Taftites in the Republican Party from abroad. When the press caught up to him as he walked to his plane with his wife, Mamie, he appeared a little sad, knowing that another chapter of his life was ending. The French defense minister, René Pleven, joined him at Orly Airfield in Paris and gave him a marvelous sendoff. "France . . . will always keep in her heart the memory of what you have done for their liberation. She will also recall," Pleven went on, "like all free people, that it is to you she owes the solid foundation of this Atlantic defense community on which depends the security and peace of Europe." This was no ordinary man leaving Paris, but a five-star general filled with good graces, having helped win World War II and then staking a claim to unify Europe for the sake of fighting the Cold War. No wonder his homecoming would be televised.[40]

Dwight Eisenhower, unlike Robert Taft, had been a career military man, ever since he left his devout, religious family and small town of Abilene, Kansas, to study at West Point. A long career it was. He almost got to serve in World War I, but as he was about to leave for France, the war ended. His military career became more about bureaucracy and management than frontline fighting. Ike served as an aide to the chief of staff, General Douglas MacArthur, and then to his real hero and model, General George Marshall. ("I wouldn't trade one Marshall for fifty MacArthurs," Ike said once, which would not sit well among some Republicans.) Eisenhower rose in stature throughout World War II, eventually serving as commander of U.S. troops in England and then leading the strike to take northern Africa back from the Italians. His biggest accomplishment, though, came with the Overlord operation and D-Day, plotting out the final liberation of Europe from Fascism. The French defense minister had been right to thank Ike for his country's liberation, and the British prime minister, Clement Attlee, did not entirely exaggerate in calling the general "the man who won the war."[41]

The transition from hot to cold war required Ike to shuttle between soldier and citizen. He served as chief of staff under Truman as demobilization began. Then, in 1948, in what some took as a curious move, he became president of Columbia University in New York City. It wasn't a good fit, this military man trundling into a world of professors and eggheads, many of whom doubted his intelligence, or at least his sophistication (Ike seemed to love western pulp novels and golf more than the world of ideas). Some Columbia faculty joked they couldn't send Ike a memo longer than a page since "his lips would get tired." The hostility was mutual, for Ike came to distrust the airy elitism of egghead professors and to hate the university's bureaucracy, something he thought he had left behind after leaving the Army. He was therefore more than happy to accept Harry Truman's offer to become an informal adviser to the Joint Chiefs of Staff in 1949 and then, a year later, to command NATO forces abroad. He accepted the task of serving his country when called upon by his "superiors." And so, while remaining president of Columbia University at least in name, he embarked for Europe, only to hear over and over how people wanted him to return home and run for president. As late as January 1, 1952, Ike could write President Truman that after leaving his perch at NATO, he wanted to live "a semi-retired life with my family, given over mainly to the study of, and a bit of writing on, present day trends and problems, with a little dirt farming thrown in on the side." Sure, he admitted that "circumstances may not permit" him to do what he wanted. Nonetheless, "the possibility that I will ever be drawn into political activity is so remote as to be negligible." That was Ike. He loved to create, in his own words, an "aura of mystery" about his intentions. Those who knew him fairly well could see through the act. Soon after World War II, MacArthur, of all people, had a dinner party for Ike in Japan. MacArthur started to josh him that one of them would become president. Ike got angry that Mac would project political ambitions onto him. He said he had no desire to run for office. MacArthur sidled up to him, put his hand on his knee, and said, "That's all right, Ike. You go on like that and you'll get it for sure."[42]

It was that aura of being a soldier above politics that drove the excitement about him back home. He could be the general on a white horse come to save the republic from ruin, plotting out his own version of D-Day-like redemption. So thought the Alsop brothers—Stewart (Stew) and Joseph (Joe), who were impeccable Establishment journalists and commentators during the golden age of the newspaper column. They had been brought up pampered and wealthy in Connecticut, raised Republican, and educated at Groton and Yale and Harvard. They lived in the posh Georgetown neighborhood of Washington, D.C., where they could hobnob with the political elite and write their sophisticated commentaries for newspapers across the country. Joseph Alsop was especially suave with a slightly aristocratic sensibility, not the traditional gumshoe style of most journalists. He was worried about the "primitives" in the Republican party, especially Joe McCarthy, who had accused Alsop of being gay (which he was). Joseph was the sort of Republican who believed Ike could save the party from its worst tendencies. With his brother, he pronounced Eisenhower "the most effective political personality to emerge on the American scene since the death of Franklin Delano Roosevelt." Ike could come back from Europe and unify the country by rising above political pressures.[43]

The man who really played this theme up was Walter Lippmann, perhaps the most famous commentator in newsprint at the time. Lippmann had grown up wealthy on Lexington Avenue in Manhattan during the early years of the twentieth century, living a pampered life of maids and caretakers in a family of assimilated Jews. He attended Harvard, but then drifted into radical orbits, becoming a young socialist. Helping to start up the left-leaning magazine the *New Republic* just before U.S. entry into World War I, he drifted to the center and tried to connect with powerful people who could win public office. He bounced from supporting Teddy Roosevelt to Woodrow Wilson and then grew alienated from the conservative politics of the 1920s. Though he liked some elements of FDR's New Deal, he distrusted the president's penchant for centralizing executive power, especially when he tried to pack the Supreme Court with supporters. By the late 1930s, Lippmann was a moderate conservative, a man who held to principles and liked to dabble in abstractions but also loved to rub shoulders with political leaders and journalists (including the Alsops) in the Georgetown social scene that furthered his insider's sensibility. Though he believed America had a role to play in the world, he worried that Truman's vision of the Cold War was too belligerent. He even called upon Dean Acheson to resign, not because he hated him the way McCarthy and Nixon did, but because "no man ought to be secretary of state who does not have the confidence of the substantial majority of Congress." It was all about having authoritative leadership. Lippmann, though, would never move from criticizing Acheson into the arms of Robert Taft's Asian interventionism. He was a moderate at heart who wanted to save the Republican Party from its own yahoos, and a believer that only a man with great leadership responsibilities in the past could unify the nation in the present. By first appearances, Dwight Eisenhower was tailor-made for Lippmann's hopes.[44]

In the spring and summer of 1952, Lippmann would admire a hero whose blemishes he couldn't help notice. The day Ike arrived in the United States, the pundit explained the historic nature of the arrival: "Eisenhower is in the unique position of being the only available public man who has a reasonable prospect of bringing about a Republican victory which will unite the Nation." Lippmann feared that the Republican Party was becoming increasingly marginalized thanks to boobs like Joseph McCarthy and Robert Taft. Ike is "not snarled up with all the issues that are dividing and embittering our people," Lippmann rejoiced. Of course, there was a danger, in that Eisenhower would be pressed to "say and . . . do all sorts of things in order to make it easier to get the necessary delegates." And Lippmann, like many others, worried that the general was not politically astute.

He recalled earlier conversations with Eisenhower in which the general asked him: "You don't suppose a man could ever be nominated by both parties, do you?" Being above politics brought dangers.[45]

So as Eisenhower's plane touched down in D.C., journalists awaited his arrival with anticipation. He met quickly with Truman to review the situation with NATO, attended some public ceremonies in the nation's capital, and then headed out to Abilene, Kansas, his hometown of about seven thousand citizens who grew overwhelmed by the press trucks and television cameras that descended on June 4. Ike would dedicate a library in his name and make a speech kicking off his candidacy. Unfortunately, just as he was about to mount the podium, buckets of rain dumped from the sky. He had to roll up his trousers and put on a bulky raincoat. He could barely read the speech as his "glasses fogged up" and dripped rain. Reading speeches was never really his forte, anyway. This one sounded like Tom Dewey, platitudinous and dull. "Political health is endangered if one party, by whatever means, becomes permanently or too long entrenched in power," Ike explained, which didn't sound like much of a passionate endorsement of his own party, more negative than positive. He took aim at the things no one liked: inflation, taxes, and bureaucracy. The *Washington Post*, a paper that would endorse Ike for the presidency later, said there was an "overgeneralized flavor" to his speech.[46]

Lippmann, too, was disappointed. But he retained his cheer and hope. One week after the Abilene performance, he argued that the general's "smiling good nature is not an act" but the "outer sign of a person who has been through the great tests of life." He may not have been wonderful at the speech or press conference that followed, Lippmann admitted, but that didn't negate his amazing potential. "What Eisenhower is offering the country is a chance to rally and gather together, and by this very rallying and gathering together to find the way to solve problems and to overcome dangers that are insoluble and overwhelming as long as the country remains so divided." Besides, Eisenhower could save the Republican Party from the Taftites, who were presently "trying to stampede the uncommitted delegates by making it appear that Taft is in such full control that he does not any longer need to pay attention to the Eisenhower men." Unfortunately, Eisenhower might not have recognized the importance of the moment; he seemed "distracted," walking into the game of politics unaware of its perils. Still, the general benefited from being above it all. He was not a "strict Republican" with a rigid "line." Ike could appeal—in a way Taft never could—to "a great popular majority in this country today who are moderate in their views and conciliatory in their temper."[47]

That was the flip side of the case Taft made for himself: that he was the real and authentic Republican who wouldn't fall prey to me-tooism or phoniness or playing to a mushy center. Lippmann would counter—as would many others who pointed to polling done on the issue—that Ike could win votes not just from conservative Republicans but from independents and some Democrats. That would be the debate the GOP would take up at their convention come July, a debate of electability versus authenticity. At this time, though, Ike didn't seem to have a lot to show for his high-road policy of being the general on the white horse reluctantly accepting political responsibility. The *Washington Post* learned on June 8 that the delegates lined up 462 for Taft, 390 for Ike.[48]

As spring turned to summer, Richard Nixon followed those delegate counts closely. He had his own problem in California. His state lined up, already by its primary on June 3, for its favorite son—Earl Warren, currently governor and earlier Tom Dewey's vice-presidential candidate in 1948. Warren had no chance of winning the nomination straight off the bat in 1952, but the governor figured if he held his own delegates and waited out what appeared an inevitable split

between Ike and Taft, he just might appear a sensible candidate and
drive up the center to mend the divide and seize the prize.

Nixon was in a rough spot but making the best of it. He had never
gotten along with Warren, who refused during his own campaigns for
governor in 1946 and 1950 to assist the young man in his own election
prospects. Warren was much more a centrist than Nixon. Indeed,
in 1951, Nixon had publicly doubted Warren was ready to put on a
"fighting drive" and "hit hard on major issues" if he ran for president.
Now, in 1952, Nixon found Warren stubborn, wasting the large number of delegates California could bring to the convention for lever-
age. But being a loyal California Republican—a good "organization
man"—Nixon had to say, at least, that he, too, was a Warren man.[49]

Richard Nixon became an "inside dopester." That was a term
coined by David Riesman, the sociologist and author of the landmark
book *The Lonely Crowd* (1950) and the follow-up, *Faces in the Crowd*
(1952). It referred to someone who enjoyed following a good horse
race in politics and gossiping about candidates. Nixon created some
of his own gossip at the time. On June 11, he sent out 23,000 copies
of a letter addressed to numerous delegates and those who supported
his campaigns in the past (he used his franking privilege, which gave
senators free use of the mail at taxpayers' expense). The letter was coy
and in the know. It asked: What should Warren do once—not *if*—he
released his delegates? To whom should those delegates go? Not whom
do you support in the upcoming election, but who is "the strongest
candidate the Republicans could nominate for president." Nixon
wanted to know who had made the better impression and who was
more electable. He assured respondents that their "reply will be for
my information only and will be held in confidence." Consider this
insider trading, he suggested. Nixon wasn't entirely honest, since once
the mail piled up on his desk throughout the month of June, he leaked
to journalists that Eisenhower was doing better than Taft (he was
convinced, as were many, that Taft was unelectable). This made

Warren seethe, Taft grow angry, and the Ike people smile. Getting
wind that Warren was miffed, Nixon calmed the situation, saying he
wouldn't release the poll numbers, keeping the inside dope to himself, but still hinting here and there that Ike was doing well. He told
one person who inquired, after ten days of being deluged with mail,
"I, of course, must remain neutral until Warren releases the Delegation." As a seasoned poker player, he knew not to overplay his hand.[50]

Richard Nixon made coyness an art form. He had already shown
off the skills when appearing with Tom Dewey at the Waldorf-Astoria.
But the informal poll and his positioning now made him a new
behind-the-scenes man—the sort who took "good fun," as David
Riesman put it, in the "hobby" of politics. The inside dopester, for
Riesman, was a man who "cannot change the others who dominate
his political attention," so his "characterological drive leads him to
manipulate himself in order not to change the others but to resemble
them." The inside dopester "tends to know a great deal about what
other people are doing and thinking in the important or 'great-issue'
spheres of life; he is politically cosmopolitan rather than parochial. . . .
He will go to great lengths to keep from looking and feeling like the
uninformed outsider." Picking up this highfalutin thinking, a writer
for the *New York Times* explained that the "inside dopester" was one for
whom "no backstage maneuver is opaque . . . no deal without its ex-
otic explanation. Like the political columnist who must elucidate all
but never be committed, they are tremendously expert but bound to
inaction." Ironically, Riesman and the *New York Times* reporter who
glossed his ideas thought that the inside dopester was usually a spec-
tator in politics, but Nixon found a way to bring the ethic into back-
room politics itself—to a game that had huge national consequences.
He had followed the horse race of politics, and he knew the players
and was ready to gossip about their strengths and weaknesses. He
was enjoying hiding his cards. He was the new white-collar man in
politics—like those he had appealed to in 1946 and the small guy

and middleman he portrayed himself to be in 1950. Their world, and his, was about making the right impression and not getting suckered by anyone. He knew how to please his potential future boss, playing his cues but not too much. Nixon was one of the "new little Machiavellians" populating America in larger numbers that Riesman's fellow sociologist, C. Wright Mills, discussed in his book *White Collar* (1951).[51]

He could head into the summer as all things to all people. Officially he was a Warren man, but he was in secret communication with the Ike people. "The Taft people tended to be organization-minded," Nixon recollected, "and they considered me to be a good organization man." That worked to keep them on board, hoping his harder-right heart might bleed their way eventually. Here was how observers recollected Nixon's positioning as spring broke to summer: "Warren didn't understand that Nixon was also working with Taft forces." Another said, "Nixon was conveying to" Senator William Knowland, the senior senator from California, "that he was for Taft. And then he was conveying to the other people he was for Ike. . . . But [Knowland] didn't grasp the situation as to what Nixon was going to do to him. See, he believed that Nixon was an honorable man." That was just how Richard Nixon wanted to come across. Not necessarily honorable, but a player who had little influence but could move behind the scenes and keep track of the horse race in order to position himself for acquiring some influence, for making it into the in-crowd. He'd keep tabs, ready for the moment to seize the prize.[52]

CHAPTER TWO

A SUMMER OF "THE GREAT SALESROOM"

Maybe it's because I sell sincerity. I can't be phony.

—JOHN WAYNE

The famous movie producer and director Cecil B. DeMille, whose days stretched back to the silent era, had traveled from Hollywood to Chicago to be at what he called "the Greatest Show on Earth." Do you mean the "*second* greatest show," a journalist asked him, playing on the title of DeMille's recent film about a traveling circus (which would win him an Oscar for Best Picture). No, "*this* is the greatest," DeMille confirmed, standing among his fellow party members at the International Amphitheatre, ready to choose a candidate for president at the Republican convention, an event that would take place over the course of the next few days, its outcome not predetermined and quite up for grabs.[1]

DeMille was joined by a slew of fellow Californians who, like the circus actors in *The Greatest Show on Earth*, made their way on a bustling train barreling through days and nights. California's Republican Party delegates boarded the *GOP*, or the *Warren Special*, as it had been christened, in the state capital of Sacramento on July 3, a day when the inside of the train felt "hotter than the hinges of hell." On Independence Day, it had conquered the Sierra Nevada and moved into the Rocky Mountains, arriving in Denver. But here it took longer than expected to pull out. A surprise guest was taken on board, one Richard Nixon, who had flown all the way from Chicago and who would return to that city on the train. He rushed aboard, brushed aside Governor Earl Warren, and then headed up and down the aisles chatting with delegates. A journalist recalled "Nixon . . . beaming and shaking hands with everybody. You'd have thought *he* was the candidate." Some wondered where he had been and why he had appeared out of nowhere. He was now sharing with the delegates on board what his personal poll had made clear: that Warren had no chance and that Ike was building steam. Having come from Chicago, he explained that Taft was going to face a fight about seating those delegates who had come to fisticuffs in Texas earlier in May. He reminded the delegates that, being so populous, California could play a huge role if it swung to Ike. He spoke like a true inside dopester, with certainty about his gossip: *I've watched this thing,* he suggested, *and I know where you want to be.* Then a backslap or handshake to make the point firmer. The inside dopester turned into an "other-directed" maven. As some watched Nixon play the delegates and heard Governor Warren fuming, they started to talk about "the great train robbery."[2]

When the locomotive finally arrived in Chicago, after days of travel, buses awaited to take delegates to the Amphitheatre or their hotel rooms. But the buses were festooned with EISENHOWER FOR PRESIDENT banners and paraphernalia. Aides swooped off the trains, ran to the buses, and ripped down those signs to put up their own reading WARREN FOR PRESIDENT. The man who had arranged for the buses was Nixon's confidant, Murray Chotiner, who personally hated Warren and had told Nixon that he had to board the *GOP* in the first place to get delegates moving in the right direction toward the convention. The events of that train ride provided smoke signals about both Nixon's and Warren's fate as they entered the Greatest Show on Earth.[3]

A revolution had occurred: For the first time ever in convention history, there'd be no sweating. A delegate could leave behind the smells of Chicago's stockyards and gasoline trapped by skyscrapers and enter a cocoon of climate control and air-conditioning. Recognizing that Republicans and Democrats would hold their conventions in succession in the same building, the Carrier Corporation ran an advertisement showing an elephant (Republican) and donkey (Democrat) shaking hands in a large convention hall, sweat-free and basking in "comfort." The comfort in the convention hall reflected the comfort in the nation as a whole. For 1952 became a year when the Carrier Corporation's sales of air conditioners ballooned to "more than one hundred million dollars" and in which "push-button weather" became the rage in many American homes. In the case of the conventions, air-conditioning not only provided ease but measured democratic energy: Some journalists read the excitement in the Amphitheatre in accord with how heavily the air-conditioning motors were pumping—when body heat went up, so did the motors to cool the floor. This was democracy in action, with the reward of cool comfort.[4]

Another revolution had occurred: A person need not be at the International Amphitheatre to catch the show. They could watch the whole thing at home. In the words of the writer Bruce Bliven, 1952 was "the year that television came to politics," the first year the entirety of the Republican and Democratic conventions appeared on screen (versus 1948, when only portions of the conventions made it on air). *Newsweek* reported: "More than 60,000,000 people were looking at the Republican convention this week—more people than have ever before seen any event while it was taking place." That caught the original excitement of America's dawning mass culture—millions of eyes focused on one thing and the possibility of a great deliberative moment moving across the nation as crowds of Americans assessed their future leaders. The politicos duly noted this. Ike's campaign strategists observed that "television sets are being purchased at the rate of a half million per month," using the passive voice perhaps to give a sense of the deluge of the tube in Americans' lives. Ike's support- ers also noticed that televisions were more prevalent in the East— where reception was much better—and thus reaching the sort of viewer more favorable to their side than Taft's.[5]

The television had already become the great rearranger in Amer- icans' lives by the summer of 1952. It had changed the ordering of furniture in most Americans' living rooms, moving front and center. Newer ranch houses in America's suburbs were built with a space purposely intended for televisions to be installed. Televisions started looking more and more like furniture themselves. Some had little cabinets below them or shelves on the side. Companies offered models with chipper names: Du Mont, for instance, offered the Milford ("con- temporary"), the Beverly ("modern"), the Clinton and the Dynasty (with their "Chippendale cabinet of mahogany veneers"). Television— with the assistance of its brethren, the modern refrigerator and freezer—even rearranged the way Americans ate. By 1951, there was something called a FrigiDinner that offered consumers frozen "vari- ety platters," kept in the freezer and then pulled out to cook, ready to be eaten in front of the television. Indeed, the Philadelphia company offering the FrigiDinner also rented television sets (in 1953, the pack- age was officially put together as the "TV dinner" by Swanson).[6]

The power of television, in its first year of domination, had already transformed the conventions. The International Amphitheatre was chosen for its ability to fit the television cameras and equipment neces- sary to broadcast live. The traditional red, white, and blue on banners now became "quiet greys and blues (which show up more sharply on TV)." Delegates who went to their seats found notes: *Don't read the newspaper* and *Don't fall asleep.* Floor participants feared "the peepie-creepie," a camera whose operator could sneak up on unsuspecting delegates and catch them shouting until they were red in the face or making physical gestures about the speeches they listened to.[7]

Journalists found the changes especially stark. Not only was there a lounge in the convention hall "with free beer, cigars, and three large television sets" available to them, but, like other Americans, they needn't go to the Amphitheatre to watch. In fact, this would be the first year Walter Lippmann decided against attending the conventions, opting for coverage on the screen. He'd occasionally call journalists who had walked the floor, when they were safely back in their hotel rooms, to get some insider information. But for the most part he found television viewing sufficient to figure out what was going on. Joe and Stew Alsop, who decided they still had to be at the site of action, didn't want to change their ways, which included imbibing alcohol while reporting. They somehow pulled this off without a hitch during the Republican convention, but when it came to the Democratic convention just a few days later, they had to rig a line upon which a friend would sling down a huge flask when requested. The Alsops had forgotten about the television cameras, and when the activity was captured live, Joe Alsop admitted to an "unbecoming posture," albeit "amusing." What the Alsops might not have noted was that there was a new key to success: how well a journalist could play to television cameras, not to print. It was during the Republican convention that a new tele-journalist gained prominence. Walter Cronkite's instantaneous commentary from the floor—which circumvented the delay of pecking out a column or story on a typewriter—made him appear more the future of the press than the Alsops or Lippmann.[8]

Some believed television made the whole idea of a journalist or commentator outmoded. What need for reporters when people could watch for themselves? Less mediation meant more truth. You couldn't *watch* politicians on the radio, just listen to their disembodied voices, but now you could scrutinize body language on the screen and read character. Orrin Dunlap at the *New York Times* concluded from this that "trickery has less chance to operate." Other optimists believed only sincere politicians would dominate in the age of television. As the perpetually optimistic *Life* magazine explained, "Television enables the performer with poise and personality to drive home his arguments as casually and as powerfully as if he were in his audience's parlor." *Life* showed this in a treatment of Senator William Benton from Connecticut—a chief critic of Joseph McCarthy and a politician with a background in public relations: "The performer who makes the biggest hit on TV may end up with the biggest political plum." The use of the word "performer" complicated the issue, of course, suggesting that authenticity might be the projection of those who wanted to win people over, those who had a stake in *appearing* authentic. More hopeful, if more cynical, was the vice president of Avco Manufacturing Corporation, who cautioned a journalist during a conference on advertising, "Don't vote for any candidate until you see the whites of his eyes." Seeing was believing, even if it was seeing a staged event where the actors had been prepped. Viewers could tell the authentic from the inauthentic, the reals from the fakes. Television created an army of inside dopesters reading the signs and figuring it out for themselves.[9]

Ironically, the big issue of the convention—the one that would determine its outcome—wouldn't get onto television in full. To seat the Taft delegates chosen by Harry Zweifel's machine-run Republican Party in the state of Texas or reopen the demands by the Ike supporters locked out from the Mineral Wells conflagration—*that* was the question. Going in, Taft pumped up his numbers and claimed he had 601 delegates to Ike's 361. He needed just 604 to seize the nomination, so this was sounding like a foregone conclusion. But not if some of those Taft delegates didn't count.[10]

The Eisenhower people saw their opening, and they played a good game of high-road politics to drive toward victory. On opening day, July 7, the chairman of the Republican National Committee, Guy George Gabrielson, who leaned toward Taft, gaveled the convention to order and asked if there were any motions on convention rules. There were. Governor Arthur B. Langlie of Washington, who had been at the earlier gathering of governors in Houston that condemned the shenanigans in Mineral Wells, rushed to the floor and pressed for what he called a "Fair Play" Amendment. Who could object to something called *that*? It stated that no delegates would be seated if there was any question about their legitimacy. Hard-core Taftites in the auditorium booed the amendment. They saw local control over delegate selection yielding to national power, and worse, they saw this procedural-sounding issue cloaking an Eisenhower coup. Ike's people said that the Republicans had to enter the general election with clean hands, making reform imperative. The Taftites recollected that the party was operating under the same procedures when Dewey won the contests eight and four years ago. Why change now? Fights broke out on the floor. People started to scream at one another; "points of order" were shouted out but faded into a background of cacophony. Throughout the battle, the Ike forces fought harder, and Taft's men failed to push back. The high-road approach won out, and the Fair Play (or Langlie) Amendment to the existing Republican Party nomination rules passed in a 658 to 548 vote. Ike, speaking from the Blackstone Hotel, where he was staying, praised the motion as a sign that the Republican Party now acted as an agency of fairness and honesty.[11]

Just how to sort through contested delegates from Texas (as well as Louisiana, Georgia, and Florida) was tricky business, requiring more in-depth meetings than could be had on the open floor of the convention. So the second morning, the Republican National Committee met in the North Ballroom of the Conrad Hilton. A member

called to have the meeting moved to the Boulevard Room, and so
the press got up and followed in tow. Suddenly there was a fracas,
more loud noises and shoving. "The video men—along with movie
and still photographers—were halted at the door." Another fight broke
out, with Henry Cabot Lodge, the Republican senator from Massachusetts who was spending more time on Eisenhower's campaign than
his own battle to preserve his Senate seat against the young Democratic upstart John F. Kennedy, arguing that the Taft people had
locked out television cameras, revealing their "public-be-damned"
attitude. Lodge asked: What didn't they want the American public
to see? Richard Nixon, too, was on hand, ready to talk to reporters.
He stopped playing his cards close to his chest and threw them on
the table. "The real issue is . . . whether the selection of the Republican candidate for President is to be determined by the will of the
people or by a small clique of politicians who happen to control the
party machinery," he said, sounding like an Eisenhower partisan and
a defender of television's democratic power. He had just knocked out
any chance that the Taftites still thought him a good "organization
man" on their side. That was okay; he was moving to the winning
side. He could feel it. The coup had begun.[12]

America's television audience couldn't watch all the debates about
seating delegates, but they could feast on large crowds whooping it
up for the party's showboats. That started on opening day, when the
choice of keynote speaker smacked back against Eisenhower's victory
on Fair Play. General Douglas MacArthur mounted the podium,
much to Ike's chagrin. Eisenhower thought Mac a vain prima donna
and loose cannon. Gossip on the floor was that the general would
serve as vice president on a Taft ticket (or run as his own man for the
nomination). It was precisely Ike's reservations about the old buzzard
(Mac was ten years older than Eisenhower, seventy-two at the time)

that attracted his party's right wing, including the Taftites, who still controlled the convention's proceedings. MacArthur, after all, had given it hard to both Truman and Acheson, in a way that many on the right could only dream of. He was the fighter who believed military victory was still attainable in Korea—if only Americans stood up and demanded victory. His love of a good fight to the finish certainly endeared him to the likes of Richard Nixon and Joseph McCarthy in 1951 (if not Ike), as it did to a number of whooping delegates on the floor now.[13]

And boy, could he give a speech, at least if a delegate or television viewer paid attention to his words. To cheers, he lashed out against the Truman administration's pursuit of the Korean War. "In war, there is no substitute for victory" was a line that Mac recycled over and over in talks he gave the year after being deposed by Truman. Meaning that Americans should *defeat* their enemies, not redraw and defend a line between South and North Korea but slam against the North and open a bigger war against the Chinese Communists. *Take them all out.* Now at the podium he condemned the Truman administration for being populated by weaklings, leaders who entered a war "without the will to win it." Truman and Acheson backed down when the "Communist armies of China struck" back against the United States. "Our leaders lacked the courage to fight to a military decision in Korea, even though victory was then readily within our grasp." After all, he explained, "no military problem is unsolvable." That sounded good now to a country witnessing a protracted war stalled in diplomatic negotiations. Why not move the war back to military action and finally kick some ass? Korea simply represented a situation of "Soviet ascendancy as a world power" and America's "own relative decline." Those were bummer lines, but Mac then turned around by hoping that Americans might return to good old-time religion. "Spiritual unity," Mac thundered, using the language of "crusade" that would ring throughout the convention (a theme that

Eisenhower would later pick up ad nauseam), could create "a purifi-
cation of the nation's conscience and a refortification of its will and
faith." Whittaker Chambers could have written this speech.[14]

When he came to domestic affairs, Mac kept steaming ahead. He
condemned "the schemers and planners who have infiltrated" the
ranks of the Democratic Party "to set the national course unerringly
toward the socialistic regimentation of the totalitarian state." So the
whole thing worked in tandem: Truman had sold the country out to
Communism abroad and at home. MacArthur then analogized the
Democrats to the corrupt British whom General George Washington had to depose (no self-referential wink was necessary on that
one). As if forgetting the time he inhabited, he railed against "the
very excesses and abuses for which the British Crown was indicted in
1776." Some on the floor probably thought they were watching a *real*
George Washington rallying for a revolution more than Eisenhower
ever could. Portions of the crowd whooped it up for MacArthur's
fiery words.[15]

But there were problems. MacArthur's speech wasn't as wonderful as his words suggested. First of all, it came on the heels of Ike's
daytime victory, meaning that MacArthur—who had hoped and
prayed that Ike wouldn't get the nomination—appeared hazier and
weaker. Worse, his speaking skills weren't stellar. Whenever he mentioned God (which he did many times), his voice would rise an "oc-
tave" and then "break." He seemed to think that if he jumped onto
his toes and pointed his finger up to the ceiling that his points would
be made clearer. And having just come through a rough battle on
the question of Fair Play, delegates on the floor seemed preoccupied,
talking so loudly about other affairs that they drowned the bellicose
general out at times. It was a sympathetic but tough audience.[16]

An audience, though, that played better to the younger showboat
and rising star in the ranks of the Republican Party—Senator Joseph

McCarthy, who mounted the podium two days later.* The delegates and television viewers now really witnessed the greatest show on earth. The Marine Hymn blared from the convention's loudspeakers: "From the halls of Montezuma . . ." Then a voice rang out announcing "Wisconsin's Fighting Marine." A set of serpentine dancers started to move through the floor of delegates, holding signs above their heads that bopped up and down. They were red and cut out to look like fish—an allusion to Harry Truman's comment that HUAC had been hunting down "red herrings"—with the names Hiss and Acheson on them. People were hollering as McCarthy approached the podium. His speaking style was a vast improvement on that of the general who proceeded him. The delegates cheered most lines, while still buzzing with debates about the delegate counting about to begin.[17]

The fanfare was all the more amazing considering that just two years ago, McCarthy was practically unknown. He had come from a hardscrabble farm family of eight brothers and sisters in eastern Wisconsin. "I'm just a farm boy" and "It's good to get away from Washington back here in the United States" were lines he often deployed in his political speeches. Elements of his biography were akin to Nixon's. McCarthy had worked once as a manager of a small grocery store. He was unattractive, "barrel-chested and short armed with thick eyebrows and heavy lips." He never made the Ivy Leagues, getting his law degree from Marquette University in Wisconsin and then settling down as a small-town lawyer (unlike Nixon, he was good at handling divorce cases). After serving in World War II, he came into his Senate position in 1946, the same year Nixon won his

---

* The night before McCarthy, the crowds had cheered Herbert Hoover, a man whose legacy the Democrats would soon try to pin on the Republicans during the general election.

first national office as part of the sweep of Republicans angry at
Truman's presidency and postwar price controls. When running
against Howard J. McMurray, an egghead who had taught political
science at the University of Wisconsin, McCarthy called his opponent "Communistically inclined." Once in office, McCarthy fought
overregulation of the sugar industry, winning the nickname "Pepsi-
Cola Joe." Recognizing his other favored private enterprise, Stewart
Alsop described him as "the big, raw-boned pride and joy of the real
estate lobby."[18]

But therein lay his problem: He was a typical Republican with no
particular identity or oomph. He needed an issue, which he got by
famously waving sheets of paper in Wheeling, West Virginia, on
February 9, 1950, very soon after Alger Hiss was convicted of perjury. McCarthy alleged that the State Department was still full of
Communists. The numbers he claimed slid around. But no matter.
Suddenly, a Republican Party star was born, the true barrel-chested
Commie fighter. It was around now that his friendship and political
alliance with Richard Nixon (and Whittaker Chambers) began.

By the time he came to the convention, though, his 1950 burst of
luster had worn off. The Tydings Committee in the Senate had investigated his claims and found them "the most nefarious campaign
of half-truths and untruths." Soon thereafter, Senator William Benton
of Connecticut was calling for his ouster. And then came lawsuits:
McCarthy sued Benton, with pretrial hearings starting in June 1952.
Joe went to court and waved copies of the *Daily Worker*, the Communist Party rag, arguing that Benton, a successful advertising
agency man in the 1920s who had worked at the University of Chicago in the 1930s before joining McCarthy in the Senate, was a Communist. Or might as well have been: "I don't accuse Benton of being
a deliberate tool of the Communist Party, but he is doing as much
damage as if he were." McCarthy would then have to shuttle to another courtroom, where he was the defendant in a suit brought by

the liberal journalist and columnist Drew Pearson, who had pressed a $5,100,000 "assault libel conspiracy suit." Pearson accused McCarthy of getting newspapers to drop his column, trying to drive him out of business. He also claimed to have persistent headaches ever since Joseph McCarthy had attacked him, striking him and then kneeing him in the groin back in December 1950. That was a fight Richard Nixon single-handedly broke up by running to the scene at the Sulgrave Club in Washington, D.C., pulling McCarthy off Pearson and yelling "Let a good Quaker stop this fight!" But it was hard to pull Joe out of fights, especially as they spilled over into the courts.[19]

The litigious nature of Joseph McCarthy's recent career made him appear murky. The convention provided an opportunity to define just who he was, to remind people he represented something more than just his lone self, that he signified a phenomenon that had ignited a movement, like that set out in his recent book, *McCarthyism: The Fight for America*. A book by McCarthy entitled *McCarthyism* was a statement in itself (and also a giveaway that others had written it). After all, no one spoke about anything called Eisenhowerism, Nixonism, Taftism, or Trumanism. But as early as 1950, there *was* something called McCarthyism, a term first utilized by the political cartoonist Herb Block just a month after McCarthy's speech in Wheeling. McCarthyism had become bigger than the man himself, probably the biggest brand in American politics at the time.[20]

If distilled to its essence and read in the pages of his book, McCarthyism meant tying the Communist conspiracy to the very highest echelons of power in America. Earlier, McCarthy had argued, much to the disgust of Dwight Eisenhower, that General George Marshall "made common cause with Stalin on the strategy of [World War II] and marched side by side with him thereafter." Now, Joe wrote in his book that the Marshall Plan "consisted of giving the maximum economic aid with a minimum of military aid" to Europe. "The Marshall Plan fitted perfectly with Communist Russia's desire for a power

vacuum in all of Western Europe." The men at the top were selling
out the small guy at the bottom, allowing Communism to spread.
This idea, combined with the use of hyperbolic language, provided
McCarthyism's followers with entertainment value. McCarthy had a
knack for over-the-top accusations that defied belief. When he attacked Acheson, for instance, McCarthy had a field day with crazy
comparisons: Acheson had never been "convicted of treason," so,
McCarthy asked, why bother attacking him? (That's how McCarthy
had others write his book: answering questions posed by himself.)
Well, there is "no more a valid argument" that men like Acheson "are
fit to represent this country in its fight against Communism than the
argument that a person who has a reputation of consorting with
criminals, hoodlums, gamblers, and kidnappers is fit to act as your
baby sitter, because he has never been convicted of a crime." Most of
all, McCarthyism meant the word found in the book's subtitle: a *fight*.
If you wanted to tear down the Communist conspiracy, you had to
slug it out, be tough, be armed if you could, or at least kick your enemy
in the groin. As one of his press releases read: "Senator Joe McCarthy
fights like a real American." The point was the fight—it mattered
more than the ends.[21]

His convention speech made clear how popular his appeal still
was (Taft pleaded for the senator's endorsement, which McCarthy
refused). McCarthy used his celebrity status to put on a marvelous
show for the delegates. As he spat out his lines, he pecked his head
into the air to accentuate his rhetoric. While the fans clapped, he
would take a break to lick the inside of his mouth, seeming to suffer
from dehydration (likely due to his high alcohol consumption). He
started by calling Douglas MacArthur "one of the greatest Americans ever born." That allowed him to rail against the Truman administration's "limited war in Korea." It was "limited, my friends, to
the area to which the Communists wanted it limited—limited as to
honor, but unlimited as to dishonor; unlimited as to the amount of

blood and agony and tears that they have squandered and will squander; unlimited as to the number of American mothers and wives who shall go so deep into the valley of darkness and despair." In contrast to MacArthur, the Truman administration was a bunch of sissies. They would hit Communists "with a perfumed silk handkerchief at the front door while they batter our friends with brass knuckles and blackjacks at the back door." He started to sound like a football coach telling his players to go out and *fight, fight, fight!*[22]

McCarthy, who knew something about political rhetoric and who was a superb campaign stump speaker, built to a crescendo. Perhaps he now remembered the mistake made in Wheeling when he committed himself to something Richard Nixon warned against—the declaration that there were hundreds of Communists working in the State Department (any *exact* number hurt his case, Nixon argued). So he moved into a refrain about "one Communist." "One Communist on the faculty of one university is one Communist too many. One Communist among the American advisers at Yalta was one Communist too many. And even if there were only one Communist in the State Department, that would be one Communist too many." This was perfect: It was a completely defensible accusation—lacking in specificity—that rang with poetic resonances of the need to fight. Every time his head pecked with the refrain of "one Communist," it was easy to envision a fist clocking the enemy's face. What was really irrefutable to anyone listening and watching were delegates applauding and jumping up and down on the floor.[23]

The same day as McCarthy's speech, the Texas delegation was seated. Usually at a Republican convention, this wouldn't be a big deal, but it was this time. The delegation included numerous Ike supporters. Working behind the scenes and on the floor, Ike's team had won its contest against the Taft machine. Fair Play paid off, and the Taftites knew it. Everett Dirksen, a senator from Illinois and a man who thought Ike a fake conservative in bed with the Eastern wing of the Republican Party, stood on the podium that evening and eyed Tom Dewey, bellowing: "We followed you before, and you took us down the path to defeat." With those words, fistfights broke out on the floor, and one man fainted and fell from his chair. This was not the sort of television coverage the Republicans wanted, but it did seem to suggest that Ike had sealed his victory, even though he could never subdue all resentments.[24]

The next day, events moved toward their inevitable conclusion. Nominations were made official. Everett Dirksen returned to the podium to nominate Taft (Tom Dewey walked out on his speech). William Knowland, Nixon's fellow senator from California and a man more loyal to his home state's interest, nominated Warren, calling the governor of California "a man to match our mountains." Governor Theodore R. McKeldin of Maryland could barely be heard above the screams of supporters to nominate Ike. There followed the more tepid announcements: Mrs. C. Edward Howard nominated Harold Stassen of Minnesota, and Fred Coogan of Oklahoma endorsed MacArthur, hoping someone would second. Things then went berserk. Each group of delegates had hired professional cheerleaders to do a sis-boom-bah routine. Banners were unfurled and paper signs were thrown into the air. People were getting knocked in the head with posters, with bodies pressing against one another in collective turmoil. Taftites on the floor took to singing "Onward Christian Soldiers!" Warren supporters broke into "California, Here I Come!" A small contingent of deluded supporters of MacArthur—a man who really wasn't in the race and had left the convention by this point—marched to the song "Old Soldiers Never Die." Finally a vote was taken that gave Ike a big lead of 595 delegates, shored up by the Fair Play delegations; he was now just nine short of the number needed to win. Suddenly, a spotlight shone on the Minnesota and California delegates. Warren wouldn't budge; his office said that "Earl is in this all the way," much to the frustration of Richard Nixon, of course. But some noticed that Harold Stassen's eyes were welling with tears at the moment; he had already told his delegates they could do what they felt was right. And now they were seeing the numbers and taking advantage of the lull that the first tabulations provided. They decided to switch and thereby pushed Ike to victory, with a final lopsided vote of 845 for Eisenhower, 280 for Taft, 77 for Warren, and 4 for MacArthur. Song and festivities broke out.[25]

Like many Americans, Ike was watching the convention festivities on television. He knew he had two things to do: shake hands with Taft and make an acceptance speech. He crossed Balbo Avenue and headed for the Conrad Hilton, where Taft's headquarters were. "I came over here to pay a call of friendship on a very great American," Ike explained to journalists. He also came, though he didn't say this, to make sure the man didn't bolt the party and take his crying delegates with him. Then he gave a rather mundane acceptance speech, taking up a central theme presented by MacArthur and McCarthy but drained of bellicosity. "I know of something of the solemn responsibility of leading a crusade," he said to the convention. "I have led one." There was a hushed silence in response to this and then suddenly a crescendo of applause, as people figured he must be referring to that war he had won. He said, "Today is the first day of our battle" with a "fighting road" ahead.[26]

By this point, it didn't take much for viewers at home following the conventions on NBC to figure out that Westinghouse was indeed sponsoring the greatest show on earth. In between the speeches, the hoopla of delegates cheering their man, the funny scenes captured by the "peepie creepie," Betty Furness ("Betty" to most Americans) would walk out, stand next to a refrigerator stocked with groceries, and open and close the door to show her viewers what a fine appliance they could purchase. Between most appearances, she would change clothes, to look sharp and well-pressed for the next. She'd stand in high heels with a big grin on her face as her hand went up and down the refrigerator next to her, stroking it seductively.[27]

Furness had been a B-movie actress in Hollywood and had done some live television appearances before starting in commercials in 1949. Westinghouse saw a promising commodity in her: She was attractive but not overly so—not a sexpot, that is (not like Marilyn Monroe, for instance, the sultry actress whose star was rising fast at this time). She had good hands that could take the up-close treatment of a television camera. She looked a little like Brownie Wise, the woman who headed up Tupperware and created its grassroots marketing campaign of holding parties at which ladies would show off plastic storage tubs to one another (a trend that took off close to this time as well). Furness herself learned to hawk a wide variety of Westinghouse products, including the Mobilair Fan, a machine that could be wheeled around the house, kind of like a portable air conditioner. The thing sold like hotcakes. She had to retain a certain calm detachment as she modeled her products; the performance was live, and on a few occasions, the product did not work (the refrigerator door might not open or the Mobilair Fan might not turn on). As viewers watched her repeat performance, they may have made a connection between the products being peddled and the political candidates who had just sold their ideas and personas for the viewers' consumption.[28]

Food didn't usually fly out of Pat Nixon's mouth. She was a calm and subdued woman, not prone to spasms, like Betty Furness in her own way. But on July 11, the day after Ike's nomination, an entire bite of sandwich sprang from Pat Nixon's mouth. She had left the convention that day to try to get away from the noise and bustle. She went to a tavern and watched "a Grade D movie on television." It was a refreshing break from hearing delegates scream for their candidates and wave their signs. And then the moment came. "Suddenly a commentator cut in with a news flash that my husband was being nominated" for vice president, she remembered. At that point, the bite of sandwich sprang onto the table in front her. *Sorry*, she said. And then she got up and bolted toward the convention hall.[29]

Pat Nixon was modest and usually described as a fine-looking, red-haired, average woman. Like her husband, she was a westerner, born in Ely, Nevada, to an Irish American family. At a young age, she moved to Artesia, California, a town close to Nixon's Whittier. Her mother passed away when Pat was in her early teens, so she wound up becoming caretaker to her father and brothers. "I had to cheer everybody up," she remembered at the time of her mother's death, so "I learned to be that kind of person." She would eventually leave home, with some aspirations to become a professional actress (she did two walk-on parts in movies), but she settled for a job as a teacher at Whittier High School. She met her future husband in a local community theater group, one of those civic organizations that Richard Nixon (who had also had some thespian training in college) joined in order to meet legal clients and make political connections. Dick latched onto Pat, and after a long period of dating, they married in 1940 and then started their family as the country entered the war.[30]

Pat was the sort of woman who stood by her man. She was a good organization woman who worked at her domestic chores as hard as Dick worked on his career. Her husband was a traditionalist. It drove Dick berserk, for instance, to see a woman wearing pants. He expected Pat to raise the kids and tend their household in their suburban-style home at 4801 Tilden Street, a house close to the more prosperous Maryland suburbs lying outside the nation's capital. He also expected her help when campaigning. She'd type letters to supporters, manage the incoming mail, get posters printed, and even travel with him in a station wagon across the state to stump in nearly every California town during his 1950 Senate run. She hated campaigning, since it tore her away from her two daughters, but Pat Nixon knew that when her husband had made up his mind about something, that was that. Right after Dick was nominated for the vice presidency, she was visited at home by journalists wondering how the campaign would affect Pat's life. She looked askance and then bemused when her daughter Patricia blurted out to a *Washington Post* reporter: "I'm tired of photographers. Reporters too." It wasn't hard for the journalists to conclude that Richard Nixon's upcoming campaign would be tough on his family.[31]

That the announcement on television took Pat Nixon by surprise hinted at the nature of the decision to put Nixon on the ticket: it was slightly impulsive, made not long before its announcement. For sure, others besides Nixon were considered, and conversations took place weeks prior to the convention and up to the last moment. Some of Ike's advisers wanted Governor Alfred Driscoll of New Jersey, a good moderate Eastern Seaboard type of Republican, but Tom Dewey, who was the man running the show, pressed for Nixon, remembering that good time he had spent with him at the Waldorf-Astoria. Nixon was young and could offset Ike's age. He was from California—a state the Republicans needed to win, Dewey pointed out. That made the decision easy, with even Driscoll saying that Nixon brought with him "zeal and enthusiasm of youth." Ike went ahead with the decision without really doing his homework. He didn't know Nixon's age or much about his run for the Senate in 1950, and he knew absolutely nothing about a small fund set up by his wealthier supporters.[32]

Once the nomination of Eisenhower was a done deal, Herbert Brownell, Dewey's campaign manager who was worming his way onto Ike's team, got on the phone and told Nixon about the choice. It was surreal for the young senator from California. The call woke him up. He had just been deep in sleep in his hotel room, taking a break from a convention that had worn him down as it had his wife. Nixon was "hot, sleepy, and grubby." He asked Brownell if he could grab a "shower or shave" before coming over to accept the nomination. No time for that, Brownell argued, the cars are downstairs and need to bring you now. So Nixon put on his old, crumpled white suit and was whisked to the convention hall looking like a dark and sweaty vice presidential candidate. Precisely what he was.[33]

Meanwhile, Pat was running from the tavern to the Amphitheatre. Dick caught her, and they moved toward the podium together. Behind the scenes, the last-minute details were sorted out. William Knowland—the senior senator from California who had nominated Warren earlier—was told he would have to nominate Nixon for vice president to give the clear message: *California, California, California.* Knowland grimaced about having to endorse "the dirty son of a bitch." Robert Taft, now realizing, like Knowland, just how much Nixon had lied about his loyalties earlier, was overheard at the same time calling Nixon "a little man in a big hurry" with a "mean streak." But this sort of anger would remain suppressed and behind the scenes during the convention. It was to be all arm waving, hugs, and kisses. Maybe the most telling moment came when Nixon arrived with Pat at the podium. He shot his arms into the air and waved to the crowds, promising "a fighting campaign for the election of the candidate for President." Perfunctory cheers followed. Pat Nixon reached for her husband and "leaned toward him for an embrace" and a kiss. Richard Nixon "turned his face away," and looked and smiled at the crowds. It was as if Pat Nixon was just a prop.[34]

The next morning, July 12, reporters were outside the convention site as delegates left for home, exhausted. They were trying to get a sense of the attitude delegates were bringing home with them. It had been a tough battle inside the Amphitheatre, but for Richard Nixon "a good fight stirs the blood." Some delegates, though, were still angry, especially dejected Taft supporters. One reporter bumped into

Joseph McCarthy as he was rambling around the Blackstone Hotel. "Are you pleased with the ticket, Senator?" McCarthy looked coy: "I think Dick Nixon will make a fine vice president." That's all he said.[35]

By July 26, the Democrats had chosen their man: Adlai Stevenson. After the midnight hour passed, he stood at the podium occupied by Ike and Nixon two weeks prior and waved to the cheering crowds as spotlights bounced a gleam off his bald, domed head. After being drafted by his supporters he was now their candidate for the presidency, and if Richard Nixon had written a fantasy novel that could project his hopes of what the the general election would look like, he could not have found a better specimen for the opposition than Stevenson. He fit the bill perfectly as the enemy to the story's hero, just the right foil for battle scenes plotted out for the "fighting campaign" in Nixon's mind.

Stevenson, like Robert Taft, came from a political family; his grandfather had been vice president under Grover Cleveland. Meaning he didn't have to work for it the way Dick had to. That was true for everything else in Stevenson's life. Things came easy to him: He had been born wealthy, gone to Choate Prep School, attended Princeton, flunked out of Harvard, and then completed his degree at Northwestern Law School. He married a wealthy debutante, Ellen Borden, and worked for the Agricultural Adjustment Administration, a key New Deal bureaucracy that regulated farm markets during the Depression. Here he first met—and this fleshed out Nixon's character portrait more fully than anything else—Alger Hiss, a man whose path he crossed again during a stint at the State Department in 1945 (Stevenson would provide favorable character testimony for Hiss later). After he entered politics on his own terms, winning the Illinois governorship in 1948, Stevenson procured a divorce from his wife. She had been a neglectful mother, and her interests in art and literature diverged from her husband's political obsessions. Now it was easy to imagine the portrait in Nixon's mind filling out: A man who couldn't control his wife, that was bad enough. Worse, as the 1952 election approached, Stevenson's ex-wife told reporters she planned to vote Republican.[36]

Here was the best characteristic for Nixon's negative portrait of his foe: Stevenson's indecisiveness. The governor from Illinois was a reluctant candidate, leading some to compare him to Ike. But Stevenson was no general on a white horse remaining skeptical about entering the dirty world of politics; he was more a smart aleck who thought himself above the prize being offered. Harry Truman had tried to get him to run, but Stevenson preferred to stand aloof and have his supporters draft him into the race. When asked what he'd do if he was actually drafted, Stevenson quipped: "I guess I'd shoot myself." But then quickly qualified that with "No politician can say he would refuse a draft." Then, when a Draft Stevenson movement materialized—the governor was seen as more electable than the front-runner, Estes Kefauver, a senator from Tennessee famous for his televised investigations into the criminal underworld—Adlai warned: "I have no fitness—temperamentally, mentally or physically—for the job" of president. Such things were said with a "flashing smile that [would wreathe] his whole face" and make his crow's-feet crinkle around his beaming eyes.[37]

Even Stevenson's supporters noted this weird dimension of his character, but they, unlike Nixon, loved it. The *New Republic* praised Stevenson's "dry wit" as well as his "elfin" and "fey" nature. Richard Nixon knew enough of the English language to follow out one definition of that word: a fairy. The contrasts in character could pile on from there. Adlai—sometimes people would call him Adelaide—played tennis, whereas Nixon and Ike both played football in college and now enjoyed watching the sport (Ike was a linebacker and sure tackler on the field, whereas Nixon was a "second-string man," according to his coach at Whittier College, known "to sit and cheer the rest of the guys and tell them how well they'd played"). Stevenson loved "wisecracking" and "fancy language," whereas Nixon was nick-named "Gloomy Gus" at Duke University's Law School and was famous for his "troubled frown" and plain, simple language.[38]

No surprise, either, for Nixon to find that Governor Stevenson, just a year ago in 1951, had vetoed the Broyles Bill, which would have administered anticommunist loyalty oaths to political candidates and schoolteachers. Stevenson believed the bill would make it difficult to recruit the best public servants by instilling a counterproductive cul-ture of fear. "We must not burn down the house to kill the rats," he explained. After winning the nomination, Stevenson just accentu-ated his pinkness to Nixon by hiring as his "personal campaign manager" Wilson Wyatt, a man who served as a national chairman for Americans for Democratic Action (ADA), a liberal (albeit anti-communist) organization. As speechwriters, Stevenson hired liberal "eggheads" who took a break from teaching at Harvard—including the historian Arthur Schlesinger Jr. and the economist John Kenneth Galbraith. Just more fodder for Nixon. *The Saturday Evening Post* called those who constituted Adlai's inner circles "well-heeled liberals with inheritances and a touch of 'social conscience.'" They "drink grand-father's scotch and sip his Vichyssoise, but have little use for the economic system which enabled grandfather to lay down a cellar and set up a family trust." No better line about his enemies could be written for Richard Nixon's plotted battle scenes.[39]

Then there was Stevenson's acceptance speech. It did not speak of a "crusade," the way Ike's had. In fact, Stevenson condemned his op-ponent for using such a zealot's word. His speech, presented in his high-pitched voice, opened with an effusion of humility. "I accept your nomination—and your program. I should have preferred to hear those words uttered by a stronger, wiser, better man than myself." He then went biblical, quoting Matthew 26:42, "So, 'if this cup may not pass away from me, except I drink it, thy will be done.'" This was passivity perfected. It's not hard to imagine Richard Nixon's eyebrows arching upward when Stevenson pleaded that his fellow Democrats not just worry about "winning the election, but how it is won, how well we can take advantage of this great quadrennial opportunity to debate issues sensibly and soberly. . . . Better we lose the election than mislead the people." Stevenson asked his party brethren to "talk sense to the American people." Then he drew out a sentence that it was hard to believe wouldn't lose everyone, especially at this late hour of the night, after the delegate counting and debating on the Democratic side: "Let's tell them the truth, that there are no gains without pains, that we are now on the eve of great decisions, not easy decisions, like resistance when you are attacked, but a long, patient, costly struggle which alone can assure triumph over the great enemies of man—war, poverty, and tyranny—and the assaults upon human dignity which are the most grievous consequences of each." Those still left in the convention hall cheered, even though it didn't really conjure the fighting spirit expected of acceptance speeches.[40]

Stevenson's opponent happened to be in an earlier time zone and heard the speech at a more reasonable hour. Dwight Eisenhower tuned in the radio and was impressed by what he heard from his cabin in Fraser, Colorado. Those were some fancy words, the general thought. Sounds like a smart guy. He was with a friend, George Allen, who provided counterintuitive feedback: "He's too accomplished an orator, he'll be easy to beat." Richard Nixon was having the exact same thought. He described Stevenson as "a man . . . who could speak beautifully but could not act decisively." The strategy was ready in his mind. The boxers had gone to their corners.[41]

The last week of July was a popular time for Americans to take summer vacations. Richard Nixon was heading for his first meeting with

Ike since the convention, a serious occasion, he thought. Little did he
know that he, too, would be expected to kick back. Dressed in a sharp-
looking suit, starched white shirt, and dark tie, Nixon might have
been surprised as the person driving him turned off pavement onto a
dirt road that stretched two miles. Looking out the windows, he could
see the Rocky Mountains in the background. Then he was told they
were heading toward a small, rustic cabin where Ike was holed up.
He shifted in his uncomfortable suit.[42]

Ike greeted Nixon at the cabin, laughing at his clothes. He told his
vice-presidential candidate to shed the suit, but Nixon had only the
shirt he had worn, so he stripped the tie off, pressed down his stiff
collars, and shoved himself into a ratty-looking fly-fishing vest that
Ike handed him. Then they headed to the nearby river. Nixon grew
more nervous; this was his first time throwing a fly-fishing line into
water. Ike showed him how to cast, to cock the pole at a certain angle
and then shoot the fly out with a pump of the arm. Nixon watched
bewildered, sometimes having to dodge Ike's line as it flew above his
head. When a photographer handed Nixon a fishing net, he asked,
"What is this?" And then he stood in the river above a bend and
riffle and caught absolutely nothing. He wore a canned smile captured
by photographers.[43]

He had come to talk about politics, but Ike was on vacation. After
fishing, Nixon was told to peel potatoes with a friend of Ike's, Senator Frank Carlson of Kansas. Photographers snapped pictures of the
two men laughing and pretending to look happy doing servants' work.
At dinner, Nixon started talking about campaign strategy, but Ike
waved him off. Still, even now, amid the laughing and eating, Nixon
made little political notes in his head. He realized that Ike *liked* to
cook the dinner they were enjoying. Later in the campaign, Nixon
would reflect on this fact and tell reporters, "Cooking shows what a
regular guy Ike is. A lot of people like to have expensive hobbies. It's
quite significant that one of Ike's real pleasures is to go into the

kitchen and cook up a great solemn meal for the folks. Even the things he cooks are a tip-off. Nothing fancy—just good clean solid stuff that built him and built this country." Only Nixon could squeeze such a melodramatic, populist political message out of the general's cooking skills.[44]

Eventually they did a little of what Nixon wanted and talked politics. Ike worried that Nixon's position on Korea was closer to MacArthur's than his own. The idea of expanding military action from Korea to China frightened the general; it might start "another war far more difficult to stop than the one we are now in." So Nixon promised to tamp down his hard-line position. Ike compromised, too, realizing that the Republican Party platform had taken a strong stance against "containment." Their mutual friend John Foster Dulles had written the Republican Party plank on foreign policy, arguing that the current administration had become "negative, futile, and immoral" since containment "abandons countless human beings to a despotism and godless terrorism" (Dulles had outlined his ideas in a May issue of *Life* magazine in an essay appropriately entitled "A Policy of Boldness"). There were *reasons* General MacArthur was a Republican and allowed to keynote the convention. Ike understood this and felt pressed to find a way to criticize Truman on Korea. He'd say the war was the right idea at the time but that the country's leaders shouldn't have gotten to the point of war in the first place. Perhaps they could suggest that if America had stood firmer against China's Communist revolution back in 1949, the Korean mess wouldn't have erupted in the first place. In essence, Ike was suggesting they might have to fudge their position.[45]

Ike wanted to attack the Truman administration on Communism, corruption, and Korea (a formula abbreviated C_2K_1, or sometimes K_1C_2). His research team was compiling files on corruption in the Truman administration, including the Reconstruction Finance Corporation, the Internal Revenue Service, and the Department of

Justice. He agreed they'd talk up Nixon's success helping get Hiss behind bars and maybe even hint that Stevenson was too chummy with
the man now in jail for perjury. But they wouldn't go all McCarthy-
like. They'd appeal to the Southwest—especially the state of Texas,
which they thought they could pick off from the Democrats—by
claiming oil found in the shallower waters off the state's shore belonged to the state, not the federal government (even if the Supreme
Court had recently ruled otherwise). And they'd talk about civil rights
for blacks down south, but not too loudly, and only through voluntary
methods rather than the force of the federal government, to appeal
to southerners wary of the civil rights planks in the Democratic Party
platform of 1948. They'd interlace all their speeches down south
with states' rights rhetoric.

Nixon wanted a "rocking and socking" campaign—one that
smacked the Democrats hard. He hoped to nail Stevenson as a weakling. Eisenhower was fine with some of that but was also taking advice
from Dewey, who said the whole thing should wait until later in
August to get off the ground. After all, there was fishing to get back to.

If Eisenhower wasn't ready to campaign full throttle, Nixon's confidant Murray Chotiner was. He was the man with a wicked sense of
humor who had arranged for those buses for Earl Warren's delegates
to be festooned with Ike banners. He was also the man who pressed
Nixon to board the train in the first place and push the delegates
toward Ike. His history with Nixon went back a number of years. He
had been marginally engaged in the 1946 campaign and then masterminded the 1950 Senate run. By the time Nixon went fishing with
Ike, Chotiner had been hired as campaign manager for his run for
the vice presidency.[46]

Chotiner was short, rotund, and, by most accounts, abrasive. He
liked to wear "loud ties and clock-face cufflinks." He was fast-paced

and slightly manic. Throughout the 1930s and into the 1940s, he served as a Los Angeles lawyer who made money defending some seedy clients in the gambling industry. During that time, he also built up his veteran credentials in the war of politics, working on numerous Republican campaigns. He carried himself with confidence built upon experience. But he didn't always have an easy in to Richard Nixon's small inner circle. Pat Nixon didn't like him one bit, finding him coarse and underhanded. Richard Nixon, on the other hand, thought Chotiner brilliant. The little man bubbled with excellent ideas. His first political principle was the importance of attack. Drawing upon the success of Nixon's brazen campaign against Helen Gahagan Douglas, Chotiner would later explain, "If you do not deflate the opposition candidate before your own candidate gets started, the odds are that you are going to be doomed to defeat." So in July, Chotiner was eager to get the campaign moving.[47]

Nixon spent the early parts of August doing small-bit stuff: visiting orphanages, attending parades, showing up at receptions, and going to Veterans of Foreign War conventions. But he was also crafting the upcoming campaign and having discussions with Chotiner about the broad themes he wanted to pursue. "The month of August is the month to plan. We don't want to start shooting too early," Nixon explained to *U.S. News & World Report*. Now with the go-ahead from the general, Nixon had decided to make "Communist subversion and corruption" the "theme of every speech from now until the election." But he and Chotiner agreed that it was the way this was done that mattered most. They had started researching Stevenson, drawing up files about his associations with Hiss and his "fey" ways. They were ready to cast an image of their opposition.[48]

Throughout August, Nixon could hear glimmerings of the sort of campaign talk he wanted as his own. He warmed to Arthur Summerfield, the GOP national chairman and onetime car dealer who ran unsuccessfully for governor of Michigan. Summerfield laid it on thick to reporters on August 2. Stevenson, he claimed, would "out-Truman the Truman regime in leading the nation down the road to complete socialism." The "ultra-leftwingers—not the Democratic Party—will have complete charge of his campaign." The next day, Senator Everett Dirksen, still remembered as the man who blasted Dewey at the Republican convention, went after Stevenson's criticism of Ike for associating with Joseph McCarthy and William Jenner, both men who had attacked General George Marshall. Dirksen retorted: "Adlai questions the right of General Eisenhower to carry on a crusade in company with such sturdy Americans as Senators Jenner . . . and McCarthy and other Republican nominees. Just how well does he think his associates look—Alger Hiss, Dean Acheson, Wilson Wyatt, the ADA, and the Lavender Lads of the State Department." That last allusion was to homosexuals, whom Joseph McCarthy enjoyed attacking as much as purported Communists.[49]

Summerfield's and Dirksen's style excited Nixon, and he worried Ike would shy away from it. That provided his job opening. During August, he drafted a hard-line stump speech that would be unveiled to the public next month. It talked about the *style* of campaign he desired as much as the issues at hand. Nixon had been conversing, since the convention, with a number of nervous Republicans—those whose memories still rattled with Dewey's tepid campaign in 1948. Nixon had received "hundreds of letters and personal messages" that asked: "Is this going to be a fighting campaign?" His answer to that question was "an emphatic YES." Oh, sure, he'd admit, there were a few (and really this sounded more like a dig at Stevenson than anyone in the Republican Party) who wanted "this campaign" to "be conducted on a so-called 'high intellectual plane'; that we should let by-gones be by-gones and not point up the countless past mistakes of the Truman Administration; that, after all, we have 'two good candidates for President.' In short, that a little nicey-nice powder-puff duel between them would give the American people a chance to make an intelligent choice." Nixon concluded: "Believe me, it wouldn't."[50]

By the time he was writing this speech, his own complaints about Stevenson's "wisecracking" persona had taken wing. The campaign headquarters received an interesting memo from one of many informal advisers (the sort who often made campaign workers roll their eyes). This one wasn't the work of a crackpot but a man whose ideas were kept in the files for further consultation. M. M. Green wrote to Nixon and suggested he center his campaign around the theme "STEVENSON THE WISE-CRACKER (Clown)." Green said the campaign "ought to make frequent references to Stevenson as a . . . gagster and smart aleck, and point out that this man of whom next to nothing is known to the public is apparently trying to joke his way into the most serious job in the world." M.M. even suggested a zinger of a line for the campaign: "Most top Fair Dealers are *flippant*. Acheson is a fop; Stevenson is both." Point out, Green suggested, that the governor's humor sounded "snobbish." Green's memo had hit upon something that Nixon had been thinking ever since the Democratic convention and was now being picked up in the press. On August 8, Malvina Lindsay, the women's page editor at the *Washington Post*, a paper that endorsed Eisenhower, wrote that Stevenson's "wit" could get "him in hot water." Stevenson had recently said, "I am beginning to detect signs of ambition in myself." Lindsay thought that sort of thing could "be misunderstood by the rank and file of voters." What she found in informal polling was that "while the American electorate likes a campaigner who can tell funny stories and ridicule his opponents, it wants this done in a direct, obvious manner. Moreover, the public is not generally accustomed to presidential candidates with the light touch." That was just the way Nixon was thinking about the matter.[51]

The stump speech template that Nixon drafted in August cranked up this issue full blast. "Let the other side continue to serve up the

clever quips which send the State Department cocktail set into gales
of giggles," Nixon wrote (he might as well have mentioned the lavender
crowd). And then he set out this contrast: "Ours will be plain, simple,
straight-from-the-shoulder language any American can understand
without recourse to Roget's Thesaurus, Bartlett's Quotations, or Web-
ster's unabridged dictionary. Wisecracks are no substitute for wisdom."
Take that, Adelaide and all you egghead intellectuals, a person could imagine
Nixon thinking. In the lines to follow, Nixon's toughness—his macho
sensibilities contrasting with Stevenson's delicate and intellectual
qualities—would be highlighted again: "If the dry rot of corruption
and Communism, which has eaten deep into our body politic during
the past seven years, can only be chopped out with a hatchet—then
let's call for a hatchet." With that line, Nixon managed to play by
Ike's rules—focusing on the themes they agreed upon—while jazzing
things up for those who worried that Ike was going to roll out another
version of Tom Dewey. He was spicing his language with rhetoric
that often sounded like Joseph McCarthy's.[52]

By the time this speech was ready to debut, Chotiner had assembled a crack campaign team. He got Congressman George Mac-
Kinnon as a research director, who was good at digging up dirt about
C_2K_1; Glenard Lipscomb, a future congressperson himself, as campaign executive secretary in charge of Washington headquarters;
and Edward (Ted) Rogers as Nixon's television and radio liaison.
Rogers was an especially big score. Before joining the advertising
firm that allowed him to take a leave now, he had been a successful
television show producer, helping to create hits like *The Lone Ranger,*
with its masked hero and sidekick Tonto riding their horses to pursue
bad guys, and *The Stu Erwin Show,* a domestic comedy about a husband and wife. Rogers would import the lessons of televisionland
into Nixon's campaign. He was Nixon's equivalent of the advertising
and public relations experts who played a large role on Ike's team.[53]

Nixon's staff formed a little war room prepping for battle. By the end of August, Dick sat in his office and wrote out a speech that crafted his campaign's style and expected tone: "Soft words and pretty phrases aren't going to win this election." The next day, Nixon told a supporter that he was going to begin "real slugging" around mid-September. He had all the pieces in place to do so, including his trusted adviser who was ready to bark out orders to the rest of the staff who were eager for a good fight.[54]

On August 12, the Selective Service System reported that it might have to start drafting nineteen-year-olds or else face a shortage of military men ready for war. Just eight days earlier, the SSS had talked about drafting fathers, seeing that some men were quickly producing babies with girlfriends or wives once they learned they had been inducted. On top of it all, the SSS announced in mid-August that it would draft middle-aged doctors to help with a growing health care crisis in Korea. There were just too many mangled bodies coming into Mobile Army Surgical Hospital (MASH) units. Major General Lewis B. Hershey, the director of the SSS, was planning a major speech for the American Legion about the general problem of manpower. It wasn't really necessary; the cause of the problem was obvious to all Americans: The war in Korea had dragged on and on and on. And it was gobbling up more and more young American men.[55]

Finally, in the last days of August, the first showdown of the presidential campaign began. The two men wouldn't debate each other directly but indirectly, in separate speeches at the national convention of the American Legion held in Madison Square Garden in New York City. Ike appeared on August 25, Stevenson two days later. What was said represented the worldviews that would continue to clash until election day.

That both speeches took place in front of an American Legion
audience was telling. This was enemy territory for Stevenson, more
friendly to Ike. Ike played to the audience, Stevenson didn't. This
was the same organization that just last spring had done everything
it could to promote the movie *My Son John*. And now, as the two men
were making their appearances, the Legion was approving its Foreign Relations Committee's report. It might as well have been written by General MacArthur and Joseph McCarthy. The Legion
called for the ouster of Dean Acheson for his failures in Korea ("Ah,
yes, the primitives are back," you could imagine the secretary of state
snickering). The committee attacked the United Nations as a weakling organization and then demanded the Korean War "be ended,
and in a military victory." The State Department couldn't solve the
protracted war, because it harbored Americans "tainted" by the "red
paint brush" of Stalin. Hunting reds at home was as important as
extending military power abroad. A year earlier, the American
Legion had sponsored the Broyles Bill that, as governor, Stevenson
had vetoed as a threat to civil liberties. Now the Legion had called
for an investigation of the American Civil Liberties Union as a Communist front organization.[56]

When Eisenhower entered Madison Square Garden, decked out in
a fine suit and wearing his Legionnaire hat, fifteen thousand delegates
rose to their feet and erupted into cheers for a solid two minutes. As he
spoke, the audience interrupted him ten times with applause. Some
of the men got so heated on the floor that they yelled out, "Give 'em
hell!" Ike tipped his hat to those screams, perhaps realizing that the
same words had rallied Harry Truman during his whistle-stop tour
against Tom Dewey in 1948. Ike proceeded to deliver on the spirit.[57]

The general gripped the podium and told the Legionnaires "we
are threatened by a great tyranny" that had built an empire throughout Eastern Europe and Asia. "Dare we rest while these millions of
our kinsmen remain in slavery? I can almost hear your answer." To

which the audience, of course, whooped up a huge and hearty "No!" The general explained that Stalin was seizing larger chunks of the world in order to pursue a course of "economic containment and gradual strangulation of America." A critical listener here might have noticed that the term "containment" was in fact a key word in Harry Truman's conception of the Cold War, an idea developed earlier by George Kennan and now practiced in Korea: Draw the line at the 38th parallel and defend it, but do not, as MacArthur wanted, cross that line in aggression. Ike was now suggesting that containment was in fact a Communist strategy and talking the language of "liberation," of *rolling back* Communism as John Foster Dulles had argued and made part of the Republican Party platform. After mentioning Poland, East Germany, Czechoslovakia, and Bulgaria, all in the Soviet orbit, Ike argued, "The American conscience can never know peace until these people are restored again to being masters of their own fate." He didn't explain just what rolling back Communism in this region would look like, but he welcomed cheers for the idea.[58]

If America was to engage this new direction in foreign policy, things would have to change. Ike worried openly that Communists "have penetrated into many critical spots of our own country, even into our Government," tipping his hat to his running mate. He then segued into a call for religious revival as the best foundation for America's fight against Communism at home and abroad. He took a page from Whittaker Chambers and the message of *My Son John*. He condemned Communism for its "paganism" and "materialism." To fight it, "we must preach and practice the truly revolutionary values of men's dignity, man's freedom, man's brotherhood—under the fatherhood of God." Only with "spiritual unity," Ike thundered, could the Cold War be won. Here he spoke the language of General Douglas MacArthur. The crowds cheered and cheered and cheered.[59]

The cheering turned to tepid applause when Adlai Stevenson entered Madison Square Garden two days later. Fortunately for him, he was fresh from a vacation in Wisconsin. He knew this would be a tough audience and he needed to be rested. He stood before them as a man who was once a "lowly . . . apprentice seaman in a naval training unit" during World War I, battling now with a "great general" who had vast "military achievements." As was his wont, Stevenson joked about the agony of being at a convention where "you have to listen to speeches," what he characterized as "punishment" that was "cruel" but not "unusual." Some in the audience laughed and started to warm up to the man a bit, but most remained quiet. And then Stevenson rolled out his "honest" campaign style that he had promised at the convention. After providing veiled support for the United Nations ("a great international system of security"), he jolted his audience. "I should tell you now, as I would tell all other organized groups, that I stand to resist pressures from veterans . . . if I think their demands are excessive or in conflict with the public interest." While Ike synched his own message to his audience and fudged some of his own principles, Stevenson looked as if he was enjoying pissing off his audience.[60]

The crescendo came when Stevenson voiced his full-throated critique of Joseph McCarthy, a hero to many audience members. "There are men among us who use 'patriotism' as a club for attacking other Americans." If that wasn't aimed directly against the senator from Wisconsin, the following lines certainly were: "What can we say for the man who proclaims himself a patriot—and then for political or personal reasons attacks the patriotism of faithful public servants?" His voice became bell-sharp: "I give you, as shocking examples, the attacks which have been made on the loyalty and the motives of our great wartime Chief of Staff, General George Marshall. To me this is the type of 'patriotism' which is, in Dr. Johnson's phrase, the last refuge of scoundrels." Stevenson's own conception of patriotism, he explained in his schoolmaster fashion, was "based on tolerance and a large measure of humility." He told the delegates who were warring against the ACLU that he believed in "freedom of the mind" and was wary of "self-appointed thought police" and "ill-informed censors."[61]

The next step each man took after the American Legion convention was just as telling as their speeches. Ike told reporters he would spend some time in New York City but then, in a feisty and bold gesture, head south. Had they heard, he asked, that Governor Allan Shivers of Texas said he wouldn't endorse Stevenson due to the tidelands oil issue? Maybe the "Solid South"—solid, that is, for the Democrats—could crack open in 1952. Nixon was pitching the states' rights ideas he thought might play well in the South. On August 23, Nixon wrote the publisher of the *St. Petersburg Independent* in Florida, "The nation owes a debt of eternal gratitude for the vigilance demonstrated in your part of the country in upholding— as much as is humanly possible—the dignity and independence of our state governments." Ike might be able to crack the South if he used language like that and projected the confidence that brought him there.[62]

And what about Stevenson? Where was he heading? In *Newsweek*'s words, he'd stay in New York and "nearby New Jersey" speaking to "audiences primarily of Democrats and members of the Liberal Party and Americans for Democratic Action." In other words, the choir.[63]

The last weekend in August saw the roll-out of a movie that would warm the hearts of Richard Nixon and the American Legionnaires. *Big Jim McLain* starred and was produced by Nixon's favorite actor, John Wayne, and it premiered August 30, just as the American Legion's convention wound down. John Wayne played the movie's hero who was employed by HUAC to go bust up a Communist ring in Hawaii. The movie's publicity poster showed the tall, lunging Wayne, his shirt flying off his bare chest and his fist punching the air. It blasted the slogan: "He's a Go-Get-'Em Guy for the USA."

Since the end of World War II, John Wayne had had a stellar rise to fame. He starred in a slew of westerns—including biggies like *Fort Apache* (a favorite of Nixon's) and *Rio Grande*—as well as World War II–themed movies—*They Were Expendable* and *Sands of Iwo Jima*— that made his leathery face and his swaggering walk immediately iconic. By 1952, Wayne was "for the second year in a row . . . the country's top box-office draw." His last feature showed off the key to his popularity. It was a typical World War II flick called *Flying Leathernecks* (1951), about Marine Corps pilots on bombing missions during the famous Guadalcanal campaign. Wayne played Major Kirby, a tough-ass officer who rallies his men, knowing they faced likely death. He perfected a combination of steel will and soft heart, the tough and the maudlin, as he wrote sad notes home to parents whose sons had been killed or injured. It was the sort of movie that would lead General MacArthur to praise Wayne as a model soldier, at least onscreen. The actor had done everything he could to avoid actual service during World War II.[64]

It was also the sort of movie that Richard Nixon loved. So much that he went into the Senate chamber and gave a speech about how every good American should see this movie that captured the "immortal achievements of our Marine Corps air arm." Much of what Nixon put into the public record had been written by the movie's publicity agents. And some might have connected the statement to the fact that John Wayne helped fundraise for Nixon's Senate run in 1950. But for Nixon, *Flying Leathernecks* was also just an honest and authentic expression by Hollywood of good American values finally making it onto the silver screen.[65]

For Wayne, the success of *Flying Leathernecks* showed off his big-name draw and justified his recent venture to create an independent company with the producer Robert Fellows. He wanted to make movies with a more explicit political message than the patriotic fare of World War II flicks or the tough male ethics found in the westerns. Wayne's politics were further right than Nixon's. He had attended the Republican convention in hopes of getting Taft nominated and was heard shouting at a pro-Ike sound truck in the streets of Chicago: "Why don't you get a red flag?" His heart wasn't in the fight for Ike so much as with the Hollywood Committee for the Re-election of Joe McCarthy, which provided the senator with some hefty cash for his reelection bid in 1952.[66]

Big Jim McLain served up Wayne's political commentary. It opened on a HUAC hearing, with Wayne narrating in character as Jim. We learn that the "good Dr. Carter"—the term "good" spoken in Wayne's sarcastic drawl—is taking the Fifth Amendment and refusing to answer questions so that he could "go back to his well-paid chair as a full professor of economics at the university to contaminate more kids." Jim explains that his partner, Mal Baxter (played by James Arness), "hates these people," because they had "shot at him in Korea." Soon, the two of them are off to Hawaii on "Operation Pineapple" to break up a Communist ring. On the way, Jim finds romance, dating Nancy Vallon, a doctor's secretary. Nancy's problem is that she's studying psychology and analyzes their relationship too much, prompting Jim to smirk: "Stop going to those lectures." Her other problem is that her boss is a Communist. The message so far: Don't trust college professors or professional doctors.

Jim and Mal go on hot pursuit of the ring, piecing together a case that proves the Communists are killing and drugging Hawaii's citizens. Mal is killed in action by the Communists, and Jim rants and raves in the morgue, now on the path for revenge. He tracks down the circle's next meeting and rushes toward the house it's being held in. One Communist sees him busting in and yells: "Hey, here's that big cop." Wayne starts slugging it out with the Communists, single-handedly smashing the ring up with his bare knuckles. Unfortunately, the leaders of the ring are dragged to another HUAC hearing, take the Fifth, and go free. Which leaves Wayne narrating about the problems of Communists using the Constitution to their benefit and implying that perhaps punching it out is a more productive route (think Joe McCarthy versus Drew Pearson). At one point Jim is asked why people become Communists, and he says, "I don't know the whys. I didn't know the whys in the war. I shot at the man on the other side of the perimeter because he was the enemy." The message of the movie could be found in those lines.[67]

No surprise the chief critic who panned *My Son John* now panned *Big Jim McLain*. Bosley Crowther at the *New York Times* admitted Wayne was "rugged and genial." But Crowther really worked up his rage toward the film. Wayne was "representative of the attitude that it is painful to think too deeply and the fist is mightier than the brain." Crowther concluded: "The overall meaning of cheap fiction with a contemporary crisis in American life is irresponsible and un-forgivable. No one deserves credit for this film."[68]

But again, who cared about Crowther? Just the highbrows and eggheads who read the *New York Times* and who shared his likes for Italian neorealist films and his dislikes of American westerns. They weren't the ones rushing to see *Big Jim McLain* and turning it into a top-grossing film of 1952.[69]

CHAPTER THREE

"A WONDERFUL GUY"?

*Dick doesn't do anything in a halfhearted manner,
so I know that we're in for a rugged time.*

—PAT NIXON, 1952

Over Labor Day weekend, one of the most famous photographs in American political history was shot by William Gallagher of the *Flint Journal*. It was released by the Associated Press and published in newspapers on September 3, 1952, making the front page of the *Washington Post* and page 16 in the *New York Times*. The photograph showed Adlai Stevenson writing up notes for a speech at a Labor Day rally in Michigan. He refused to "make the same speech twice," and thus often penned his thoughts at the last moment, working down to the wire. The photograph captured a man who looked deep in concentration. But what it depicted more clearly than anything else, having been shot from below the stage on which Stevenson sat cross-legged, was a huge hole in the sole of his shoe. The hole appeared in the lower left corner. A viewer could trace a finger in an arching line to the top of Stevenson's domed head in the upper right corner, making the photograph perfectly balanced in composition. Indeed, it would go on to win the Pulitzer Prize for photography the next year.[1]

The image became all the buzz at the time. Reporters and viewers debated its meaning. It was worrisome to a Stevenson supporter, this early in the campaign, that the *New York Times* entitled the picture "Worn Out," suggesting exhaustion on the part of the governor. But the *Washington Post* said it showed off how much shoe-scuffing Adlai had done on his "whirlwind tour." Viewers could read the man's determination and energy in the sole's hole.

The image inspired other questions: Maybe Stevenson couldn't afford new shoes? Maybe he was a frugal man who eschewed spending money on new items? Maybe he didn't know how he appeared in public, maybe he didn't care? Some pondered if Stevenson *wanted* to project an image of frugality and disdain for appearance—to tease out sympathy from a critical audience—making the photograph seem almost sinister. For his fans, it was further testimony to the fact that here was a man who cared more about what he had to say than about how he looked. For his opponents, it showed a man abstracted from the real world, too ethereal and in the realm of ideas to realize what a dork he looked like to millions of newspaper viewers. All of these interpretations floated around, it must be said, because so few Americans knew just who Adlai Stevenson really was.[2]

In contrast to Stevenson's image, Pat Nixon was hammering home to readers of the *Saturday Evening Post* that her husband was a normal, down-to-earth man. On September 6, her article "I Say He's a Wonderful Guy" appeared and was quickly added to a growing number of promotional materials the campaign used (including a puff piece written by Victor Lasky and published in *Look*). Nixon's election team knew there were questions about Stevenson's divorce (he had never married again), so they wanted to put Pat out front and center. Here was an average housewife who loved her husband, despite the fact that the last time most Americans saw her was when she tried to kiss Dick on the podium and he turned his cheek.

Pat never stepped out of her subordinate role but did say she was part of a fighting team. "Perhaps we both feel strongly about" his campaign, she explained, "because we come from typical, everyday American families that have had to work for what they got out of life." She dished on details about her domestic scene: "I run a suburban household, and by that I mean I do everything, because we've never had a full-time maid until the week before the Chicago convention." She depicted her husband as the type who had no desire to hobnob with the Georgetown social set. "Dick simply cannot stand Washington cocktail parties. . . . He'd much rather stay home and play the piano for the children." Then there was this line about their humble means that would turn into trouble around the corner: "We have never done much entertaining in Washington because a senator's salary, which is all we have, runs out amazingly fast. . . . Last year I went to school to learn how to make draperies and slipcovers." Little did she know, these lines would both imperil and then save her husband from an imminent crisis.

Pat emphasized Dick's hair-on-the-chest qualities. He was no Adelaide. She pointed out that "he follows all sports events." Knowing that politics was really Dick's favorite sport, she predicted the near future by playing up her husband's real-man status and his love of a rough campaign style: "Dick doesn't do anything in a halfhearted manner, so I know that we're in for a rugged time."[3]

The day after Pat's article appeared, Richard Nixon stood among fans in Boston's Woodland Park and rang out his own he-man qualities. He told his listeners that Adlai Stevenson would continue the "policy of appeasement" begun under Dean Acheson's "wishy-washy

State Department." Nixon barked out the language of liberation over
containment: "Mr. Stevenson tells us we must be satisfied for genera-
tions with a shameful sort of 'uneasy coexistence' brought by concessions and negotiations. To me this smacks unpleasantly of 1938 and
1939 when another dictator was temporarily appeased by the world's
greatest giveaway program." The largely Catholic and McCarthy-
supporting crowd whooped at this language of tough determination.[4]

No surprise to hear McCarthyite rhetoric from Dick, but it *was* a
surprise that the next day, Ike would trundle into similar territory.
The general had come to Indiana to campaign on September 9. After
having laid low for the most of August, Ike had kicked into high campaign mode now with the speech at the American Legion conference
late that month and was now starting a flurry of autumn activities.
After touching down at the Indianapolis Airport, Ike exited the plane
only to meet Senator William Jenner, who bounded up to greet him.
The senator's hand shot out like a dart, pumping the general's. And at
that moment, Ike grimaced and wondered what he was doing here.[5]

Joe Alsop, writing from Indianapolis at the time of Ike's visit,
described Senator Jenner as "the local imitation of Sen. Joseph R.
McCarthy." Some thought him even more bellicose. When Jenner
opposed Truman's appointment of General George Marshall to secretary of defense, he did it with panache. General Marshall, Jenner
argued, was "a front man for traitors" and a "living lie." He was responsible for consistent defeat: "Everything he has been a party to
during the past ten years has helped to betray his solemn trust and to
set the stage for the staggering Soviet victory that is sweeping across
the earth." Marshall was a "stooge" and "co-conspirator" and "an
accomplice in a deliberate conspiracy against the American people."
Amazing logic, that—a five-star general and hero who was actually
a puppet of Communist plots. After World War II, according to Jenner, Marshall followed the Acheson "line" and sold out the national-
ists in China to the Communists. Because of that failure, "our boys

are dying in Korea." And yet "General Marshall is still proud of this role he played as the inaugurator of the 'sell-China-down-the-river' line." Jenner's language was so bold that Senator Karl Mundt—a man who cosponsored failed legislation with Richard Nixon to outlaw the Communist Party and who was proud of his own HUAC activities—called it "the most venomous, the most diabolical, the most reprehensible, the most unfortunate and irresponsible speech I have ever heard made on the floor of the Senate or of the House of Representatives." Well, that was Jenner.[6]

And now Ike was sitting in a car with him, driving from event to event, where the general implored his audiences to vote a straight Republican ticket. Jenner was right next to him, all smiles. The senator "kept grabbing [Ike's] arm and poking it up through the air during the whole trip." After the day passed into evening, Ike told his friend and lawyer Bernard Shanley that when "he pushed my arm up twice . . . I just didn't get up" to wave anymore. Ike tried to slip out of a bear hug that Jenner gave at another point. But while most of the day wore on, Ike sucked it up. He laughed at Jenner's jokes during a lunchtime meeting and grinned his grin as much as possible. And it seemed to work the other way. Jenner told reporters after their shared speaking engagements: "I agree with the general one hundred percent—one hundred percent." Somehow, a man who thought Ike's favorite boss and mentor was a Communist stooge now saw eye to eye with him.[7]

Joe Alsop, who planned to vote for Ike in November, explained why Eisenhower should have doubted the "one hundred percent" comment. He reminded the general of what Jenner had said about him after the convention. The Indiana senator "bitterly and semi-publicly complained that the nomination of General Eisenhower had 'cut the rug out from under him,' because he and Eisenhower disagreed about everything." So how now this? Alsop couldn't quite answer that question. Maybe it was just Ike's way of showing off the

Republican Party as a big tent. Alsop, much like Walter Lippmann, had started to grow suspicious about the war hero's ability to remain a noble soldier above politics.[8]

As if this wasn't bad enough, September 9 brought more bad news to Joe Alsop and others who wanted Ike to transform the Republican Party: Senator McCarthy won the Republican primary of Wisconsin. It was a resounding victory, because the senator from Wisconsin did very little to win. After all, he was a busy and distracted man. Not only did he face two lawsuits, but soon after the convention in July, McCarthy entered Bethesda Naval Hospital for an operation on a herniated diaphragm. He figured he'd lie low, except to talk once from his hospital room with reporters, standing in his shorts, pulling up his shirt to show off surgical stitches while slurping warm martinis. He admitted slight trepidation about his chief Republican opponent, Leonard Schmitt, who had opened up a "talkathon" campaign by going on the radio and answering telephone callers for a whopping twenty-six hours. Schmitt was a fairly progressive Republican who called Senator McCarthy a demagogue and hoped crossover voting in the Republican primary might allow Democrats to push him over the edge to victory. It didn't work. The Republican Party in Wisconsin had moved definitively to the right and embraced McCarthy. The senator won without lifting a finger.[9]

Moving from Indiana to New York City must have been a culture shock to the general. Especially now that he was sitting in the Transfilm Inc. studio in midtown Manhattan the morning of September 11. Ike wore a suit and shot his eyes over to huge cue cards. These had two sentences printed on them that he read into a camera. Then a technician would say "Next," and he'd do another two sentences. The man responsible for making Ike endure this sat in a room next door pounding on a typewriter. He'd produce more two-line sentences and hand them to Ike's brother, Milt, who would sign off on them and send them to the general.

That man pounding the typewriter was Rosser Reeves, and he was one of the biggest names in American advertising. He had entered the profession at a difficult moment—during the Great Depression, when products weren't exactly easy to move. He worked first for Cecil, Warwick and Cecil and then jumped to Benton & Bowles, where he met Ted Bates. A friendship formed. They broke from B&B and started their own agency called Ted Bates and Company. They managed to have some pretty big clients, including Colgate-Palmolive with its line of health and soap products and Continental Baking, maker of Twinkies and Wonder Bread. Reeves had started to experiment with different techniques of persuasion and developed the central idea he became known for during his life: the "hard sell," based upon the "Unique Selling Proposition." Reeves believed in telling people what a product would do for them—a singular thing, usually—and then repeating that over and over in "spots" on television and radio, busting through saturated markets by the sheer force of one's own focused deluge.[10]

Reeves believed his advertising methods could assist in the world of politics. In 1952, he had attended the Republican convention and sat next to the journalist Drew Pearson. They both listened to General MacArthur's keynote speech and came to different conclusions: Pearson thought it strong (though he disagreed with its content), but Reeves found it diluted, flowery, and "lousy." He did some informal polling and found that many delegates—even those who cheered their lungs out for MacArthur—didn't remember much from the speech. He was now inspired to bring the hard sell—simplicity, unified message, directness, emphasis on the product's best features—to political campaigning. He approached the Eisenhower team.[11]

When he first caught wind of this idea, Eisenhower balked, much as Dewey had about radio spots in 1948. The general thought advertising techniques undignified. But Reeves pressed: Advertising would get his message out there, even if in simplified form. Besides, anything that Dewey had rejected looked good to a candidate who wanted to win in 1952. Eisenhower caved, and Reeves started to write up short spots in which citizens would ask questions and Ike would quip a retort: "WOMAN: The Democrats have made mistakes—but aren't their intentions good? EISENHOWER: Well, if the driver of your school bus runs into a truck, hits a lamppost, [and] drives into a ditch, you don't say: 'His *intentions* are good.' You get a new bus driver." Long on metaphor and short on substance, this was just the sort of message appropriate for the growing medium of television. The payoff was obvious. A colleague of Reeves explained, "The general's answer would be his complete comprehension of the problem and his determination to do something about it when elected. Thus he inspires loyalty without prematurely committing himself to any strait-jacketing answer." In other words, short, sweet, but not necessarily to the point.[12]

The main advertising agency working with Eisenhower, Batten, Barton, Durstine and Osborn, gave a nod to Reeves's proposal. Bruce Barton, a major *B* in BBDO who had spent a life in public relations stretching further back than Reeves (to 1918) and who'd also had a brief career in Republican politics, encouraged Ike to stop reading speeches on television and instead speak extemporaneously from notes. That way Ike could talk "to people, as one frank, unassuming American to his fellow Americans." The model he suggested Eisenhower follow was Fulton Sheen, a Catholic bishop who had a weekly television show, *Life Is Worth Living*, in late 1951 and early 1952, in which he walked around and smiled while speaking about religious issues in front of a blackboard on which he wrote key terms (Sheen was awarded an Emmy as the "most outstanding television personality" in 1952). Barton thought Sheen looked and sounded authentic, not canned the way a person reading from a page did. Though Ike would still be reading cue cards in Reeves's spots, he wouldn't *appear* to be reading cards but rather to be saying things that sounded as if they had just come to his mind.[13]

Trusting the advice of his advertising men, as usual, Ike read the cue cards over and over, and they managed to film around forty "spots" on September 11. Then, after Ike was gone, Reeves hunted down ordinary-looking citizens around Rockefeller Plaza and brought them to the studio to read questions printed on cue cards (he searched for an authentic Korean veteran for one). The two performances were grafted together and a short introduction was filmed with the words "Eisenhower Answers America" flashing onto the screen.[14]

As far as Ike knew, his performances on September 11 would be put in storage for about another month. He had found it slightly demeaning, this answering of unheard questions. Between performances, someone in the studio heard him mumble, "To think that an old soldier should come to this."[15]

The next morning at his Morningside Drive home, Eisenhower had a breakfast meeting with Senator Robert Taft. The two men hadn't said much to each other since the convention. After packing up from Chicago, Taft had headed to the northern woods of Canada to stew about his defeat. He blamed the "power of the New York financial interests" and the "four fifths of the influential newspapers in the country" that opposed him. He seethed about polls that showed his supposed unelectability. He figured this would be the last time he'd run for the presidency, and he was still upset at Ike about his defeat.[16]

But not after the two-hour breakfast. Taft, beaming, walked out with a statement for reporters. Eisenhower had supposedly agreed with Taft that the chief issue of the campaign should be "liberty against the creeping socialism in every domestic field." Taft got Ike to promise some radical budget and tax cuts to shrink government if he won office. They also agreed that there were only "differences of degree" when it came to foreign policy. This may have been an understatement; it was on the issue of NATO that Ike had decided to run against Taft in the first place. Taft said he'd campaign for Ike with no hesitation and was looking forward to the general's upcoming visit to Ohio. The two shook hands and smiled at each other. Critics called the whole event "the Surrender at Morningside Heights."[17]

As much as Ike might have wanted a big tent, some were starting to think about pulling up stakes. Senator Wayne Morse of Oregon, a moderate Republican who was originally enthusiastic about Ike, decided he couldn't stump for him after hearing about the Taft breakfast meeting and the hand-pumping sessions with Jenner. "Whenever one compromises with principle there is no principle left," Morse explained. Walter Lippmann, who still hoped against hope that the general might commit to "healing and uniting the nation," worried openly in his columns that Ike was getting too close to Taft and sounding the trumpet of "liberation," an idea he found "seriously wrong and dangerously misleading." A picture of the general was starting to fill out: a man who would condemn the hard right but curry its favor, who would worry about hard-line foreign policy but speak its language to the faithful. In other words, Ike the general on the white horse was starting to look blurry.[18]

Now the fun would begin. Nixon was getting ready to embark upon what he called "the most intensive vote-getting drive in U.S. political history, from the standpoint of miles traveled, speeches delivered, and citizens visited." It would be, in poetic language, "an intensive train-plane-auto campaign" that would bring Nixon to the masses. Finally, the rocking and socking started. It would begin September 17 on a train called the *Nixon Special*, replete with multiple cars for staff, the press, and the candidate himself (the most beautiful of them all, with big separate beds for Dick and Pat). The vice-presidential candidate wanted his whistle-stop tour to make Harry Truman's 1948 journeys look like kid stuff. Remarkably, Governor Earl Warren, still seething with anger about Nixon, a man he considered a traitor, would come out to the Pomona railroad station to send him off on his merry way up through California and into Oregon. Everything was finally coming together.[19]

To start rolling out some of the themes he'd develop on the back of train platforms, Nixon went on *Meet the Press* on September 14. The show had been on the air since 1947, offering a dry interchange between reporters and politicians, a kind of public service amid all the commercial entertainment television offered. Nixon wanted to explain how he and Ike saw eye to eye on foreign policy—something a whole host of journalists doubted at the time. Reporters asked him about the language of "liberation" creeping into his and Ike's rhetoric. Nixon squirmed a bit, knowing that liberation sounded to some— including Walter Lippmann and moderate Republicans—like opening up World War III. "General Eisenhower has never advocated, nor have I, the liberation of the so-called Iron Curtain countries by force. We have advocated a policy of liberation through means other than force." The reporters looked slightly quizzical and asked him to explain. He was talking about "psychological warfare, economic pressure . . . internal warfare." Tough stuff: kind of mysterious-sounding, even creepy, but not traditional warfare.[20]

After the lights were turned off and the microphones killed, Peter Edson, a columnist on the show who liked Nixon and pitched him softball questions, took the opportunity to ask a question off the record: "Senator, what is this 'fund' we hear about? There is a rumor to the effect that you have a supplementary salary of twenty thousand dollars a year, contributed by a hundred California businessmen. What about it?" Nixon explained no, it wasn't a salary but a campaign treasure chest for the most part. The number Edson had on his fingers sounded a bit high as well. You can see a guy named Dana Smith about the thing, Nixon told him; he'll explain it. He figured that was that. Edson said he'd look the guy up.[21]

Dick left Washington, D.C., the next day. Before embarking, he okayed a memo to his research director to look into how well Stevenson knew Alger Hiss at the Agricultural Adjustment Administration. Then, walking through the bustle of National Airport en route to catch his flight, he spoke to journalists and blasted Stevenson's "wisecracking" ways: "When we discuss our boys dying in the Korean war, the prices we have to pay, and these crooks down here in Washington, it is no laughing matter." He then flew to Denver, stopping in at Eisenhower headquarters, and then to his wife's hometown of Ely, Nevada, on September 16. Whisked downtown in front of the Nevada Hotel, they had a hometown-girl-makes-good ceremony in which the mayor presented Pat Nixon with a copper key to the town. Dick gave a stump speech. Then he and Pat flew to California to start their big journey and engage their war against Stevenson's humor.[22]

Ike had already begun his own whistle-stop tour, leaving Manhattan's Pennsylvania Station on September 14 aboard the *Look Ahead, Neighbor! Special*. He wanted to make it back to the Midwest, now that he had penetrated the South and Dick was covering the West. Ike's tour wouldn't be as hyperkinetic as Nixon's, but he planned to make seventy speeches during it. The first leg would bring him through Indiana, across Illinois, and then up to Iowa and Minnesota. From there, he'd fly back to New York City to speak at the American Federation of Labor (AFL) convention on the first day of Nixon's whistle-stop tour, September 17. The speech there would be symbolic of his confidence that he could not only crack the Solid South but could get some northern urban union members to vote for him, even if he was now chummy with Senator Taft, the architect of landmark antilabor legislation. He was feeling confident, and it showed.[23]

The day of his departure, Ike made two public statements to get the show rolling: one against Truman's call for nationalized health care (he opposed "regimented, assembly-line treatment"), and a more telling one about his views on faith and politics. It showed that as the general tiptoed toward the language of liberation in foreign policy, he also moved closer to the positions of Nixon's conservative intellectual friend, Whittaker Chambers, on the sources of national domestic unity necessary for a bolder foreign policy. Ike explained that American democracy rested upon the bedrock of "God-fearing families" (he, after all, had come from one). He pointed out, "You can't explain free government in any other terms than religious." The language he had imbibed and then unveiled at the convention—the language of "crusade"—started taking sharper form. For Ike, religion was now central to victory in the Cold War, as it was for Chambers. Ike explained, "What is our battle against Communism if it is not a fight between anti-God, and a belief in the Almighty?" His call to arm Americans religiously didn't take on any particular theological hue—there was no talk of Christ or mention of any particular sect, just a generalized belief in God. But it was for the sake of gaining "courage to make . . . decisions" and "the confidence to leave the result to a higher power" that should inspire religious faith. It's what got Ike through the difficult times of World War II. Confidence grounded in faith.[24]

As his train moved farther west, Ike began sounding more like Nixon. Stepping to the rear platform of the train in Fort Wayne, Indiana, on September 15, Eisenhower ripped into Stevenson for his humor. "As we face the issues of the campaign," he explained to the large crowd gathered, "I see nothing funny about them and no way to make them amusing." Then, in South Bend, Ike railed further against Stevenson's "funny" speeches. What was humorous about the Cold War or the corruption in Truman's administration? Ike asked his fans. "It wasn't a laughing matter when I had to make the decision to leave the service in which I had served for forty years because I became convinced that there was another duty that I had in this country and in the political world." Stevenson wasn't presidential material; he was a wiseass.[25]

If Stevenson was the smart aleck and nerd in high school, Ike was the tough football player. Every chance he got, Ike celebrated the virtues of football on the campaign trail. When in South Bend, Indiana, he made a stop at Notre Dame's famous field house, praising the school's legendary coach, Knute Rockne, and his vision of athletics joined to religious faith (captured in the iconic 1940 movie *Knute Rockne, All American*, that starred Ronald Reagan as a young player named George Gipp). Ike then backslapped Frank Leahy, the current coach at Notre Dame. Then he moved through Illinois and Iowa up to Minnesota, where he requested a handshake with Coach Wes Fesler of the University of Minnesota, who happened to be bringing the team out for a practice near where Ike was speaking. Ike said that when he played football at West Point, he remembered University of Minnesota players being twenty feet tall. The players cheered, the coach smiled, and then Ike took off for the next stop.[26]

As much as he loved talking the virtues of football, Eisenhower stayed on the C_2K_1 message. He'd talk about the Truman administration's pursuit of "an aimless sort of . . . fumbling course abroad," especially in Korea, believing this the central theme of the upcoming election. He also condemned "three Internal Revenue collectors who between them collected five and a half billion dollars in one year" and "who had to be relieved for crookedness and some of them put in the penitentiary." The government was corrupt down to the bone, he suggested. All of this wrapped around to the broader theme of a crusade—*run the money changers out of the temple!*—to be fought on the rear platform of a train that would charge across country through day and night. His crowds kept growing larger and more enthusiastic at almost every new whistle stop he made.[27]

Recognizing that Stevenson had covered some of the same ground as Ike, James ("Scotty") Reston, a Pulitzer Prize–winning reporter at the *New York Times*, made some acute observations published the day Richard Nixon began his tour. Ike used his campaign trip, Reston argued, to get around newspaper columnists like Lippmann and Alsop and to talk directly to the masses. "Dwight D. Eisenhower may be losing ground with the intellectuals and the independents—as many persons on his own campaign train think—but he still is an immensely popular figure in the villages and cities of the Middle West." By counting heads in the crowds, Reston figured that Ike was trouncing Stevenson. But the slaughter wasn't just numerical, it was qualitative. Reston believed the contrast could be painted this way: "It is the difference between the crowd at a concert and the crowd at a football rally." Ike's events are "larger and more enthusiastic," Stevenson's "quieter and more attentive." When Ike would go back onto the train and talk with journalists traveling with him, Reston noticed they snubbed his platitudinous statements. When he went back to the rear platform and addressed the thronging crowds, he received applause. As Ike said in Minneapolis, "I gather determination to carry on the job" when speaking to a crowd. "When this many people are here gathered in this great field to hear a fellow American express his views, they are showing a seriousness and a determination that cannot be denied." Ike's whistle-stopping looked like a pep rally for a football game and return to God.[28]

Another trip was about to take place—this one, too, bringing good news to Richard Nixon. The day the vice-presidential candidate left for his whistle-stop tour and Ike flew back to New York to speak at the AFL convention, the sixty-three-year-old movie star and director Charlie Chaplin left America for England on the *Queen Elizabeth*. Even though Chaplin was one of America's best-known celebrities before World War II, there was no fanfare at his departure. His friend, the movie critic James Agee, couldn't even locate him at the dock (Chaplin was madly waving his hat at him out a porthole of the boat). The comic artist was leaving, in part, because the FBI was compiling background about his left-wing politics and following up HUAC's earlier investigation of him (fortunately, Chaplin never appeared before the Committee). Now Truman's attorney general, James McGranery, was pursuing his case. Chaplin figured his native soil of England would prove more hospitable for the debut of his latest film, *Limelight*. When he arrived in England, he learned that the U.S. attorney general had already denied his reentry into the United States, forcing him into exile. Disgust and disgrace entered his voice as he told the British press while embarking for shore, "This is not the day of great artists. This is the day of politics." He was not a man who checked his own pretensions.[29]

It was a victory for one of Richard Nixon's closest friends in Hollywood, Hedda Hopper. She was known for wearing crazy hats and breaking gossip in a town that ran on gossip. Her journalism and reportage—which usually moved fast from telephone conversations with celebrities to words on paper—were must-reads for anyone in Tinseltown. She had a mean streak, too, one she shared with Dick Nixon. They had agreed a year earlier that it would be wonderful to deport Chaplin to England. Hopper hated the man, in part because his leftist politics—he supported the Progressive Party and Henry Wallace in 1948—offended her conservative sensibilities, but also because he had a paternity suit filed against him and all sorts of allegations of loose living (including a boatload of affairs and divorces). Besides, he wasn't even an American but a Brit, never having acquired American citizenship in the whole time he spent in Hollywood acting in his "tramp" movies and piling up his celebrity income. Nixon felt indebted to Hopper; she had appeared in radio advertisements for him during his Senate run of 1950. The senator wrote Hopper on May 29, 1952, "We aren't able to do much about it when the top decisions are made by the likes of Acheson and McGranery. You can be sure, however, that I will keep my eyes on the case and possibly after January we will be able to work with an Administration" that could nail Chaplin. Fortunately for Hopper, she didn't have to wait that long. Learning the news of Chaplin's lockout, she wrote, "I abhor what he stands for . . . I would like to say, 'Good riddance to bad company.'"[30]

What Hopper could not have known at the time was that the movie Chaplin had recently completed and planned to debut overseas was profoundly anti-American. It wasn't politically explicit, it was just a real bummer. Set in London in 1914 (the year World War I erupted), the movie centered on an old clown and performance artist, Calvero (played by Chaplin), who rescues a young woman, Thereza (or Terry), from committing suicide. He's a vaudeville and comedy performer who has lost touch with his audiences. While allowing Thereza to recuperate in his apartment (something it wasn't difficult to imagine would make Hopper cringe, the sight of a gray-haired man and a youthful beauty living together), Calvero proceeds to confess that he's "all washed up." He has a drinking problem, and his agent can get him only crappy gigs. He puts on a show and everyone walks out. "It's no use, I'm finished," he concludes. He gets philosophical: "As a man gets on, he wants to live deeply. A feeling of sad dignity comes over him, and that's fatal for a comic." And then, as Thereza starts to fall in love with him, she regains her health and becomes a great and famous dancer. With her success, she gets him a show where he performs his traditional shtick and finds audience approval, only to fall to a heart attack. As he dies, his last act is to lie on a couch and watch her dance, recognizing her youthful beauty in contrast to his elderly demise and tragic fate.[31]

This was just the sort of fare that an intellectual like Bosley Crowther—the man who slammed both *My Son John* and *Big Jim McLain* (a favorite movie of Hopper's)—would like. And he did. First, he came to Chaplin's political defense. The great artist was victim, Crowther would argue a week after James McGranery rescinded his return papers, to "the sort of pressure and harassment that are being applied to many artists and creators in the movies as a result of the present Communist fear." What danger could this man pose to the United States? Crowther wondered. He was once the little "tramp" whom Americans loved to watch toddle onscreen and perform his slapstick. This was no dangerous radical. When Crowther eventually saw *Limelight*, he gushed, "It is a brilliant weaving of comic and tragic strands, eloquent, tearful and beguiling with supreme virtuosity." The movie took on the difficult theme of "fate" and "natural inevitability." No wonder the film would do well in Europe but not in America, where it finally came to the screen later in October only to face angry American Legion pickets.[32]

Crowther's highbrow appreciation of the film and its explorations of tragedy didn't resonate much. In 1952, Hopper's "good riddance" resonated more. There was no room for talk about fate or the limits of the body overcoming desire. This was to be the year of positive thinking and confidence about America's prospects. And Chaplin was better off exiled to Europe, precisely where he would stay for years, to the applause of Hopper and Nixon.

A day after Nixon's appearance on *Meet the Press*, Peter Edson tracked down Dana Smith, who was more than ready to talk. Edson reached him on the phone and had gotten some details about Nixon's fund.

That same day, September 15, three reporters sat in Smith's law office in Pasadena. They were Ernest Brashear of the Los Angeles *Daily News*; Richard Donovan of the liberal-leaning *Reporter*, who was writing a portrait of Nixon eventually published as "Birth of a Salesman"; and, most important, Leo Katcher, a West Coast writer for the liberal *New York Post*. Katcher had caught wind of Dana Smith's activities from a disgruntled Earl Warren supporter who had given money to the fund and grown miffed at how Nixon positioned himself behind the scenes to get onto the national ticket.[33]

Dana Smith appeared to the reporters like an owl with popping eyes framed by circular glasses. He was in his fifties, balding, and comfortable in life, having inherited his family's riches made in the lumber industry. When not talking to the reporters in his office, he would hover over the shoulders of secretaries to see what they were doing or take phone calls at his desk about tax cases. He was a man of connections, who knew the world of businessmen Dick Nixon wanted to tap. He was also as much of a personal friend to Nixon as a man could be and chaired Nixon's finance committee during his 1950 Senate run. Smith had recruited the donors and then set up the fund in the First Trust and Savings Bank of Pasadena. Proud of the work he had done, including a careful documenting of expenses and revenues, he talked openly to the reporters, sometimes with little thought as to what he was saying. He basked in his brief flurry of fame.[34]

Smith explained that he lined up a number of funders rather than one big bundle of money. That would look better. "We limited contributions from any one source or any one family to five hundred dollars a year so that no one could say that we were buying a senator or accuse us of owning one," he explained. To this, either Brashear or Katcher asked: Could they have a list of the funders? Smith looked nervous suddenly and balked. The thing wasn't secret, but now that reporters were involved, Smith worried about giving away too much information. After all, when Nixon, a month back, was asked by the

Kansas City Star about finances, he said that he had "no other sources of income except" his "salary as senator." Smith changed the subject from the donors to the way the money was spent, which made it sound innocuous. Smith detailed costs for stationery, travel, mailings, and radio and television advertising. The reporters also learned that Dick Nixon had a penchant for sending out Christmas cards to his supporters, a whopping twenty thousand to twenty-five thousand the previous year.[35]

Smith was remarkably open about the political philosophy behind the fund. After gathering together a group of men angry at the legacy of the New Deal and the increased power of labor unions, Smith set out what they wanted: "Our thinking was that we had to fight selling with selling, and for that job Dick Nixon seemed to be the best salesman against socialization available. That's his gift really—salesmanship." It was Katcher, likely, who asked a follow-up here about Earl Warren: Why no money given to the governor? "Frankly, Warren has too much of the other point of view, and he never has gone out selling the free-enterprise system. But Dick did just what we wanted him to do." Smith's loose lips here made the thing sound a tad troublesome, as if the man running for vice president had been a puppet on strings for angry businessmen. But it also represented Smith's opinion—and those of the men he organized— that Nixon played the authentic conservative to the phony Warren.[36]

Soon after the meeting with journalists and his own phone call with Smith, Peter Edson wrote a story that played down controversy surrounding the fund and told Nixon that he should have Smith list out the donors to get rid of any lingering sense of secrecy. Smith did. It read like a who's who of regional businessmen: Rea L. Eaton, "San Marino stock broker"; John Garland, "San Marino real-estate man"; Henry Kerns, "San Gabriel automobile dealer"; Earl Gilmore, "Los Angeles oil man"; Earle M. Jorgensen, "Los Angeles steel manufacturer"; Fred Bixby, "Long Beach rancher"; Thomas Knudsen, "Glendale dairyman"; Thomas P. Pike, "San Marino, oil drilling"; R. R. Bush, "Pasadena oil"; Tyler Woodward, "Los Angeles oil"; E. B. Miller, "Long Beach contractor"; Walker Smith, "Pasadena mortgage business." There were sixty-four more, mostly men with real estate, ranching, oil, or other economic interests driving them to find a man who could articulate the gospel of the free market. Direct correlations between these men's desires and the policies Nixon pressed for as senator were fewer than some might have expected. Nixon consciously avoided the appearance of currying favor. His own study of the fund concluded that there was a "total of 65 letters regarding cases or legislation from the 76 contributors. . . . No appointments or pressure brought to bear in any instance. 10 letters regarding legislation—which were answered, glad to have your suggestions, will keep them in mind; or giving them information on pending legislation." A legal firm working with Nixon to clear his name pointed out: "In two instances the contributor advised us that subsequent to his contribution he had contacted Senator Nixon to request his assistance in connection with matters pending before a department or agency of the Government, but that in each instance Senator Nixon declined to take any action or render any assistance in connection therewith."[37]

And yet: Some of the contributors had obviously *tried* to get the ear of the senator. And Nixon *did* consult with Smith regarding some tax cases. He introduced S-1029, a bill that opened military property to private oilmen, something that benefited two contributors to the fund who wanted to drill at Camp Roberts in California. And he *did* oppose public housing nearly every chance he got—something that pleased the real estate men on his list. "Last June Nixon voted to cut the public housing program from 75,000 units a year to 5,000," a representative of organized labor pointed out. "In the same month he also voted for an amendment permitting rents on housing around military installations and defense plants to be increased."[38]

The problem of connecting funder to legislation was that Richard Nixon would have voted the way he did with or without the money. It was a matter of ideological principle for him. Smith was right to choose Nixon in the first place: The young senator really was a salesman for the free market and a devotee of antiregulation. Those who went looking for a smoking gun—a specific deal that paid off a contributor with favor—were likely to find only smoke. Nixon would channel the ideas of these angry men even without taking cash from them. These were, after all, *his* people.

Still, the fund had cracked open one of the most difficult problems in American politics: how to finance campaigns ethically. America had a long history of trying to get "money out of politics," going back to the Tillman Act of 1907 and the Federal Corrupt Practices Act of 1910—both passed during the Progressive Era when reformers, upset at the influence business had over politics, tried to clean up political decision making. The Tillman Act had made it illegal "for any national bank, or any corporation organized by authority of any laws of Congress, to make a money contribution in connection with any election to any political office." The Federal Corrupt Practices Act required politicians to report contributions and put limits on spending for House and Senate seats. Later, the Hatch Act of 1939 put a limit ($5,000) on individual campaign donations. Though all of these acts might have sounded sweeping, they were also, as the *New York Times* notes in 1952, riddled with "generous loopholes" and aimed mostly at political party activity, meaning donations to individual candidates were much less policed. Considering this, there was nothing illegal about Nixon's campaign funding per se. But that didn't mean Nixon's donations from businessmen passed the proverbial smell test.[39]

Just a month before the fund crisis erupted, Senator Paul Douglas, a man elected to the Senate as a Democrat from Illinois the same year Stevenson won the governorship, had published an article entitled

"What It Costs to Run." As he traced his own political biography, moving from City Council to U.S. Senate, Douglas described his campaign expenses ticking upward. Especially bad were the costs for radio and television advertising. Senators inevitably found themselves asking for money from "big contributors," and these men usually "want something in return." Douglas suggested that public financing of political campaigns was the best solution, an idea that his fellow Illinois friend, Adlai Stevenson, also toyed with. Maybe Nixon's fund could prompt a wider discussion about the problem of campaign finance, but that would suggest that Stevenson's deliberative conception of the presidential election—and his role as what the op-ed writer Marquis Childs called around this time "schoolmaster"—could set the tone.[40]

Instead, the issue of Nixon's fund zinged back into the dynamic of the campaign: *Defend, smash back, attack.* Three days after his first meeting with the man who managed Nixon's fund, the journalist Richard Donovan attended a follow-up press conference with Dana Smith. The balding owl was all confidence: "I'm glad this story got out, because there wasn't anything wrong about it." Smith reiterated that it didn't matter that businessmen gave money, they just wanted to get their ideas out there. This wasn't pay to play. "But, Mr. Smith," Donovan interjected to make a point about special influence, "supposing members of a labor union had made a contribution to . . ." Smith waved his hand and cut him off. "Oh, that's different. A labor union is a special interest."[41]

SECRET RICH MEN'S TRUST FUND KEEPS NIXON IN STYLE FAR BEYOND HIS SALARY. Thus rang the headline accompanying Leo Katcher's story in the *New York Post* on September 18. That word "style" suggested something more than what Katcher really had on the vice-presidential candidate. It made it sound as if Nixon was taking the money for himself rather than for his project of free-market sales-manship. Katcher wrote, "A contributor to the fund, a state official in California, said the appeal to him was based on the fact that Nixon needed a larger home, as befitted a Senator, and that the Nixons could not even afford a maid." Then Katcher wrote, "In the past year, Nixon has purchased a two story house in exclusive Spring Valley, a suburban section of Washington." Readers of this urban Democratic newspaper were, of course, supposed to put two and two together and say: *Well, these rich bums are buying this guy a goddamn house.* Unfortunately for the *Post*, there was little evidence to suggest that.[42]

When he first learned that the story was spreading, Nixon panicked. He dispatched his research team to look into the *New York Post*. Nixon smelled a rat: The paper's editor, James Wechsler, had been a Communist in the 1930s and was now a liberal who published in 1951 a series on Joseph McCarthy entitled "Smear Inc." The articles that made up the series rang with this sort of line: "Like a drunk at a party who was funny half an hour ago but now won't go home, McCarthy is camped in America's front room trying to impress everybody." Nixon's team made contact with Alfred Kohlberg, an ally of Joseph McCarthy, to see what he could dig up on the paper. He told them that "under Wechsler the Communists have taken over the place completely," which was wrong—actually, Wechsler had been purging Communists from the paper. Nixon searched his own papers from HUAC for anything that leaped out about James Wechsler. Nixon's advisers knew people who had contacts with a janitor who worked inside Stevenson's operations; they had already gotten long distance phone call records from Stevenson headquarters to the *New York Post*. It was common knowledge that James Wechsler was writing some of the governor's speeches, and the *Post* was one of the few newspapers to support Stevenson (Wechsler estimated 75 percent of dailies were in favor of Eisenhower). So Nixon's team felt confident having Karl Mundt tell reporters the *New York Post* was "a left-wing smear sheet."[43]

That might have calmed the nerves of the vice-presidential candidate pursuing a manic whistle-stop tour of California. The day the *Post* blasted its headline, Nixon turned into a whirligig. He started in Bakersfield, giving a rear-platform speech at 9:00 A.M., another at Tulare, others at Fresno, Madera, Merced, Stockton, and Sacramento. During this last stop he started commenting on the case cracking open. "This is another typical attempted smear by the same left-wing elements which have fought me ever since I took part in the investigation which led to the conviction of Alger Hiss," he told crowds. And then he was whisked away to the airport, to fly to Reno, Nevada, where he motorcaded through town and then spoke in front of the courthouse. He then zipped back to the Reno Airport and arrived trainside in Sacramento a half hour before midnight, just in time to crash into the large bed next to Pat's in their private car. Such would be Nixon's life as the fund scandal ratcheted up—days of manic publicity and then falling into bed with an aching neck.[44]

At the crack of dawn the next day, the *Nixon Special* pulled out of Sacramento and traveled to Marysville, a small lumber and mining town, where the vice-presidential candidate had his first speech of the day. It went as planned until a group of men ran toward the train, one of them screaming, "Tell us about the sixteen thousand dollars!" (That was the number associated with the fund at this point.) The conductor had started pulling the train out of the station, and Nixon yelled to his back, "Hold the train! Hold the train!" It screeched to a halt after making it just one hundred yards. The crowds ran toward it, hecklers and fans alike.

Nixon gripped the rear guardrail and then pointed at the man who had shouted about the money and glowered. He thought to himself how he was going to "let him have it." He blasted back: "You folks know the work that I did investigating Communists in the United States." The crowds cheered at that. "Ever since I have done that work, the Communists and the left-wingers have been fighting me with every possible smear. When I received the nomination for the vice presidency I was warned that if I continued to attack the Communists in this government, they would continue to smear me." The lines of conspiracy had now been drawn by Nixon—this was a plot against him. Behind the men running and yelling about the money there was something more sinister, something directed by the forces of Communism massing in the world and the nation. This wasn't just routine political heckling. And then Dick segued from conspiracy into legalese: "Rather than charging the American taxpayer with the expenses of my office, which were in excess of the amounts which were allowed under the law, what I did was to have those expenses be paid by the people back home who were interested in seeing that information concerning what was going on in Washington was spread among the people of this state." Amazingly enough, the crowds cheered that, too.[45]

Nixon walked back into the train as it pulled out of Marysville, this time for good. The cheering crowd he left behind contrasted with the gloomy message Murray Chotiner and William Rogers, a lawyer with good Republican connections and a friend to Nixon, started to share with him. They were finding the press all a-jitter about the fund. Nixon would slump in a chair and receive the news and then go back outside and give another rear platform speech, first in Chico, and then Red Bluff, Redding, and Dunsmuir. Eventually, later in the day, he'd head out of California into Oregon, doing some evening platform speaking there. Hecklers would call out about the fund; Nixon would respond, and the crowds would cheer him when he shouted that he'd never let up on his "attacks on Communism and corruption in the administration." He would continue to pursue the "battle cry for a crusade." But then he'd return to gloomier and gloomier conversations on board his train. Eventually Chotiner let on that the *Washington Post* and the *New York Herald Tribune*—both papers that endorsed Eisenhower for president—would feature editorials the next day calling for Nixon to resign. That really threw Nixon for a loop. He knew that Bert Andrews, a key Washington writer who worked for the *Herald*, was on the train with Ike. He also knew the paper's owner, Bill Robinson, was close friends with the general and likely talking crap about him. It sounded to Nixon like Eisenhower's men were ganging up on him via newsprint. Chotiner called the general's inner circle "stupid," while Rogers looked nervous.[46]

In fact, Ike hadn't even heard the entire story about the fund until this day. His advisers wanted to protect him from bad news as he went through the rounds of a trying whistle-stop tour on September 18. The next day, Eisenhower's *Look Ahead, Neighbor! Special* moved from Omaha, Nebraska, to Kansas City, Missouri, with numerous stops along the way. During this time, the full story was broken to him. He knew right away it meant trouble: A campaign crusading against corruption now had ties to a "secret fund." But if he kicked Nixon off the ticket, it would make him appear to have exercised bad judgment in the first place. Most of all, Ike didn't want "emotion" to replace "fact and justice." So he turned to a skill that had worked for him so far: evasion. He had done it on Korea, criticizing yet supporting the war. He had done it on Jenner, condemning "un-American" comments about Marshall and then campaigning for the man who made those comments. Now he had to turn his evasive nature on high. Speaking from Kansas City, he said, "I have long admired and applauded Senator Nixon's American faith and his determination to drive Communistic sympathizers from offices of public trust. There has recently been leveled against him a charge of unethical practices." Then from that passively worded construction, he explained:

"I believe Dick Nixon to be an honest man." But anyone listening to his words would notice that believing wasn't the same as being true. Ike said he'd have a phone conversation with Nixon some time in the near future to sort this thing out. He suggested, let's see where this goes.[47]

For Ike it went immediately to the Muehlebach Hotel in Kansas City, where he stayed the evening. Protesters gathered there holding signs that read DONATE HERE TO THE FUND FOR POOR MR. NIXON, with pro-Eisenhower groups screaming at them. It went to the front page of the *St. Joseph News-Press* published just north of Kansas City, a paper that endorsed Eisenhower and that now printed this doggerel:

We have often heard the shout
We must turn the rascals out
The rate they're leading us to ruin isn't slow
But cleaning up their own backyard
May be just a wee bit hard
When millionaires are slipping them the dough.

It's hard to imagine that this wouldn't fray Ike's nerves. More and more his inner circle—especially his brother, Milt, and *New York Herald Tribune* owner Bill Robinson—were saying that Nixon should be kicked off the ticket.[48]

The night of September 19, Richard Nixon had more conversations with Chotiner and Rogers. Murray was pretty sure they could turn this thing around. "Dick," Chotiner explained, "all we've got to do is to get you before enough people talking about this fund, and we will win this election in a landslide." He noticed how the whistle-stop crowds contrasted with the newspaper editorials. Nixon just grew gloomier, exhaustion hitting him hard. Go to bed, both Chotiner and Rogers suggested, as the clock struck two. So Nixon trundled into his private room and woke up Pat. He told her he was consider-

ing quitting. She shot up in bed and said, "You can't think of resigning. If you, in the face of attack, do not fight back but simply crawl
away, you will destroy yourself. Your life will be marred forever and
the same will be true of your family." Her "wonderful guy" would
have to man up.[49]

Saturday, September 20, started glumly for Nixon. The *Washington
Post* and *New York Herald Tribune* printed their calls for his resignation,
the papers hitting Eastern Seaboard towns before he was out of bed.
The *Post* explained that "Eisenhower's principal domestic issue—
and one with which we completely agree—is that new leadership is
needed to return high moral standards to Government. Obviously,
this issue would be seriously compromised by Senator Nixon's remaining on the ticket." That hurt. So did the Herblock cartoon
printed next to those words. It showed a dark, shadowy Nixon slumped
over, holding one suitcase brimming with brooms, brushes, and
toilet bowl cleaners and another with "$16,000" on it (still the figure
most thought the fund to be). The title of the cartoon: "Death of a
Salesman."[50]

The Eisenhower-Nixon Research Service readied a telegram for
Sherman Adams that morning. The staff had read newspapers with
growing despair. Eastern papers had gone negative on the fund
situation, and Ike needed their support to win the election, or so the
researchers thought. Consider the list: Nixon had "poor judgment"
(*New York Times*); he was "lacking in both discernment and sensitiv-
ity" (Baltimore *Sun*); the vice-presidential candidate faced "serious
ethical questions" (*Washington Star*). The conclusion the researchers
drew was: "The only mistake Ike can make in this situation is to ig-
nore the verdict of a pro-Republican press that Nixon has completely
disqualified himself as a possible successor to the presidency."[51]

Meanwhile, on the West Coast, the *Nixon Special* had made it over the state line into Oregon the night before. On Saturday it lurched from Roseburg to the college town of Eugene, arriving late in the morning. There to greet the *Nixon Special*, standing amid cheering fans, was Charles Porter, a member of Americans for Democratic Action (ADA), who held a sign that read on one side NO MINK COATS FOR NIXON—JUST COLD CASH. (That referred, in Nixon's words, to a "mink coat accepted by a White House secretary" that "had become a symbol of all the corruption of the Truman administration.") The other side of the sign read: SH-H-H . . . ANYONE WHO MENTIONS $16,000 IS A COMMUNIST. Nixon pulled in, and the crowd of about two thousand heaved forward. Porter was surrounded by whooping fans as the candidate stepped out on the platform. Seeing the sign, Dick glowered: "That's absolutely right. There are no mink coats for the Nixons. I am proud to say my wife, Pat, wears a good Republican cloth coat." The crowd cheered. It suddenly came to Nixon at that point: "They were not only listening to what I had to say and believing it, but also they were willing to fight back." Literally in this case, with the crowds yelling to "tear" the sign "down" and calling Porter a "Dirty Communist" as they descended on him with fists flying. The police moved in, and Porter carried out a citizen's arrest on Sinclair Sutton, a Nixon fan, who wound up in jail. The *Washington Post* described the incident as a "near riot."[52]

That same morning, Robert Humphreys sat bolt upright in bed, with a big thought burning in his mind preventing sleep. He was head of the Republican National Committee's publicity department, in charge of coordinating media messages for the campaign. He was blessed with knowing the world of the print media—having attended Columbia University's school of journalism before going to work with *Newsweek*—but also having cut his teeth with the publicity department of the Indiana Republican Party during the Depression.

He moved back and forth from journalism and partisan publicity, finding both worlds to his liking. Forty-seven years old but boisterous and tightly wound, he was respected as a writer but also a man who appreciated the growing power of television in American life. Humphreys was "fairly slight, dark, with a small, sharp face and darting eyes" and "made of springs." The fund crisis and Ike's handling of it had started to incense him to the point of insomnia.[53]

His thought right now was: *Get Dick off the whistle-stop and out of the newspapers and onto television.* He wanted to help the vice-presidential candidate because he shared Nixon's desire to make the campaign of 1952 "aggressive" and "militant," providing voters with the stark choice missing in 1948. Back in July, when he moved into his new position, Humphreys had mapped out a campaign "based on attack." But he tempered this idea by noting that "both Republican candidates have warm and winning personalities" and a "high degree of salesmanship in their manner." Most Americans would want to welcome them "as visitors" in their "living rooms," and the best place to do this was television. Not through advertisements, which were stilted (the way Ike's spots would still appear to some as he read the cue cards), but "informal, intimate television productions" that could address "directly" the "individual American and his family." More emotion could be projected via the screen—more than made it through individual words printed in black and white on paper. The fund scandal could be solved by putting Nixon into Americans' living rooms and showing off his likeness to ordinary people. Now all Humphreys had to do was sell the idea to the man in charge.[54]

Humphreys already had the ear of Arthur Summerfield, then GOP chairman, and had forged an alliance with Murray Chotiner, who was coming to the same conclusions about his boss's prospects. Chotiner had explained to Nixon: "What we have to do is to get you before the biggest possible audience so that you can talk over the heads of the press to the people. The people, I am convinced, are for you but the press is killing you." All three men envisioned an act of telepopulism—direct communication to the people that circumvented the columnists and journalists in newsprint. It was this idea that awoke Humphreys on September 20 and structured his existence over the course of the next three days.[55]

The *Nixon Special* made it out of the near riot in Eugene up to Albany and then Salem, the state capital, where Nixon was welcomed by a friendly Governor Douglas McKay. Then the train barreled into Portland, where problems awaited. This was "the ugliest" crowd Nixon had seen. His fan base was thin, but the hecklers were out in full force. Members of the Portland Young Democrat Club acted as beggars, waving tin cups and holding signs that read GIVE NICKELS FOR NIXON. When the Nixons disembarked from the train into automobiles, young protesters tossed pennies at them, forcing Dick and Pat to duck loose change flying through the air. When at 5:30 they arrived at the Benson Hotel, where they planned to stay the next two nights, crowds raged. "Pat and I were shoved and jostled as we got out of the car," Nixon recalled. With help from a bodyguard, they made it into the hotel.[56]

Meanwhile, Eisenhower talked to reporters on his train. He pounded his fist into his hand and started to grandstand. He had just been told that the press had aligned against Nixon, the vast majority thinking the vice-presidential candidate would be booted off the ticket. "I don't care," Ike told the reporters. "I am taking my time on this. Nothing's decided, contrary to your idea that this is a setup for a whitewash of Nixon." Then the general added: "Of what avail is it for us to carry on this crusade against this business of what has been going on in Washington if we, ourselves, aren't clean as a hound's tooth?" Nixon would hear this comment later in the day and figure it meant Eisenhower wanted him to prove himself worthy of the vice-presidential position—a threat of sorts. "I must admit that it made me feel like the little boy caught with jam on his face." With hecklers popping up every stop and Ike remaining aloof at best, Nixon was starting to get angrier and angrier, when not growing morose.[57]

It showed in a set of remarks he made later that day in Portland and then put out in a press release for the morning of September 21, Sunday. Nixon had reflected on how his team was "one-third of the way along the rugged, difficult campaign road." He admitted it had not been "an easy journey." The conspiracy had mounted and grown more furious: "Powerful forces, aligned against our cause, are exerting every possible pressure to still our attacks against the little men, the unscrupulous men, the misguided men and the blindly selfish men who make up the present Administration." He assured his listeners that the campaign would not break apart under pressure, and it was hard not to hear the following words aimed directly at Ike and his inner circle: "Any weakening in our ranks, any disunity, any surrender to the divide-and-conquer technique of a determined opposition will seriously endanger our righteous cause." He went through the typical stump stuff about corruption and Communism and Korea, but then he took note of where he was—"the Pacific Northwest." And he drove up the tension full throttle: "Let me tell you that other Koreas could come even closer. They could reach right into our country's heartland. They could bring the bombing and the carnage right *here* if our drift toward disaster isn't halted." Only Dwight Eisenhower could stop a Communist invasion via "the mouth of the Columbia River" or one staged close to "Anchorage, Alaska." Talk of invasion and a country crumbling into disunity reflected Nixon's state of mind as he went to sleep Saturday night. He was now at the stage of nightmare.[58]

Sunday was set aside for layover, rest, and religion. In St. Louis, Ike and his wife attended the large and upscale Second Presbyterian Church for services. The Reverend James Clarke delivered a sermon entitled "How to Climb Out of the Depths of Despair." The congregation clapped at Ike's entrance and departure. After sleeping in, Dick and Pat went to First Friends Church in Portland. When Dick returned to the Benson Hotel, he sounded as if he had attended Clarke's service. "I'm not worried anymore," Nixon told Thomas Bewley, an old family friend and lawyer on the scene. But by early afternoon, his God-inspired high had worn off.[59]

By now, Dick's right flank had shown its support. Karl Mundt had trashed the *New York Post*, and Robert Taft had answered the charges of corruption, arguing a typical libertarian defense: "I see no reason why a senator or representative should not accept gifts from members of his family or his friends or his constituents to help pay even personal expenses which are not paid by the government." Besides, Taft argued, "those who contributed to the fund probably agreed one hundred percent with his legislative position anyway." Then, on September 21, word came from Joseph McCarthy. He rallied, too: "The left wing crowd hates Nixon because of his conviction of Alger Hiss, the man for whom Adlai Stevenson testified. The Communists know that Nixon's election will be a body blow to the Communist conspiracy. Dick Nixon has given a complete answer to this new smear invented by the *New York Post* whose editor admits he once was a member of the Young Communist League." Though Nixon might have enjoyed these comments, it's hard to imagine they did anything to sway Ike or his men.[60]

Nixon used his day of rest to read through telegrams and news reports and then held a staff meeting. He had a brief conversation with Tom Dewey, and they started to talk about the idea of a major speech on national television. Then a message came from Harold Stassen, the man who had helped swing the Republican convention to Ike by releasing his Minnesota delegates. It was not heartwarming: *Tender your resignation to Ike and let him decide how to proceed.* Nixon panicked. Then another message came, this one from his mother in D.C., where she was babysitting the kids: "This is to tell you we are thinking of you and know everything will be fine." That was a coded Quaker message that she was praying for her son. And at that point, Nixon broke down and cried.[61]

It was like a voice drowned out by deluge, barely audible in the hoopla. "When I've got something to say about it, I'll say it," snapped Adlai Stevenson to journalists' questions about Richard Nixon's fund scandal. Here was a man who disliked loose accusations and preferred the high road: "Condemnation without all the evidence, a practice all too familiar to us, would be wrong," he explained on September 19. Then on Sunday, Stephen Mitchell, Stevenson's choice for national chairman of the Democratic National Committee, said that Nixon should quit and that he had "more facts" about the case than Stevenson.[62]

The Democratic response to this whole mess seemed muted. Murray Chotiner explained this from his vantage point of cynicism. He told Nixon that he "smelled a rat" and concluded that Stevenson "is afraid of something here. . . . I bet he has something to hide." Of course, it could be that Stevenson really wanted to take the high road and allow the facts to come out and clarify the case. Or maybe both takes on the matter—Chotiner's cynicism and Stevenson's high-road approach—reflected reality.

Just how important was this whole fund thing? Robert Humphreys knew he didn't have much time to answer that question. He did a quick informal poll. His conclusion was drastic: Concern about the fund was "confined to the Washington and New York press corps, the Eisenhower train, the Nixon train, a few top-level party leaders and friends of Ike's, and a few editorial writers who called for Nixon's resignation." Versus this small group, "the public generally was not paying a bit of attention." Meanwhile, Sherman Adams had gotten Robert Burroughs, an RNC committeeman who had done some polling in the past, to sort through things. Burroughs thought the situation more pervasive than Humphreys did; nonetheless, he hit upon a regional breakdown in levels of concern. In "the Eastern Seaboard States . . . and the Southern States" many citizens "feel Nixon should resign." In "the West Coast States" the majority "feel that Nixon should be kept on the ticket and defended." In the Middle West, where Ike currently was, the people "are more open-minded on the subject and less violent in their reactions. But seem to show a majority opinion who favor keeping Nixon on the ticket and defending him." Though Humphreys might have oversimplified the situation, both informal polls provided an opening for Nixon to go in front of the people and explain the situation. On that, consensus reigned.[63]

On Sunday morning, Arthur Summerfield called Robert Humphreys and told him to get to St. Louis to present his idea of having Nixon speak directly to the American people on television. Summerfield would meanwhile scrounge money to block out network time. So Humphreys grabbed one of four phones on his desk and called TWA for a flight, booking a puddle jumper from Washington, D.C., to West Virginia, Ohio, and Kentucky. When he landed in Louisville, Kentucky, a flight attendant told him to get off the airplane. He refused, delaying the flight, but made it to St. Louis, arriving just after Eisenhower had left for a dinner event.[64]

Humphreys started his evening by having it out with Sherm Adams, the cold-blooded man who served as a shield between Ike and the outside world (including Nixon). Arthur Summerfield was there, too, still unsure about the money for TV time. The conversation between Adams and Humphreys came on "hot and heavy." Adams wouldn't lay his cards on the table, but he did let on that there had been discussion about throwing Nixon off the ticket. Humphreys erupted: "What do you plan to do, change every piece of literature, every billboard, every campaign poster, every sticker in the land with Nixon's name or picture, and how the hell do you think we are going to do that?" Adams glowered but knew Eisenhower doubted that booting Nixon would do much good. Humphreys kept circling back to the idea of a televised speech. He pressed Adams: "On Friday morning in Nebraska the general said, 'I intend to talk with him at the earliest time we can reach each other by telephone.'" Humphreys thought the general evasive and called Adams on it: "Do you mean to tell me we can convince the American people that for the last sixty hours Dick and Ike have not been able to get together on the telephone when anyone knows that all the general has to do is pick up the phone and call him?" Adams gave way on this point, recognizing Humphreys's eye for public relations, and said he'd have the general call Nixon when he was back from his dinner event.[65]

Humphreys and Summerfield took this as a sign that Ike's team was softening, giving a green light for the speech. They scurried around to find funds, contacting Leonard (Len) Hall, head of the GOP Congressional Campaign Committee. Hall committed $25,000. Then they called Everett Dirksen, the Taftite who now headed up the Senate Congressional Campaign Committee, for another $25,000. But they couldn't reach him. So they went back to Len, who said he'd pledge Dirksen's money (much to the chagrin of the senator once he found out). With these commitments and others finagled from the RNC, Summerfield and Humphreys had what they needed. Nixon could make his speech.[66]

Meanwhile, back at the Benson Hotel, things were in a flurry with meetings and phone calls. As the afternoon wore on, Dick took a call from the man who had done so much to get him into the position in the first place, Tom Dewey. Throughout the course of the crisis, Dewey had transformed himself into what Dick Nixon had been in the spring—the inside dopester. Dewey opened with ominous words for Nixon: "Did Ike tell you that he went to lunch with a lot of his old friends today, and that every one of them except one thought you ought to get off the ticket?" As Dewey told Nixon this, Eisenhower was at a dinner meeting where he was hearing the same opinion. Nixon got nervous and depressed, knowing that conversations were taking place behind his back and now expecting another Stassen-style betrayal. After all, Dewey was one of those Eastern Republicans who took newspapers seriously. Instead, Dewey doled out his advice: "I think you ought to go on television. I don't think Ike should make the decision. Make the American people do it."

What better way to allow Ike's evasiveness to solicit a solution to the problem? Dick got excited about the prospect. But how to make it work? Dewey had more to say on that: "At the conclusion of the program ask people to wire in their verdict to you in Los Angeles, and you will probably get over a million replies and that will give you three or four days to think it over. At the end of that time you can say that it was 60 percent against you and 40 percent for you— say you are getting off as that is not enough [support]. If it's 90 to 10, stay on." This could serve as a moment of direct democracy, the people's voice being heard, which sounded strange coming from such a stiff and Establishment man as Tom Dewey. But it appeared the best way to solve the problem without hurting Ike. Dewey explained, "If you stay on it isn't blamed on Ike, and if you get off it isn't blamed on Ike. All the guys here in New York agree with me."[67]

Nixon, ever the "organization man," took a great-minds-think-alike approach, saying that he was considering a television appearance just as Dewey outlined. Chotiner and Humphreys had been pressing the idea, too. Then Nixon looked at his watch and told Dewey he had to leave for the Temple Beth Israel for a dinner speech. Maybe they could talk again in the near future as things got closer to the actual televised talk. Dewey suggested they'd be in touch. Though Dewey was sounding nervous, he still had a warm spot in his heart for his young recruit, at least at that moment.

Nixon returned to the Benson Hotel after his dinner speech, hoping to find a message that Eisenhower had called. No luck. Then around ten o'clock, meaning midnight in the Midwest, Ike followed Sherm Adams's advice and called his vice-presidential candidate. It had been a few days since they last spoke, so Ike opened up with a cheery "Hello, Dick. You've been taking a lot of heat the last couple of days." Dick replied, "Yes." Ike asked, "Has it been pretty rough?" Dick said, "Yes." Recognizing the strain in Nixon's voice, Ike said, "You know this is an awful hard thing for me to decide." Nixon grew angry at those words. Then Ike explained that he had been "to dinner tonight with some of my friends and they just don't know what is to be done, but they thought some way you ought to get your story across to the country." Those words suggested that Dewey had spoken with him or that Sherm Adams had said something about what Robert Humphreys was proposing. Nixon's mind was racing to figure out where the general was going with this.[68]

"I don't want to be in the position of condemning an innocent man," Ike said. Did that mean he thought Dick was innocent, or just that Ike was nervous and felt rushed to judgment? "I have come to the conclusion that you are the one who has to decide what to do. After all, you've got a big following in this country, and if the impression got around that you got off the ticket because I forced you to get off, it's going to be very bad. On the other hand, if I issue a statement in effect backing you up, people will accuse me of condoning wrong-doing." Ike's midnight ramblings led to the inevitable conclusion: "I suggest that you ought to go on a nationwide television program and tell them anything there is to tell—everything you can remember. Tell them about any money you ever took." Dick was coy here, like the employee who nods at his boss's ideas even though he's already thought of them. He pressed for resolution on the matter. "Well, general, do you think after the television program then an announcement should be made one way or the other?" Then old smiley blue eyes went back to his typical evasiveness: "Well, I am hoping that no announcement would be necessary at all—that maybe we could tell after the program what ought to be done." This pissed Nixon off. "Well, general . . . there comes a time in matters like this when you've either got to shit or get off the pot." Silence. "The great trouble here is the indecision." That comment was a tad less harsh but still suggested Nixon believed Eisenhower had more in common with Adlai Stevenson than hoped.

The general stiffened, repeating that he thought Dick should go on television but that he couldn't commit to a decision. Then Ike changed the subject: "How have your crowds been to date?" Nixon got excited. "I have been told they have been twice as big as Dewey's in 1948." Ike recognized, as did Dick, that such fanfare might be a good sign in the face of the crisis. "Well, keep your chin up," Ike told him. And before putting the receiver down, Nixon responded with an inconsequential "Best of luck." He hoped to have a promise from his boss that he was secure in his position. Instead, he got the green light to go in front of millions of Americans and spill his guts on television.

The suspense and tension of the situation had hardwired themselves into Dick Nixon's mind. His neck throbbed with pain, he cried at startling moments, he'd move from manic meetings to slumping in a chair. And then late at night he confessed his doubts to his wife. She of course bolstered him every chance she got. After his conversation with Ike, she had told him: "You have to fight it all the way to the end, no matter what happens."[69]

That inspired Dick to call a press conference at the crazy hour of 1:00 A.M., West Coast time. He turned up the drama quotient. On the eleventh floor of the Benson Hotel, Dick Nixon opened up to journalists with: "I've come to announce that I am breaking off . . ." And he let those words resonate and fall like a thud to drive up the blood pressure of the reporters. *What, his run for the vice presidency?* And then he came back with: "I've come to announce that I am breaking off my campaign trip tomorrow for the purpose of going to Los Angeles to make a nationwide television and radio broadcast." The groggy journalists asked if they could know what the nature of his comments would be. *No,* Nixon thought. "I knew that any advance notice of what I was going to say would cut down the size of my television audience. This time I was determined to tell my story directly to the people rather than funnel it to them through a press account." So he let the drama rise and got ready for his upcoming flight back to Los Angeles.[70]

CHAPTER FOUR

"CHIN UP"

Secretary Acheson and President Truman will never forgive me
for being what I am—a rather ordinary middle-of-the-
road American—not well off and yet refusing to follow
the blandishments of the left-wingers to join the
American gold rush.

—RICHARD NIXON, IN A DRAFTED BUT EVENTUALLY
CUT PORTION OF THE CHECKERS SPEECH

Who *is* Richard Nixon? That question came to him buoyed up in the air, on a plane, in a state of sleep-deprived surreality. Flying from Portland to Los Angeles on Monday, September 22, Dick Nixon knew he would face the who-he-was question soon after landing. When those television cameras started to whirl, they would expose his soul to those millions of faceless Americans sitting in their living rooms. Ike said it was up to him, that he must face the nation on his own terms, so the general wouldn't have to make the decision himself but let others pass judgment. Even one of Nixon's bigger fans, Robert Humphreys, refused to help him, feeling that Nixon had to perform his defense on his own terms without coaching, or else the performance wouldn't be authentic. Though Arthur Summerfield requested Humphreys fly from D.C. to L.A. and put his public relations skills to the test, Humphreys said no, explaining Nixon had to be "a man telling his own story in his own way." So Dick was now forced back on his heels to explain who he was. He'd ponder his identity, drift to sleep, his head propped into the alcove of the airplane window or onto Pat's shoulder, and then wake in a state of panic and write down some notes on postcards stuffed into the seat pocket in front of him. Or he would awaken to a photographer snapping his picture, if Murray Chotiner (sitting close by) didn't intercept the cameraman.[1]

Figuring out who he was required Nixon, as it would more and more Americans at the time, to think about the things that made up a man, namely, his possessions. A country stabilizing its abundance and prosperity had started to define people by what they owned. So to *connect*, to talk about what he held in common with his fellow citizens, he was forced to think about what he *had*.

First, his house, the thing all Americans longed for in the 1950s. His was a two-story white brick, perfectly ordinary. It placed him in the middle of the bell curve. He was a World War II veteran in his thirties, with a wife, two children, and a dog—but he would come to that last point later. The house had seven rooms and, in the words of his daughter Julie, a "bright California look with its cheerful aqua walls, peacock blue draperies and a touch of spring green in furniture covering." It sat in Spring Valley in Washington, D.C., a neighborhood a bit pricey for the Nixons. The house had originally cost $41,000; the Nixons had taken out a mortgage on which they still owed $20,000. Nixon wrote down some numbers on a postcard that he figured he could check once he was back in Los Angeles. But this he knew on the plane already: Living slightly beyond his means, scrimping and saving, just made him feel all the more average. It would allow him to connect.[2]

He had his car, a 1950 Oldsmobile. Pretty basic. It was simple and sleek, with whitewall tires. It wasn't too large, but it had enough room to put two kids in the backseat. If he took vacations, which he never did, they could fit some beach chairs in there, too.[3]

And yes—he had a dog. He'd have to remember to talk about

Checkers, a cocker spaniel with big floppy ears, black and white (hence the name). Checkers had been sent to the Nixons soon after the Republican convention by Lou Carrol, a Texas businessman and fan of Nixon's, who had heard Pat say something about the kids wanting a dog. He telegraphed Nixon's secretary to ask if he could pack up the pooch in a crate and send him along, and she said sure. The dog surprised Nixon. He never had a pet growing up, even though he was raised in a rural setting where many families did. Dick wasn't all that affectionate with the dog, more awkward than anything else. But now that he thought about Checkers, he considered the dog a political asset. It filled out the picture of the average household. By 1952, acquiring a dog constituted a democratic rite of passage, no longer the exclusive possession of America's wealthy aristocrats, who were known to prance around with their purebreds in places like the Upper East Side of Manhattan. Now, a dog brought workingmen their slippers at night and served as a "lovable companion" or "Man's Best Friend," as magazine advertisements put it. In the 1950s, a dog's quality of life followed upward with its owner's. With the end of World War II's regulations, rubber was cheaper, hence chew toys were readily available; the cost of steel went down, making canned dog food more affordable, replacing table scraps.[4]

Yes, Nixon would have to talk about his dog in order to connect to his fellow Americans. The last time a major political figure discussed a pet was when FDR talked about his dog Fala while campaigning against Tom Dewey, exactly eight years ago to the day that Nixon would make his speech. Republicans had spread the rumor that FDR had his Scottish terrier rescued from the Aleutian Islands by a destroyer that "cost [the] taxpayers . . . two or three, or eight or twenty million dollars." In his mellifluous voice, FDR had complained that "Republican leaders have not been content with attacks on me, or my wife, or on my sons. No, not content with that, they now include my little dog, Fala." The president went on to explain that Fala's "Scotch soul was furious." It made for a wonderful defense, humanizing FDR even more than his crippled body would. Nixon remembered the speech and thought it a work of genius. FDR, though the leader of the Democrats, was really the closest thing to an aristocrat that America could produce, raised in wealth and a product of the best schools. But the president was talking about his cute little dog in a way that made him seen like an ordinary person. This was a masterstroke played by the master, and now if Nixon stole a page from his opposition, it could "irritate my opponents." He was taking this page from his opposition just to tweak them. It was a safe bet. Who could hit a man when he was down, especially if he talked about his dog?[5]

These thoughts ran through Nixon's head as he went in and out of sleep on the flight back to Los Angeles. Then with a sudden *clomp*, the wheels hit the ground, and he was back in reality. The plane taxied and then unceremoniously deposited the vice-presidential candidate and his wife onto the tarmac. About five hundred people awaited them, chanting "We want Nixon." Nervous and exhausted, Dick told the crowds, "It's wonderful to get back and get this welcome from our friends. It's wonderful to know that our friends are sticking with us during this difficult time when one finds out who his friends really are." And then he ducked out of the scene into a nearby car, in hopes of getting to his hotel room. He was driven to the Ambassador Hotel, where Pat and Dick had separate rooms booked. He needed to be alone.[6]

Meanwhile, the *Look Ahead, Neighbor! Special* had made it from Kentucky into Ohio. Taft had been campaigning in his home state for Ike a number of days by now, though his heart didn't seem in it. In Cincinnati, Ike took the stage and Taft sat next to the podium and "looked up at the ceiling, fiddled with his fingernails, and made it pretty clear by his whole demeanor that he regarded the Republican presidential candidate as an errant amateur." He might at least have appreciated

Ike's tone, with the general almost parroting his vice-presidential running mate. Earlier that day in Kentucky, Ike had complained about
Stevenson's "aristocratic explanations in Harvard words." Now, next
to a Harvard Law School graduate, he attacked Stevenson for his
"faintness at heart" and his "elaborate indecision." Little did Ike know
that his own indecisiveness was something his vice-presidential candidate was planning to employ to his own advantage.[7]

Dick Nixon would have to present himself as authentic and honest
through the medium of television, which was easier said than done.
In 1952, people could still believe television promoted honesty—the
ethic of seeing as believing. But Americans also knew that things
were staged in the land of television, that artifice mattered as much
as honesty. Viewers knew televisions were there, in part, to sell them
things like Betty Furness's refrigerators and dishwashers. It was impossible to disassociate the tube from its hucksterism. Nixon's speech
would have to enter this strange world of authenticity battling the
great salesroom ethic. One of the more interesting questions that
Nixon's men had to ask—earlier on, before things got down to the
wire—was what they wanted as a warm-up act to their man's speech.
That translated into the question: Lucy or Miltie? In other words,
Monday or Tuesday night for Dick's speech, following *I Love Lucy* or
the *Texaco Star Theater*? The contest between the opening shows illustrated how quickly things had changed in the course of the last
few years in televisionland, with *I Love Lucy*'s new dynamism displac-
ing *Texaco Star Theater* in short order.

Nixon's people wanted to follow *I Love Lucy*, the younger and more
popular of the two shows broadcast Monday nights at 9:00 P.M. It
happened to be the Eisenhowers' favorite, and by the spring of 1952,
it was the favorite of millions of Americans, with Nielsen placing it at
number one. It was a situation comedy both fresh and cutting-edge.

It focused on Lucy (Lucille Ball), a housewife who often chafed at the limits of the domestic sphere and drove her husband, Ricky Ricardo (Desi Arnaz)—a Cuban big-band leader and nightclub entertainer— absolutely nuts. Audiences loved her antics and slapstick routines, providing the show with a loyal following and making Ball "Miss Monday Night" among millions of viewers (stores would put up WE LOVE LUCY TOO signs to explain why they closed early the first day of the business week). The show's June 1952 ratings trounced those of the political conventions on television during the summer.[8]

Much of *I Love Lucy*'s energy and appeal came from its unspoken tensions. It looked spontaneous yet was scripted. It appeared live—as many shows on television still did in 1952—but was filmed in a studio where employees would flash cue cards to the audiences that read AP- PLAUSE. CHEERS. LAUGHTER. Three cameras would take in the perfor- mance, their footage spliced together during editing. The two major characters—Lucy and Ricky—were husband and wife not just on camera but in real life, with Arnaz an actual Cuban, and a big-band leader, too. By the spring of 1952, as the show soared to number one, Lucille Ball became pregnant, and by the end of that year the show introduced Lucy as being pregnant (her new baby would appear the next year). When it was discovered in spring of 1952 that Lucille Ball had registered as a Communist in 1936 (due to pressures from her grandfather, who was a socialist, or so she claimed), HUAC didn't come down hard on her as it would in other cases but investigated quietly behind closed doors, fearful about blowback, giving the show a strange power few others had. Whom would HUAC have been in- terrogating, its members might have wondered, Lucille Ball or the wacky housewife Americans had come to love?[9]

I Love Lucy's content reflected a strange play on reality versus artifice. Consider "Lucy Gets Ricky on the Radio," an episode that aired in the spring of 1952 when the show was skyrocketing to the top of the ratings. It began with Lucy and Ricky sitting down with

their neighbors, Ethel and Fred Mertz. They get set to watch television. Then Lucy—playing her usual nutty self—says they shouldn't
watch television that night but do something else. The three others
exclaim, *"Don't watch television?!"* The bewilderment reflected the idea
that television already dominated their lives, and the audience couldn't
help notice that the television was placed just where the audience in
the studio watched them, at the center of the stage. Lucy insists on
having an adult conversation and opens with "How about those elections?" The three others look nervous, unsure of what to say. Of
course, elections in spring were hard to imagine, but it's more hard to
imagine this foursome wanting to talk about politics at all. So they of
course do what the audience expected: They grow silent and then
admit they have no other option than to turn on the television, only
to complain about the quality of the picture. As they do, it was easy to
imagine viewers in the studio and home reflecting on what they had
just watched: A television show about people watching television, inca-
pable of thinking of any other thing to do with their evening.[10]

The show's freshness had carried it above the other choice for a
Nixon warm-up act—*Texaco Star Theater* with Milton Berle, who was
sometimes called Mr. Television or Uncle Miltie. His show first aired
on television back in 1948. The format—a succession of vaudeville
stage performances—appeared antiquated in contrast to *I Love Lucy*.
Berle would come out every Tuesday, often in a wacky costume (sometimes in drag), and entertain his viewers with an opening monologue
rife with jokes. Then he'd introduce a guest star—a singer or fellow
comedian. There'd be time for a comedy skit and then a buildup to a
grand finale that often involved a big band and some dancing. The
live audience would whoop and laugh.

From 1950 to 1951, *Texaco Star Theater* was "the top-rated show on
every rating system," including Nielsen. But the show grew stale
for Berle and soon there was slippage in its rankings. By 1951, Uncle
Miltie was already losing viewers to Fulton Sheen, the Catholic bishop,

who hosted *Life Is Worth Living* (the show Bruce Barton wanted Ike to model his "spots" on). Many critics thought Sheen's straightforwardness, his simplicity and directness, lifted his show above Milton Berle's formulaic shtick. Berle, at least, was good-humored about losing ratings to Sheen: "If I'm going to be eased off the top by anyone, it's better that I lose to the One for whom Bishop Sheen is speaking." Sheen would go off the air after the first part of 1952 (returning later), but he was only one competitor for ratings. Between January and June 1952, Berle's show "slid from No. 1 to No. 20" in rankings.[11]

In the end, Nixon had to settle for Uncle Miltie as his warm-up act. The vice-presidential candidate could not move from Sunday's thumbs-up from Ike and his announcement of the speech at a press conference in the wee hours of the morning to a successful speech the same day. Nor did Nixon's managers have open pickings; there was wheeling and dealing to do to get their slot, as Humphreys and Summerfield scurried around at the last moment. When they secured Tuesday night, they called Murray Chotiner. "Dick's got a speaking engagement for Tuesday," Chotiner told Summerfield. "Then get someone else to fill it," Summerfield scoffed. Tuesday may not have been their number one choice, but they'd take what they could get, assured that the tension and drama had built enough that Nixon might even pull up Berle's ratings.[12]

There are times during a crisis when a man can see more clearly. That happened when Dick was on the plane back to Los Angeles. Chotiner had suggested during the flight that he thought Stevenson wasn't attacking him because he had similar problems, and Chotiner was proven right around the time they took off. Details started to come out about Stevenson's own pot of money dedicated to political purposes. While Nixon started working on his speech, Stevenson was having his staff document what they could about his private fund.

It turned out Stevenson's fund supplemented the low salaries of state employees. It came from monies left over from the Stevenson for Governor Committee, the organization that propelled him into office in 1948. The money—about $18,700 at the time of his election—had been given by anonymous donors, and Stevenson wanted it to remain that way so that officials never felt beholden to any particular individual. He also wanted to replenish the fund and hired a man named Dutch Smith (the parallels to Nixon's case became remarkable at this moment) to raise more money in order to replenish the pot. Once again, the donors would remain anonymous. As with Nixon's fund, there was nothing illegal—that is, by the letter of the law—about Stevenson's fund, but it just didn't look good, and it certainly leveled the playing field of the debate about the fund crisis.[13]

The news broke just at the right moment for Nixon. *Everyone* looked guilty now, not just Dick. Stephen Mitchell—the head of the DNC—looked silly having called for Nixon to resign over a fund that looked remarkably similar to his own boss's. Just as Chotiner expected, Stevenson had played softball for sinister reasons. Or at least it could appear that way. The *Washington Post*, having already called for Nixon to resign, now opined: "The Stevenson fund does not in any respect minimize Mr. Nixon's transgression, but it does rob the Nixon incident of much of its potential value as a campaign issue." That's all that mattered to Nixon. The day he flew to Los Angeles to make his speech, the Illinois Republican national committeeman C. Wayland Brooks called for Stevenson to resign. Nixon now could smell the opening to his comeback.[14]

The *Look Ahead, Neighbor! Special* had pulled into Cincinnati the evening of September 22 and then pulled out the next morning, heading north and east up to Cleveland with stops along the way. Before disembarking from Cincinnati, a new guest came on board: Bill Robinson, an old golfing buddy of Ike's and, more important, the man behind the *New York Herald Tribune*. His newspaper had already spoken for him three days ago by calling for Nixon to resign. He was on the train to press that case harder, and he was ready to push the issue.[15]

Arthur Summerfield caught wind of this development. He now felt relieved that Robert Humphreys had refused his suggestion to go to L.A. He called Humphreys and told him to get to the airport so they could fly together to Cleveland, figuring that after a day of Robinson's pummeling, the vice-presidential candidate would need all the friends he had in making his case. Humphreys leaped out his front door with no bags, joined Summerfield at the airport, and flew to Ohio. He knew this was make-or-break time for his man Nixon.

Summerfield and Humphreys arrived in Cleveland in time to secure a suite at the Carter Hotel. Ike was done with his daytime events, reclining on his bed, ready for debate. Humphreys decided his role was to be Dick's attorney. Jerry Persons, who was an assistant to Ike when he was abroad in Europe in 1951 and made the transition to campaign worker smoothly, started to press Humphreys. He had new allegations about the vice-presidential candidate. "We have been told that the Nixons redecorated their house and retained a Georgetown decorator to do it for ten thousand dollars. When the work was completed, Mrs. Nixon paid the entire amount in cash." Humphreys pushed back: "I was over at the Nixons' a week ago Sunday night and Pat was in the living room with Dick when I arrived. . . . I said to her, 'That is a stunning circular couch, where did you get it, Sloane's?' She answered: 'We brought it from Whittier.'" And then Humphreys thought about some of the best publicity the campaign ever garnered about Nixon and talked about the infamous household drapes. "I said: 'Those beautiful drapes—don't tell me they didn't come from Sloane's?' Pat answered: 'No, the material came from Lansburgh's and I made the drapes myself.'" Just as she had said in the *Saturday Evening Post* piece about her "wonderful guy" (*Reader's Digest* was just about to reprint the story in its October issue).[16]

The debate settled down for a moment, and Humphreys figured it safe to go for a late dinner with Summerfield. But the conversation in the general's suite raged on, with Bill Robinson continuing to trash Nixon. The only thing that stopped the incessant bickering was the need to get to the Cleveland Public Auditorium, where Ike had an evening rally he had postponed so people could watch Nixon on television. When Humphreys arrived at the scene, he hiked up what seemed "endless stairs" to an upper-level suite. There in one corner the manager had placed "a TV set, angled out," giving the place the feel of an American living room. "About fifteen feet away, along the left wall from the TV set," there was a "sofa for Mr. and Mrs. Eisenhower at right angles to the wall." The moment had come. Ike sat on the sofa with a yellow pad of paper, Mamie at his side.[17]

For Richard Nixon, Tuesday, September 23, began with a morning swim. Perfect activity for an isolated man, to push his body through water, feeling resistance and listening to the blood thump in his ears. Then he went for a walk with his friend and campaign volunteer, William Rogers. They returned to the plush Ambassador Hotel, and Nixon started to gather what he had—postcards from the plane, reports from lawyers, notes from conversations with friends, memories of things he had said while whistle-stopping—to fashion something that looked more like a speech.[18]

Nixon enjoyed pushing to the wire, working full tilt, eyeing the clock and feeling the pressure. He considered drafting the speech an "intense preparation for battle." He remembered the way he had felt during the Hiss investigation—"keyed up, mentally and emotionally" in such a way that he could face a "crisis." He was going through mental calisthenics now, building up the confidence that he needed to face the biggest audience he had ever met. "I had to go for broke," he thought. The speech had to be a "smash hit" that would "inspire" viewers to give him "enthusiastic, positive support." This would be the performance of a lifetime. He tried to get his mind into a state of controlled panic. He was a man in a jam, for sure, but he had to convince himself to be the confident salesman he knew himself to be.[19]

At 4:30, just two hours before showtime, Nixon was talking through some details about the speech with Chotiner and Rogers. Suddenly, the front desk told Dick that a "Mr. Chapman of New York" was on the phone. *Christ, that's the code name for Tom Dewey,* Nixon thought as he picked up the phone. Dewey sounded nervous. He had bad news: "There has just been a meeting of all of Eisenhower's top advisers. They have asked me to tell you that it is their opinion that at the conclusion of the broadcast tonight you should submit your resignation to Eisenhower." *What?!* Nixon thought to himself, without saying a word. "Hello, can you hear me?" Dewey asked into the silence on the other side, jiggling the phone in his hand, figuring he had lost the connection.

Nixon finally spoke up. "What does Eisenhower want me to do?" Well, Dewey suggested that Ike didn't know, exactly. Nixon pressed: "It's kind of late for them to pass on this kind of recommendation to me now." Then Dewey gave his own advice: "What you might do is announce not only that you are resigning from the ticket, but that you're resigning from the Senate as well. Then, in the special election which will have to be called for the Senate, you can run again and vindicate yourself by winning the biggest plurality in history." That sounded absolutely nuts to Nixon, a complete abdication of political power, something he couldn't contemplate. But Dewey insisted on pressing and asked what he should tell Ike's friends about his proposed plan. "Just tell them," Nixon blurted out, "that I haven't the slightest idea what I am going to do, and if they want to find out they'd better listen to the broadcast. And tell them I know something about politics, too!" Then Nixon hung up on the man who had helped him reach this point in his career.[20]

Nixon didn't know if he had just bucked his boss or not. Maybe Dewey had made the phone call on Ike's behalf, maybe Dewey acted on his own. Maybe now by ignoring Dewey's advice he was going over Ike's head and appealing directly to the public. Whatever, the conversation made Dick's blood boil. *All of this, less than two hours before the damn speech*, Nixon thought.

Less than an hour after slamming the phone down on Tom Dewey, Dick was heading to the El Capitan Theater with his wife, a body-guard, two staff members, and his friend Representative Patrick Hillings, the man who took over Dick's congressional seat when he ran for the Senate. The team rode in a Cadillac limousine with five motorcycle policemen leading them through the streets of Holly-wood. When they arrived at the studio, Nixon headed for Dressing Room B, where he applied "beard-stick" to his face, worried his five o'clock shadow would make him look sinister. Then he moved to the set and passed a mass of empty seats. He had requested the place be vacant, and now it looked dark and empty, providing him with a finer appreciation of just how alone he was. The only people around, besides those who accompanied him, were the technicians and camera-men, and they made Nixon nervous. In his paranoia, he thought they were likely union members who might despise his right-wing politics and try to screw up his performance.[21]

Ted Rogers met Nixon at the studio. He had wanted the vice-presidential candidate to come earlier so they could rehearse and map things out, but Nixon refused in order to preserve enough time to prepare the speech in privacy. Rogers had gone early to the studio and decided on the "GI bedroom den" for the speech's setting. It was replete with a desk, shelves stocked with prop books, and a plump armchair where Pat would sit. Just right, thought Rogers: simple and plain, with a touch of the ordinary. Rogers worried about what the camera could capture on the set, and so he had, in Nixon's own words, "used a salesman who resembled me" to serve as a "stand-in." He had figured out how far Nixon could get up and walk around without going out of camera range and drew a circle around that area. Rogers also prepared a booth where Chotiner and other friends could sit while the action was filmed. Drawing upon his background and expertise in television, Rogers informed Nixon of his parameters and then asked what he planned to say. Nixon told him that he was just going to glance at his notes when he spoke. He wanted to retain the "spark of spontaneity so essential for a television audience." Or, as his wife explained later, in slightly exaggerated and more dramatic terms, "He discarded his notes and talked from his heart." In other words, he wanted to be more Fulton Sheen than Milton Berle.[22]

Three minutes before the speech, Nixon went wobbly. He turned to Pat and said, "I just don't think I can go through with this one." Once again, she buttressed him: "Of course you can." There was "confidence" in her voice, Nixon remembered. He prayed for guidance, bolstering himself further. Pat sat ramrod straight in the chair, looking somewhat unnerved and uncomfortable. He sat down at the desk in the GI den set and imagined a sea of faces that he could not see but that could see him.[23]

The cameraman's fingers spread out into a fan and then closed as they counted down, finally pointing to Nixon. Television viewers couldn't see him yet, as they watched an American flag blowing in the wind and heard a voice-over: "You are about to hear a report from Senator Richard Nixon," brought to them by the RNC. Then Nixon appeared, sitting at a desk, dressed in a gray suit, white shirt, and black patterned tie, looking around nervously.[24]

The speech started off a bit rough. "My fellow Americans . . . I come before you tonight as a candidate for the vice presidency and as a man whose honesty and integrity has been questioned." Nixon pointed out that a cover-up was the usual way to respond to scandal, but he would have none of that. "The people have got to have confidence in the integrity of the men who run for . . . office." And then he started to stumble, showing signs of exhaustion. He announced the fund and then said, "Now, was that wrong? And let me say that it was wrong—I am saying, incidentally, that it was wrong, not just illegal (because it isn't a question of whether it was legal or illegal; that isn't enough; the question is, was it morally wrong?)—I say it was morally wrong . . ." At this point, viewers no doubt grew confused; it sounded like a muddled confession of wrongdoing. But then Nixon pulled it out, saying that the money wasn't for his "personal use" and that his "contributors" didn't get "special favors." He had started to find his groove.

Nixon then segued into establishing his credentials as a senator of limited means. "Not one cent of the eighteen thousand dollars . . . ever went to me for my personal use." He trailed into a story about how senators weren't overpaid, earning only "fifteen thousand dollars a year in salary." His mind raced to his whistle-stop speeches as he rearranged the papers on the desk and came up with a line from his stump speech against the charge of corruption: "Do you think that when I or any other senator makes a political speech, has it printed, should charge the printing of that speech and the mailing of that speech to the taxpayers?" He knew that when he said that at whistle-stops, crowds would scream out "No." He couldn't hear the "no" now, of course, but he imagined it to make himself feel better. Of course, the statement was crafty. He never asked a legitimate follow-up to it—that is, whether or not Americans thought that wealthier Southern Californians should pay for such a thing. Instead, he said there were other ways to pay for campaigning.

"The first way is to be a rich man," he said. He looked puzzled at this moment and then seemed to refer to Stevenson and himself simultaneously: "I don't happen to be a rich man; so I couldn't use that one." Or he could have put his wife "on the payroll," as his opponent for the vice presidency, John Sparkman, did. But he wouldn't do that. As he built his own populist credentials, he took digs at his opposition—highlighting his own virtues against his enemies' misdeeds. Then the camera pulled away from Nixon, making him look smaller.

Here was a chance to introduce his wife, who looked so intensely and steadfastly at her husband that she could have been one of the props on the set—inactive, stiff. Like the rest of America, she had no idea what he would say next and hung on every word with anticipation. Nixon talked about how Pat Nixon had worked as an unpaid "stenographer" for him during "many hours on Saturdays and Sundays in my office," never on his "payroll." The camera had scanned out from the desk and then panned across a strange-looking bowl on top of a stand, finally focusing on the armchair where Pat sat. She stared at her husband, then stared some more.

Nixon then discussed the audit done on his fund, waving the reports in his hand and arguing that nothing bad was found. "Nixon did not obtain any financial gain from the collection and disbursement of the fund by Dana Smith," Dick read blandly from the report. He remembered at this moment that it was him alone on television—that his audience might be rooting for him but might be cynical about watching a salesman. "I recognize that some will continue to sneer," Nixon had written down, even though it came out "smear." He posed another rhetorical question: "Well, maybe you were able, Senator, to fake this thing. How can we believe what you say?" Here Nixon had confronted the challenges of the medium he appeared on—admitting that perhaps all of this came across as phony and staged. Maybe a viewer looked at the books on the shelves to his side and thought: Hmm, wonder how many of those he's read or even cracked open? Then Nixon looked at the camera, and it was hard not to imagine a drumroll playing in the background. He was now going to do something "unprecedented in the history of American politics." He would tell everything about his personal financial situation and bare his soul.

He started with his humble beginnings. His "family was one of modest circumstances." They owned a "grocery store, one of those family enterprises" where he and his brothers helped out. He talked about working his way through college and law school—showing off his aspirations to move into the white-collar classes—and then marrying Pat, "the best thing that ever happened to me." They scrimped and saved, and then he went to war. But he was no big shot in the military, just a midlevel guy. "I got a couple of letters of commendation, but I was just there when the bombs were falling." Then he entered politics.

At this point, Nixon started to detail his earnings and his debts, emphasizing that he and Pat "lived rather modestly." He told of his $41,000 home and the $20,000 remaining on his mortgage and their house in Whittier, on which they owed $10,000. There was his $4,000 "in life insurance." And there was his "1950 Oldsmobile car." There was some furniture but no "stocks and bonds of any type." He offered the other side of the picture—the debt. Not just the mortgages but also a loan from his parents for $3,500, which he paid with 4 percent interest, "because it is part of the savings they made through the years they were working so hard." The good father was a good husband and a good son. Looking at the possessions that constituted the man, Nixon said, "It isn't very much."

Then it was time to go for broke, to turn up the populist meme all the more with some whistle-stop-tested lines and a new one about his dog. What better than the oratory that had worked on live crowds? "I should say this, that Pat doesn't have a mink coat, but she does have a respectable Republican cloth coat; and I always tell her that she'd look good in anything." After smiling at this line, Nixon then pinched his nose and looked almost exasperated, to drive up the drama of the next lines. "One other thing I probably should tell you, because if I don't they'll probably be saying this about me, too. We did get something, a gift, after the election. A man down in Texas heard Pat on the radio mention the fact that our two youngsters would like to have a dog; and believe it or not, the day before we left on this campaign trip we got a message from the Union Station in Baltimore saying they had a package for us." That background set the dramatic tone Nixon took now. "We went down to get it. You know what it was? It was a little cocker spaniel dog, in a crate, that he'd sent all the way from Texas; black and white spotted, and our little girl, Tricia, the six-year-old girl, named it Checkers." Then Dick ratcheted the story up: "The kids, like all kids, love the dog; and I just want to say this right now, that regardless of what they say about it, we are going to keep him." His voice even quavered a bit at this moment.

From here Nixon turned to a populist attack on the Democrats. He named "Mr. Mitchell, the Chairman of the Democratic National Committee," who had said "if a man couldn't afford to be in the United States Senate, he shouldn't run for the Senate." Such sentiment—which sounded plutocratic—didn't "represent" the way most Democrats looked at it, or, more important, "the thinking of the Republican Party." Sure, it was fine for "Stevenson, who inherited a fortune from his father," to run for president. But American democracy allowed "a man of modest means" to run for office, too. And then Nixon looked on his desk for a quote his college professors from Whittier had hunted down. "Remember what Abraham Lincoln said, 'God must have loved the common people, he made so many of them.'"*

---

* Lincoln in fact never uttered these words, as documented by Paul Boller and John George in *They Never Said It* (New York: Oxford University Press, 1989), 84.

He moved to attack Stevenson's fund, saying the man should open up the way he himself just had. He went after Sparkman again, arguing he should explain how his wife had gotten onto his payroll. He threw the whole thing open at this time—calling for everyone to share "their financial history." Nixon needed to pull the spotlight off himself before rushing back into it.

Having sat in the chair behind the bland-looking desk for the majority of the speech, Nixon suddenly rose. The cameramen might have gotten nervous at this moment, but Nixon could look down and see the circle Ted Rogers had drawn on the floor, so no need to worry. Nixon stretched his arms out to his imagined audience and pounded his fists into the air and started to express his emotions. "Why do I feel so deeply? Why do I feel that in spite of the smears, the misunderstanding, the necessity for a man to come up here and bare his soul as I have?" Nixon leaned on the desk and shot his fist out toward the camera: "I love my country, and I think my country is in danger." He hammered on Korea, with its "117,000 American casualties!" It wasn't just Truman but the State Department that mattered here—what Nixon called the "Truman-Acheson administration." We need to clean out the State Department, Nixon implored. As he walked around and blasted Stevenson and Truman—recollecting the latter's "red herring" comment during the Hiss case—he started to look offstage, maybe for a clock to figure out how much longer he had. Now he had no notes, and the speech became disjointed. As usual, he segued from Communism to corruption at home and then let out a clumsy gibe at Stevenson, referencing his ties to Truman: "You can't trust the man who was picked by the man who made the mess to clean it up, and that is Stevenson." Then he flew back to the Communist issue, arguing that "Mr. Stevenson pooh-poohed and ridiculed the Communist threat in the United States—he said that 'they are phantoms among ourselves,' has accused that of us of attempting to expose the Communists, or looking for Communists in the Bureau of Fisheries and Wildlife." As he started to fray a bit here, Nixon thought it best to move back to the desk. He picked up a letter he had received from a nineteen-year-old wife whose husband was in the "Fleet Marines in Korea." This young woman called herself one of many "lonely Americans" hoping that Dick and Ike would win office, even offering a check for $10, which Nixon quickly explained he would "never cash."

Now the clock was really ticking. And he hadn't answered the question his viewers brought with them to the show: "Whether or not I am going to stay on the Republican ticket or resign." The nasty phone conversation with Dewey likely zipped through his mind at this moment. Here it was: He was about to go over the head of his boss and throw open the election to the forces of telepopulism. "I am not a quitter," he told his audience. "And, incidentally, Pat is not a quitter. After all, her name was Patricia Ryan, and she was born St. Patrick's Day—and you know the Irish never quit" (perhaps he intended tones of Knute Rockne here). The camera panned to Pat, who almost smiled, or maybe just pursed her lips with anguish about how much her husband had revealed about their finances (or the fact that she hadn't really been born on St. Patrick's Day or christened Patricia). Then Nixon explained, "But the decision, my friends, is not mine." He placed that in the hands not of Eisenhower but the Republican National Committee, the organization that had helped foot the bill for this speech. "Wire and write the Republican National Committee whether you think I should stay or whether I should get off; and whatever their decision is, I will abide by it." But instead of providing an address or telegraph connection or phone number, Nixon ended by talking about how Ike was a "great man." He leaned toward the camera, as if trying to reach out to the crowd he couldn't see, and then a voice from the network spoke over him, "You have just heard a report from Senator Richard Nixon . . ." Fade to black.[25]

Nixon stumbled off the set looking dazed. He realized he had forgotten to give out the information about how to contact the RNC. Chotiner rushed out of the booth he sat in and said he had done a great job. Nixon doubted that, but if he had taken the time to over-come his fears of the unionized cameramen, he might have noticed a tear trickling down one of their faces. If he could be transported across the country to the Cleveland Public Auditorium, he would have heard a crowd of seventeen thousand breaking into the chant: "We Want Nixon! We Want Nixon!" Or heard Eisenhower perched up high in the suite above the auditorium turning to Arthur Sum-merfield and saying, "Well . . . you certainly got your $75,000 worth tonight." Or have seen the general's wife, Mamie, tear up and feel "a lump in [her] throat." Or he might have witnessed Bill Robinson—his archfoe—swing around full circle to praise Nixon, or seen Har-old Stassen, wherever he had watched the speech from, scribbling out a note of congratulations and endorsement for the vice-presidential candidate he had just recently told to get off the ticket. And he might have heard conversations erupting among the sixty million who had tuned in to watch the show—a good number of whom were looking up ways to contact the RNC.[26]

Robert Humphreys watched from atop the Cleveland Public Audito-rium as Ike wrote out statements furiously on a yellow pad of paper. And then he watched the general leave to go downstairs and address the crowds chanting "We Want Nixon!' Humphreys stayed in the suite, turned off the television, and called RNC headquarters. The operator told him, "We are simply swamped with telephone calls—every light on this board is lit up; I've never seen anything like it." Then Humphreys learned about the telegrams pouring into the office; Western Union had to call in extra help to keep up with the traffic (by four in the morning, twelve thousand telegrams had already been sent). The next morning there'd be a huge mound of them piled up on a desk, big enough for a person to hide behind. The regular mail would soon add to the size of the pile.[27]

The responses rang like a chorus, singing praise in unison. Type-writers pounded, fingers held pens that wrote furiously, telegraph machines spilled out a staccato of words: Richard Nixon "is actually one of us little people." "Senator Richard Nixon is a man of the people." "The white collar man is all for Senator Nixon." Viewers gushed about the "straight forward, from the heart talk by Senator Nixon." The idea of "heart" featured prominently in many citizens' telegrams and letters (even a hard-ass politico like Everett Dirksen said that "Nixon's speech will go deep into the hearts of the Ameri-can people"). So, too, "tears . . . running" down viewers' faces. One wife, who had helped out on a number of anticommunist campaigns run by the American Legion, reported that her husband cried when Nixon read the letter from the nineteen-year-old woman whose hus-band was serving in Korea. There were even comparisons between the Checkers speech and Jesus Christ's Sermon on the Mount. Some became downright loopy in praise. A woman writing from Los Ange-les rang out: "Omnipotent, Omnipresent Divine Love quences [sic] all the fiery darts of the wicked. We need to keep an honest, fearless thinking American like you in Washington." The theme of honesty leaped out of almost all the responses. A writer from Ohio said bluntly, recognizing the force of the medium: "I think you are honest—you look it . . ." Almost all of the telegrams, letters, and phone calls wound around to the theme that Richard Nixon was an authentic American who deserved to stay on the ticket. After reading a number of the tele-grams, Senator Frank Carlson of Kansas, good friend to Ike, said that the speech followed by the response constituted "the most dramatic thing that has happened in American politics in my lifetime."[28]

Obviously, the speech as a whole, but Checkers especially, had been the smash hit Nixon had hoped for. Beyond the telegrams, letters, and phone calls, Nixon received dog collars, cans of dog food, dog blankets, and even a small kennel for Checkers (as they drove away from the El Capitan after the speech, an Irish setter trotted up to their car, and Nixon, in rare humorous form, said, "Well, at least we got the dog vote"). There were other responses: A whole horde of insurance salesmen—distressed by his meager insurance plan—wrote to offer services. Nixon had opened himself up to the American people, and they had responded in full force back, in whatever way they could. Most agreed with Darryl Zanuck, the great movie producer, who called Nixon right after the speech and praised "the most tremendous performance I've ever seen." But for the millions who wrote in, this wasn't a movie, all phony and scripted. It was a man who managed to convey sincerity, honesty, and authenticity to a faceless crowd.[29]

Murray Chotiner had been right: It was smart of Nixon to go "before the biggest possible audience so that [he could] talk over the heads of the press to the people." Once the speech landed at the offices of magazines and newspapers, the glowing tone of the commentary changed.[30]

It was easy to imagine the eyes rolling in the offices of the *New York Post* as reporters watched Nixon speak. They often had a bottle of Dewar's out this late at night and would trade jokes. Jimmy Wechsler called Nixon's speech a "soap opera," an analogy that was taken up by other outlets. "There was . . . a moment when it looked as if the family dog would scamper across the screen, but he never quite made it." (Even one of Ike's friends, Tom Stephens, said the next day on the *Look Ahead, Neighbor!* that the only thing missing from the speech was "where Chequers [*sic*], the Nixon dog, crawled up on Dick's lap and licked the tears off his face.") The speech for Wechsler became a "sentimental saga of 'Dick and Pat.' . . . The corn overshadowed the drama." What Nixon had pulled off was a massive evasion of a fundamental question: "Whether it is ethical, defensible or desirable for a member of the U.S. Senate to accept an 'expense fund' from members of wealthy special-interest groups that have a direct stake in the legislative business of the Senate." The editors of the *Post* pointed out that Nixon "conspicuously omitted comment on yesterday's disclosure that his office had rendered its services to Dana Smith—head of the Nixon fund—in a tax refund case." The *Post* would consistently trace a direct connection between Nixon's politics and the sort of man who was providing payment to Dana Smith. Having witnessed what they considered a great con job, their only hope was to compare the speech to Douglas MacArthur's in 1951—when the old general talked about his vision for the Korean War and about his fate of fading away—that won accolades and "great throngs" in the streets but never clinched any political victory. Maybe Nixon's comeback was a flash in the pan. The *Post*'s editors offered the only thing they could: a liberal prayer for the glow to wear off.[31]

The entertainment press riffed on the themes found in the *New York Post*. *Variety*, coming out a week after the speech, usually didn't comment on politics, but the editors knew it was now impossible to disentangle television from elections (they had run a series of articles around the televised conventions earlier). The editorial about Checkers was entitled "Just Plain Dick." In his televised speech, Nixon had spoken "in the best tradition of the American soap opera. It was as slick a 'production' as anything off the Anne Hummert belt line, parlaying all the schmaltz and human interest of the 'Just Plain Bill'–'Our Gal Sunday' genre of weepers." This referred to the many soap operas that Frank and Anne Hummert had produced and that had reigned on radio for the past twenty years. *Variety* continued: "The only thing missing was the organ background music as Nixon, appealing for a commutation of sentence with a faithful wife as the major prop, turned in a performance that would have gladdened the hearts of the . . . soaper fraternity." Nixon had just showed that television had a future in the world of politics: "With a good script, good casting and topflight production, you can't miss." After all, though *Variety* didn't note the fact here, *The Guiding Light*, one of the most popular radio soap operas ever, known for its omnipresent organ music and sponsorship by Procter and Gamble, had moved to television just the previous July. Noting that this trend was fast winning the domestic housewife market during the day, *Billboard* had already labeled the Checkers speech "Dick's Other Income" and suggested the magazine's jadedness about politics: "Critics have castigated young Nixon on the grounds that he brought the soap opera to politics. Radio and television people, nevertheless, are aware that soap operas have, for quite a long day, racked up the most consistently substantial ratings known. And there is no reason to assume that the Senator's saga did not have a like attraction to the nation's viewers."[32]

The two leading opinion writers who had trumpeted the cause of Ike—Walter Lippmann and Joseph Alsop—struggled with Checkers. They could not wallow in the cynical conclusions of the *New York Post*, *Variety*, or *Billboard*. They still needed to believe in the general, but Nixon's speech made it harder. On the evening of September 23, Walter Lippmann had the British newspaperman John Miller and his wife over for dinner. They turned on the television and watched the speech in silence. Lippmann, usually a rather calm and reflective man, turned to his guests after the speech was over and spat out, "That must be the most demeaning experience my country has ever had to bear." The next day, he wrote up his thoughts in one of the more stinging columns he had penned.[33]

Lippmann admitted that watching the show was "a disturbing

experience." Ike had allowed Nixon to appeal to the public directly when in fact he should have reviewed the facts on his own and pursued what Lippmann called a "judicial process." Lippmann reasoned from his own elitist assumptions. "The first judgment" on this matter "cannot be made by the public." Unfortunately, "the General has been showing an alarming disposition to improvise his great decisions" rather than being a firm leader. Now he allowed his vice presidential candidate to use "the magnification of modern electronics" in order to pursue "mob rule." Lippmann had seen the future of telepopulism and drew back in horror.[34]

Joseph Alsop concurred to a large extent. "The Republicans have handled the matter of Sen. Richard Nixon's special fund badly." He concluded that "the affair is bound to hurt Gen. Dwight D. Eisenhower's chances, although no one knows how seriously." Alsop also blamed Nixon, who did more bad than good when he started to scream about a "smear." For sure, the speech might clear the man, but a "very real question of principle remains." That Eisenhower sat on his hands, waiting for the situation to clear itself up, riled Alsop (much like Lippmann), who wanted to see more leadership from the general. Still, Nixon was the source of the trouble. "There is a tragic irony in the fact that a man whose personal integrity is his most immediately striking characteristic should have been hurt in this way, through no fault whatsoever of his own." It still wasn't about the general himself, as far as Alsop wanted to believe.[35]

Joe's brother, Stewart, had a slightly different take. He seemed to have a better feel for the future of American politics. Stew ruminated on how important "eggheads" became in Stevenson's campaign (he meant people like Arthur Schlesinger Jr. and Bernard DeVoto, two men Nixon's onetime legislative aide and general campaign worker Jim Gleason called "intellectual snobs"). Stew noted that Springfield, where Stevenson's headquarters were located, now felt like a "university town" populated with so many professors and intellectuals. Then he contrasted the egghead feel of Stevenson's campaign to Nixon's Checkers speech, which was "certainly not calculated to appeal to the intellect." He elaborated: "Certain of Nixon's assertions, like his claim that he was really 'saving the taxpayers money,' were hardly complimentary to the intelligence of his audience. . . . Nixon tapped, in a new way and almost for the first time, the vast store of accumulated skills of the entertainment and advertising industries." Alsop compared Nixon's performance to that of Jimmy Stewart in Frank Capra's melodramatic and populist movie, *Mr. Smith Goes to Washington*, in which a hayseed senator filibusters against corruption and graft in order to preserve a camp he wants to build for young boys.* Stewart Alsop might have sounded wary and cynical at these moments, like the writers at the *New York Post* or *Variety*, as he moved toward opposite conclusions from his brother's: "The Nixon episode may turn out to be a net asset to the Republicans." Nixon had tapped into something potent. After all, he and Ike were drawing bigger crowds than Stevenson. Why did citizens feel drawn to Ike? There's a "sincerity and essential goodness of the man." Stewart didn't say so but he might as well have: That sincerity was missing from the wisecracking Stevenson and the Harvard phonies who surrounded him. And Nixon had learned to play upon it for his own advantage, too. He had just used television to do so.[36]

One critic of Nixon who remained surprisingly silent about the speech was Adlai Stevenson. He hadn't watched the Checkers broadcast. He didn't own a television, as if confirming all the eggheadedness Stewart Alsop depicted in his campaign. Besides, Stevenson was

---

* To make Alsop's comparison more resonant, it's important to note that Capra's movie was as much about a cynical press corps as about the corrupt ambitions of political bosses. Mr. Smith faced down hard-boiled journalists who balked at his naïveté and refused to take him seriously.

scrambling to explain his own fund; he had no time to comment on anyone else's.[37]

The person who really mattered was less certain than either the fans or the critics in the press. He remained an enigma. For sure, Bill Robinson did an about-face and decided Nixon should stay on the ticket. And the telegrams, phone calls, and letters pouring into RNC headquarters appeared incontrovertible. But Ike remained aloof and evasive, still the man of indecision looking for wiggle room and a chance to postpone a decision already postponed.

He was willing to listen to his advertising men, as usual, and they kicked into high gear. They had a good handle on the Checkers speech, because they appreciated the power of television. Bruce Barton, the wise old man of public relations who had counseled presidential candidates from Calvin Coolidge to Tom Dewey, entered the picture. He sent a cable to Ben Duffy, the current president of BBDO and close friend of Ike's, to make suggestions about what Eisenhower should do: "Ben, tonight will make history. This will be the turning point of the campaign." Barton had nailed the moment with those words. He went on: "The general must be expertly stage managed and when he speaks it must be with the understanding and the mercy and the faith of God. My suggestion is that at the conclusion of Nixon's speech the general come out with the following memo in his own handwriting: 'I have seen many brave men perform brave duties. But I do not think I have ever known a braver act than I witnessed tonight, when a young Marine private [Barton got that detail wrong—Dick had served in the Navy] lifted suddenly to the height of national prominence, marched up to the TV screen and bared his soul.'" This could send a message of courage and confidence but also appeal to Ike as it left open questions about Nixon's fate.[38]

Ike trusted Ben Duffy and almost channeled Bruce Barton's script as he penned a response to Nixon's speech. In front of the audience at Cleveland, Ike said, "I have seen many brave men in tough situations. I have never seen any come through in better fashion than Senator Nixon did tonight." The crowds continued whooping "We Want Nixon." What Ike had just said was me too, *but . . .* [39]

Ike wrote out a longer statement that highlighted his evasion. He started by giving credit where credit was due, sharing his belief that Summerfield had gotten his money's worth: "Your presentation was magnificant [*sic*]." He injected vague looseness into his feelings: "Whatever personal admiration and affection I have for you—and they are very great—are undiminished." "Undiminished"—that suggested little had changed, either positive or negative. Eisenhower played that theme out: "While technically no decision rests with me, yet you and I know that the realities of the situation will require a personal pronouncement which so far as the public is concerned will be considered decisive." On that point, Ike seemed to mimic Adlai Stevenson's inability to commit, or the bureaucratic language that organization men used in large corporations. The general descended further into bureaucratese and passive language: "In view of your comprehensive presentation, my personal decision is going to be based on a personal conclusion. To complete the formulation of that personal decision I feel the need of talking to you and would be most appreciative if you should fly to see me at once. Tomorrow evening I shall be at Wheeling, West Virginia." The great performance hadn't seemed to persuade the man on top, or so his opaque language suggested.[40]

Nixon was celebrating in his hotel when he heard about Ike's note. Dick moved from exhausted celebration back to exhausted anger. He couldn't believe Ike really needed to meet face-to-face in order to decide his fate. "What more can he possibly want from me?" Nixon asked as he threw his arms up. *That's it*, Nixon thought: "I'm not going to crawl on my hands and knees to him." *For Christ's sake*, he thought, Ike had turned it over to him, he had dribbled the ball for a slam dunk, but now the general wanted to pull the ball back into his corner of the court and just sit there. Reporters close to Nixon were astounded to hear him cuss out the general. At this moment, it looked as though everything would collapse.[41]

Wednesday, 6:00 A.M., the Carter Hotel in Cleveland. In a suite, dressed in a loaned pair of pajamas, Robert Humphreys was scurrying around, writing notes for Arthur Summerfield, who was also in the suite, or making calls to Ike's and Dick's handlers and numerous Republican Party leaders. There was a manic, frantic feel in the room. Journalists stood in the hallway outside and cupped their ears to the door, hoping to find an answer to what remained a mystery: What had Ike decided?

Murray Chotiner was on the line with Humphreys and sharing big news: Dick Nixon had written out a resignation from the ticket. Chotiner had ripped it up without Nixon's knowing. But there was no sense of what Nixon was going to do; he was on a plane heading for Missoula, Montana, where he planned to resume his campaign schedule. He was exhausted and cranky. A thought occurred to Humphreys: What if Nixon lets on about quitting while in Montana and there's press present? Summerfield was trying to get hold of Dick. Humphreys scrawled a note as Summerfield talked on the phone: "Art . . . intercept Dick before he says something to press. . . . Dick should hold at that airport until you have talked to Ike."[42]

Finally, after Nixon's plane landed in Missoula, Summerfield got him on the phone. He pleaded with him: Please, please come to West Virginia and see the general. The *Look Ahead, Neighbor!* had left Cleveland at 2:00 A.M. and now barreled south through Ohio and into

West Virginia, planning to arrive in Wheeling around 6:00 P.M. Please break off the campaigning—did the underpopulated state of Montana really matter anyway?—and fly to West Virginia for that face-to-face meeting with the general. Nixon balked: Only if he was assured that he was still on the ticket would he rearrange his schedule. Summerfield got off the phone and placed an immediate call to the general's men.

At that instant, Humphreys heard scuffling at the door to the suite. He opened it to find a group of journalists and photographers hanging around. He chased them down the hall, knowing the moment of decision was nigh. Meanwhile, back in the room, with the door shut, Summerfield reached Ike's men. He discovered something that a few people had surmised but had never been confirmed: Ike had already decided to keep Nixon on the ticket. The general's original fear that he couldn't win by shucking Nixon remained with him through the crisis. And now there were the telegrams and letters and the informal polling that Summerfield and Humphreys had done on the phone with Republican Party leaders who backed Nixon. In certain ways, Dick had succeeded in going over Ike's head and making his appeal directly to the people. So the general said, yes, Dick's still on the ticket, but he'd really like for him to come to Wheeling all the same.[43]

What a score. This could be the perfect end to a dramatic story, almost like a father and son reuniting after years of youthful rebellion and mutual misunderstanding. Summerfield now had what he and Humphreys needed. Only one problem remained: Could the Wheeling airport handle Nixon's DC-6 airplane? A few phone calls cleared that up. The plans were set: Dick would fly first to Denver for a brief stop, then to Wheeling to meet the general and find redemption. The script had been written. Summerfield felt deep in his heart that he and Humphreys had just witnessed a "turning point of the campaign."[44]

CHAPTER FIVE

"AMERICA HAS TAKEN DICK NIXON TO ITS HEART"

*There is never a time when it is safe to relax or let down. When
you have won one battle is the time you should step up your effort
to win another—until final victory is achieved.*

—RICHARD NIXON, *SIX CRISES*

The Reverend John Welch was livid. He gathered his flock from
Ravenswood, West Virginia, to come see the man expected to be the
next president of the United States. His congregation constituted
part of a three-thousand-person crowd, which also included local
schoolchildren gathered with anticipation and excitement in chilly
and wet weather. The *Look Ahead, Neighbor!* pulled into town. Then it
stopped. But there was no Ike waving from the rear platform. The
mood among the crowd turned gloomy. Welch left after the train
pulled out of the station and his disappointed brethren dispersed. He
went back to his office and wrote an angry letter to Ike's headquarters: "It was indeed very rude treatment." Did they know the local
paper is owned by a "rabid 'Democrat'" and that the editors would
have a "field day in next week's edition"? Just what were they thinking by not putting in an appearance and leaving the crowd bewildered?[1]

What Pastor Welch didn't know was that Ike's train had to hurry north, first to Parkersburg, but more important, to Wheeling, the town where Richard Nixon's plane would land that evening (and the city where Joseph McCarthy had made his first historic speech two years ago). The general was busy figuring out how to reconfigure the upcoming event in Wheeling, which could no longer be a standard stump speech. Ike was gathering notes, writing up ideas, and rehearsing his thoughts. His men fed him some stuff from Nixon's team. There was no time for stopping and waving to the crowds in Ravenswood.

Ike arrived in Wheeling before Nixon. The vice-presidential candidate's plane was delayed. So the general waited in his car with Mamie at the airport. The two candidates had not met in person since the fund crisis had unfolded. Anyone considering what had changed in that time didn't need to look far. A few days ago Ike couldn't find time to reach Dick on the phone and rumors spread that he would kick Nixon off the ticket; now the general sat in the rain and waited for Nixon's arrival. Ike, the calm cool general, was now anticipating the man who seemed to have shown him up by taking to the airwaves and displaying his special powers of persuasion. Right after Dick's DC-6 landed, Ike bounded out of the car. Nixon was shocked: "General, you didn't have to come out to the airport." To which Eisenhower flashed a big grin of redemption and said: "Why not? You're my boy."[2]

Then it was out to Wheeling Island Stadium, where crowds of thousands faced a "cold and miserable night" with intermittent rain. The general stepped to the podium, spreading his arms into a V shape and waving his hands to cheers. He praised Nixon's courage in baring his soul during the Checkers speech. The people had spoken, the general declared. "Western Union is swamped trying to handle the telegrams of people who think Dick Nixon is just all right, and by golly, we are going to tell the National Committee I think he did a most courageous and wonderful thing." He explained that they had polled leaders of the RNC and found they wanted Nixon to remain on the ticket. "He is not only completely vindicated as a man of honor but as far as I am concerned he stands higher than ever before," Ike explained, elevating his running mate to lofty heights. He even read a note sent to him by Nixon's mother testifying to her son's honesty, as if to play upon the sentimental mood set by Nixon's speech. He thundered his theme home: "America has taken Dick Nixon to its heart." Then he quieted his voice for a moment and said, "And now I give you Dick Nixon," and the crowds rejoiced.[3]

Nixon began his off-the-cuff speech with glowing words about a man he had been cussing out in front of journalists just the night before. And then he proceeded to revisit the recent past in a way that defied his own feelings. You see, Nixon said, Ike could have said "at the outset . . . 'This is just a smear; I am not going to listen to any of these charges; and, as far as I am concerned, I am not even going to wait until the evidence is in before I make up my mind.'" Which, of course, is exactly what Nixon had hoped and pleaded for in private meetings. "I am glad General Eisenhower didn't do that, because there has been too much of that in the present administration," Nixon explained. He was playing his part now, turning from supplicant to attack dog. "There is too much of this business of cover-up, too much of this business of clamming up whenever any charges are made against those in high places." He then shot out: "I want you to know that this is probably the greatest moment of my life." The man who had been stuck in purgatory now stood vindicated. Arthur Summerfield described Nixon at this moment as "a truly great American who walked unscathed through the valley of despair."[4]

And then, as he had before during the fund crisis, Richard Nixon cried his eyes out. He turned and put his head on the shoulder of Senator William Knowland, who happened to be standing near by, and wept. The irony could not be missed. The man whose shoulder

Nixon chose had called Nixon a "dirty son of a bitch" at the convention and had been considered a potential replacement for the vice-presidential candidate when the fund crisis reached its apogee (he was rumored to be on Ike's train to serve as substitute for Nixon if necessary). But all of that went unspoken. This was a time of redemption, not of ill feelings. A *Life* reporter and photographer captured the moment: "'And strong men wept' is a strictly cornball phrase in these cynical days. Yet at Wheeling, W. Va. one night last week one U.S. senator put his head on the shoulder of another and wept . . . before 6,000 people, and few thought it strange." This was no act, but serious "pathos and candor" for all to see. "Hollywood might have hesitated to accept" Nixon's recent story as a "script." With those words, *Life* had just reconfirmed the bizarre mix of authenticity and performance art that the fund crisis prompted. The magazine, of course, was Henry Luce's photo-centered equivalent of *Time*, and thus moved with the story line that Ike's campaign wanted, meaning that it endorsed the Hollywood-style happy ending.[5]

After the big event, Nixon and Ike ducked into a car and drove off to the *Look Ahead, Neighbor!* so that Ike could show off the train to his boy. Nixon's dream came true: The two of them talked about political strategy, the way they hadn't back in Fraser, Colorado, in late July. Nixon was hopped up, like a son who could finally talk hombre to hombre with his dad. Ike wanted to talk about how the whistle-stops were going, feeling the energy among the fans and eager to return to the show of "shouting and waving at people," activities he had come to enjoy more than he had expected to in the beginning. As Ike went on, Nixon looked right at him and blurted out: "This is just like war, General. Our opponents are losing. They mounted a massive attack against me and have taken a bad beating." Now's the time to take the offensive, he suggested. Nixon wasn't sure Ike understood what he was getting at, but that didn't matter. Nixon had drawn his own battle plans. In effect, he had outflanked the famous general of World War II.[6]

Now that the crisis had passed, it was time to return to the flurry of campaigning. Just after descending into Wheeling to come out of his valley of despair, Nixon flew to Salt Lake City, Utah, Thursday evening, where he spoke at the Rainbow Rendezvous Ballroom, as well as live on radio and television. The next morning the Nixon team drove north to Ogden, Utah, for a speaking engagement at the City-County Building and then chartered a flight to Grand Junction, Colorado, and then Colorado Springs for events. From there it was to Amarillo, Texas, where he brought up the tidelands oil issue in his speech, and then off to to Oklahoma City, where morning events were scheduled for Saturday, September 27 (they had even considered squeezing in a stopover in Muskogee).[7]

So it seemed Nixon had moved back to his manic business as usual, except that something had changed since the speech. There was, of course, Nixon's own war footing. He started sounding sharper in his attacks, and this would continue as the last month of the campaign built to a crescendo. In Salt Lake City, just off the celebration of Wheeling, he railed: "The party in power will go down in history as the party which is dedicated to the principle of cover-up. Cover up so that people won't know what's happening. Cover up to keep in power." His fists would start flailing to the beat of his own words as he continued: "Cover up the tremendous waste in our federal expenditures. Cover up the truth about inflation. Cover up the Communist infiltration in Washington. Cover up our foreign policy mistakes, even if the lives of American boys and the security of the country are involved." He would condemn Stevenson's own fund crisis on a regular basis, projecting a feeling of moral superiority now. He was dynamic, hopped up, charged with energy.[8]

But there was something more going on. A message had emerged from the telegrams and letters sent in the wake of Nixon's speech, and they empowered him mightily. It was similar to the way that lingering anger from Taft's defeat at the convention carried over and culminated in the senator from Ohio's subsequent victory at the "surrender at Morningside Heights," when Taft had appeared to win so many concessions from Eisenhower. For as much as viewers praised Nixon's honesty in his speech, many also derided the way Eisenhower and his men had handled the crisis that preceded it. A typical response to the speech came from Colorado: "Frankly we are disgusted with the way Eisenhower's campaign managers and advisers have handled this and also Eisenhower's campaign. We personally think they are a bunch of half wits and if the Republicans lose the election this Fall, they will be responsible." A man who ran Kilgore Hardware and Auto Parts Store in Florida spelled it out more bluntly: "I am for Nixon. Why don't Ike kick off of his bandwagon all weak kneed reporters advisers and enemies and replace with Americans." Others asked for Ike to resign, pondering: "What kind of a person is he that he can't stand up for honest and true Americans? First Taft, then McCarthy, and now Nixon." Plenty of letter writers complained about Tom Dewey, remembering his double defeat and assuming (accurately, perhaps) that he was coaching Ike to push Nixon off the ticket. Some drove all the way to the logical conclusion: "From now on, let Nixon do the campaigning. Put a muzzle on Eisenhower."[9]

Many of these citizens' letters and telegrams channeled the thoughts of Fulton Lewis Jr., a radio commentator and Nixon ally. Lewis was the equivalent of Joseph McCarthy on the airwaves, not only because he supported McCarthy but because he used the same punctuated iterations that McCarthy loved—his words pecking the air with brutal resolve. When he first learned of the allegations about the fund, Lewis went on the airwaves and called the accusations "filthy,

slimy, and thoroughly vicious." Lewis was pitch-perfect the evening
after Nixon's speech: "There is many an American today who saw
and heard that presentation of his last night who will rate it as a companion piece to the address of General Douglas MacArthur before
the Congress a year ago last June . . . It has left a terrific recoil on the
traducers and the cheats, the smear artists who made the attack, and
that goes for his enemies inside the Republican Party just as well as
outside." He saved his best rhetoric for the circle of men surrounding
Ike who were doling out bad advice. Ike's advisers went into a "frenzy
of schoolgirl panic" instead of facing the situation like grown men.
Lewis railed against the "pinheads and amateurs" on Ike's train. He
derided the "pip-squeak tyrants" and "fox-terrier little men." The
general needed to get more "fire of attack" into his speeches and get
rid of people like Sherm Adams, "a small town, small visioned, pouter
pigeon intellect." He should throw out Dewey's "plants" on his team.
Implied in all this was that "Dick" should take the lead on the campaign in the future. Many of those who wrote Nixon in support took
their words directly from Lewis and counseled him to step out in
front.[10]

Nixon took up the charge of Lewis and fans as much as he could.
As he turned to campaigning, his crowds grew in size. So, too, did
the energy felt at his events. Jim Murray, a reporter from *Time*, recalled attending a Nixon rally in Nashville, Tennessee, on September 27, when the spirit of Checkers was still fresh: "My God! I can't
believe this. It looks like they think Nixon is running for president."
That was the point. Nixon felt in the lead now; the postspeech comeback meant the campaign had changed. He had moved to the center
of things, and Ike had allowed it. When in Oklahoma, he continued
with his Checkers strategy by moving to the podium for a speech
and then ignoring journalists who wanted to ask follow-up questions. A newspaperman, Wheeler Mayo, publisher of the *Sallisaw
Times* in Oklahoma, complained: "Never in my 20 years of owning

and operating newspapers and as past president of the Oklahoma Press Association have I witnessed the snubbing that Nixon gave the press." As he moved into the spotlight, Nixon saw no reason to bother with anyone intervening between him and his people.[11]

Speaking solely to his fan base, Nixon upped the heat of his rhetoric. Truman had recently come out to whistle-stop for Stevenson, injecting the vigor he had shown in 1948 and charging Ike with being a stooge for special interests and even being soft on Communism back in 1946. Nixon pushed right back, recognizing that Dewey's response to the president of the United States in 1948 had been too wimpy. Dick no longer felt hamstrung by a disapproving bureaucracy or Ike's snickering inner circle. Having been out west in Utah, Colorado, and Oklahoma right after the speech, he came east for the first few days of October. On October 3, speaking in Wilmington, Delaware, Nixon slammed Stevenson as a coward: "If the umbrella is the symbol of appeasement, then Adlai Stevenson must go down in history as the Umbrella Man of all time. For he has been attempting to spread a shadowy political parasol over the great issues of foreign policy, Communism, corruption, and cost of living." This was just perfect: the image of a parasol conjured visions of British snobbery and aristocratic effeteness. To put a fine point on it, Nixon bellowed about a man who would never have been seen with a parasol: "These harsh times call for a man. For a real man . . ."[12]

That "real man," Dwight Eisenhower, spoke three words with bitterness and disappointment the very same day: "Take it out." Meaning the section of his speech in which he condemned the senator he would stand next to on the back of the *Look Ahead, Neighbor!* as the train made its way through the state of Wisconsin. What he really wanted to say was: "I know that charges of disloyalty in the past have been leveled against General George C. Marshall. I have been privi-

leged for thirty-five years to know General Marshall personally . . .
And this episode is a sobering lesson in the way freedom must not
defend itself." But Sherm Adams, who didn't disagree with the words,
insisted they sounded extraneous, not organic to the rest of the speech
the general planned to give. Ike backed down in the face of Sherm's
protest, gritted his teeth, and prepared to spend the rest of his day
with Joseph McCarthy, a man who had trashed Marshall and who
appeared, soon after the convention, happier with Nixon on the
ticket than Ike.[13]

The night before, in Peoria, Illinois, Joseph McCarthy had
bounded onto Ike's train unannounced. The senator talked and glad-
handed. It was easy to imagine McCarthy asking if Ike was going to
take on old "Ad-lie" or "Alger," using the purposeful slips of tongue
that peppered his speeches now. Ike said, actually, he thought of saying something critical about Joe in Milwaukee the next evening. Not
a good idea, Joe said; the crowds wouldn't like it. Governor Walter
Kohler Jr. of Wisconsin, who was also aboard the train, encouraged
Ike not to do it. Ike just stared silently after hearing this. He knew
Wisconsin had gone Democratic in 1948 and that McCarthy had
just won his primary in a landslide without lifting a finger. He left
the issue open as his train barreled ahead from Illinois towards Wisconsin. He was still an expert at evasion.[14]

Their first stop the next day was Green Bay, Wisconsin. Ike enjoyed a cool, crisp autumn morning and receiving a blanket from the
Green Bay Packers football team. But he also felt "groggy," having
thumped his head the evening before as the train jolted through Illinois. As he prepared his remarks, photographers asked if they could
get a few shots of the general and McCarthy together. Not going to
happen, Ike's men announced as the general started moving onto
the rear platform. McCarthy jumped up and grabbed Mamie's
hand, holding it aloft much to Ike's disgust. Ike then started to talk
up to the crowd assembled "party strength" and asked people to vote

a straight ticket to form a "team" to go to Washington in January. Then Ike shifted and started to talk about "differences" between "me and Senator McCarthy." They shared the same ends—to clear the government of Communist traitors—but differed on the "method." That was an odd endorsement. So odd that afterward, numerous journalists asked McCarthy about his relations with Eisenhower. McCarthy described them as "very fine" and then changed that to "perfect." But the journalists weren't convinced and commented on his strained expression.[15]

Ike's train moved south to Appleton, a town close to where McCarthy grew up. The senator bounded to the rear platform to address a gathering of seven thousand, calling Ike "a man who is an outstanding general" and "who will make an outstanding president." Recognizing the leanings of this local audience, Ike left out any talk of "difference" from the morning, slowly moving toward grudging if unspoken support of McCarthy. In fact, Ike didn't mention McCarthy at all. Instead, he said: "You need every single man we have got on the ticket here in Wisconsin from the governor himself through the Senate and the House. Please give us the whole works, and we will do the job, we promise you." That was about as full an endorsement of the senator from Wisconsin as Ike could give.[16]

The day culminated with an evening gathering in Milwaukee. A crowd of 8,500 showed up at the Milwaukee Arena, and Joseph McCarthy came out to cheers. But in his opening remarks, he slipped up a bit: "So long as I represent you I shall continue to call them as I see them, regardless of who is president." A few boos broke out at what sounded like a who-cares-who-wins-the-presidential-election statement. Hecklers even hooted him, and McCarthy tried to look dignified by saying, "Don't worry about one or two trouble-makers in the crowd—I'm used to troublemakers." Ike might have grimaced at that line, but instead he approached the podium to give a speech that resonated with those of his vice-presidential candidate.

He condemned "men" who were "advisers in a foreign policy that . . . weakly bowed before the triumph in China of Communists hailed as 'Agrarian Reformers.'" He mentioned Truman's "red herring" comment about Hiss. Then he stole lines from the Checkers speech, lines aimed right at Stevenson's large domed forehead: "There are those who dismissed the quest for Communists as a kind of silly game being played in the Bureau of Wild Life and Fisheries." The general parroted another Nixon line about Stevenson's equation of Communists with "phantoms." Those "comedy touches," Ike argued, showed just how foolish Stevenson was. The whole time, McCarthy sat on the stage and beamed, smiled, clapped, and made a big "OK" sign with his thumb and forefinger.[17]

Two days after Ike's tour of Wisconsin, McCarthy was asked again by journalists what he thought of the general. McCarthy gave a full endorsement, even suggesting he might call off his one-man Communist hunt if Ike won, especially if Ike would really "clean house." But then Joe said he had to stop taking questions since he had work to get back to. His job wasn't over yet. Seems he was researching Stevenson and planned to do a television show toward the end of the month about the governor's Communist associations.[18]

On October 8, Dean Acheson gave a press conference to catch reporters up with the situation in Korea. He sounded and looked hopeful, his trademark mustache arching upwards with his words. A "humanitarian solution" to the prisoner-of-war crisis was still possible, Acheson explained. At the same time, though, the United States had not backed down from its position of voluntary repatriation. "We shall not trade in the lives of men," he said, "or forcibly deliver human beings into Communist hands." He cited that the United Nations backed that position as well. Acheson knew full well that the POW situation was the last string to tie up before a truce could be declared. But he also knew the other side wasn't budging on the issue. It was now "entirely up to the Communists" to move. Which meant that very little had changed with the situation in Korea since spring, no matter how chipper he might have looked. It was a strange performance, especially amid an election campaign that was heating up. The journalists then asked Acheson about Eisenhower's criticism of U.S. policy in Korea, and he dodged the question.[19]

The day after Acheson's press conference, the *Nixon Special* barreled from Pittsburgh to York to Harrisburg, Pennsylvania, where the vice-presidential candidate spoke at Capitol Plaza, arriving via motorcade at 10:45 A.M. Twenty thousand people showed up; the police labeled the crowd the "largest ever to attend a political rally at Harrisburg" (not bad for midmorning on a weekday). Confetti and balloons filled the air, as if this was a hero's homecoming. Nixon appeared on the podium, where he lambasted Stevenson for criticizing Eisenhower's recent campaign trip with Joseph McCarthy. Adlai suggested the general showed lack of "backbone" against right-wing loons. The vice-presidential candidate belted out: "I haven't seen any evidence of backbone in . . . Stevenson, Truman, and Acheson except when like little boys in a mud fight they attack that great American, General Eisenhower." Stevenson was just "a graduate of Dean Acheson's spineless school of diplomacy" that was failing in Korea, as even Acheson himself seemed to admit the other day. The huge crowd roared with applause.[20]

Nixon then boarded his train, visiting solidly Democratic and unionized steel towns along the way before arriving the next evening in Erie, Pennsylvania. He had been honing and editing his speech, to be held at the Gannon Auditorium in a city his handlers called "predominantly Catholic" and where the "leading campaign issues" would be "Communism and the Korean War." He looked at his drafted speech, admiring its opening whack against the Truman

administration: "If the Russians had been running our State Department during the last seven years of Trumanism, they wouldn't
have developed a better—or more successful—Asiatic foreign policy
from the Soviet viewpoint. Dean Acheson, Harry Truman's architect of striped pants confusion, managed to lose for the Free World
half the continent of Asia and one-fourth of the entire globe's population." That was good, Nixon thought as he combed further through
the speech on the train and then the automobiles that took him to
the Auditorium. He liked how he called Stevenson Dean Acheson's
"pupil." But then he got to a line about Stevenson "looking at the
Communists through Acheson's rose-colored State Department
glasses . . ." *Not bad, but not good enough,* he thought. He crossed out
"rose" and wrote in "pink." Now, that was perfect.[21]

It was right about now, during the second week of October, that the
first Eisenhower "spots" rolled out on television. They would flash
onto the screen with the words "Eisenhower Answers America" and
then flashed to ordinary-looking citizens asking questions. A young
married couple in one wondered, "General, the administration tells
us we never had it so good." Ike came on looking stern, like a man
who had been sitting through a morning of being on camera saying
two sentences over and over, and retorted, "Can that be true when
America is billions in debt, when prices have doubled, when taxes
break our backs and we are still fighting in Korea? It's tragic and it's
time for a change." That was it.[22]

They were now all over the television networks, costing a whopping two-million dollars. *Variety* declared it "the most intensive satu-
ration spot campaign in the annals of American broadcasting."
When hearing about them, Stevenson reacted with sour grapes. "I
don't think the American people want politics and the presidency to
become the plaything of the high-pressure men, of the ghostwriters,

of the public relations men . . . This isn't Ivory Soap versus Palmol-
ive." That sounded like what a man who refused to buy a television
set would say, like a man who *Time* would describe as littering his
speeches with references to "Shaw, Disraeli, Oliver Wendell Holmes,
William James." Stevenson asked, "How can you talk seriously about
issues with one-minute spots?" (Let alone, it could be added, in thirty-
second spots.) Of course, if he had to ask, he didn't know (or perhaps
he didn't care to admit that his side ran short advertisements with
silly jingles, though not nearly as many since his campaign was more
cash-strapped.) Whatever motivated the comment, it was another sign
that his view of the election as a deliberative assembly—a serious
quadrennial conversation—had never materialized. And only two
weeks remained.[23]

The eggheads had revolted. On October 16, a full-page ad ran in the
New York Times paid for and written by "Volunteers for Stevenson
and the Columbia University Faculties and Staff." It was a scathing
indictment of the president of Columbia University, a position Ike,
who had just celebrated his sixty-second birthday two days earlier, still
officially held. The professors opened by praising Stevenson's "character," "humility," and "dignity." They saw themselves in him. Then
they segued into complaints about their university's president. They
admitted that some of them "once thought that our beliefs and principles were in large measure shared by General Eisenhower. Even as
late as July we hoped that we might witness a campaign between two
candidates who would debate the issues at the highest levels of political responsibility." Good-bye to that now with Ike shaking hands
with Taft on Morningside Heights and with McCarthy on his recent
trip to Wisconsin. Ike had "surrendered to the most unsavory elements of his party," including McCarthy and Jenner, while Stevenson
had consistently opposed "Communism and McCarthyism." Even

worse was Richard Nixon, whose Checkers speech did not answer "questions about his financial support" but only provided a "dramatic monologue insulting to the intelligence." On this topic, they concluded: "We are alarmed at the thought that a Republican victory would put Richard Nixon next in succession to the White House." The signatures on this manifesto numbered over three hundred.[24]

The ad's sponsors had an executive committee chaired by Allan Nevins, the Dewitt Clinton Professor of History at Columbia University. He was the author of big books about big subjects, with works on Grover Cleveland, the Civil War, and John D. Rockefeller. Before joining the Columbia faculty in 1928, he had been a journalist who had worked under Walter Lippmann at the New York *World*. Nevins was that rarity who felt comfortable writing scholarship and political commentary simultaneously. He was an egghead who had connections, with close personal feelings toward Stevenson but also toward his brother General Arthur Nevins, who had helped Eisenhower write his memoir about World War II, *Crusade in Europe*. Though he respected Eisenhower, Nevins had grown increasingly distressed watching the general pal around with Jenner and McCarthy, especially disgruntled that Ike had edited his defense of Marshall out of his Milwaukee speech. Nixon's Checkers speech made Nevins ill; he believed it "so essentially dishonest and emotional an appeal that" the vice-presidential candidate "confused a great many people as to the issues involved." Nevins thought of himself as one part citizen, one part Columbia University man. He wanted to make it clear that an important constituency at Columbia didn't support Ike's run for the presidency. Some of his colleagues suggested the slogan: "Keep Ike for Columbia or don't let them take him away." Whether he wanted Ike to stay on as university president after observing his behavior during the campaign was probably a more open question now for Nevins. But he certainly agreed that Ike didn't deserve to enter the White House.[25]

Nevins recruited a younger historian, Richard Hofstadter, to help draft the statement that appeared in the *New York Times*. Hofstadter was perfect for the job. He had grown up in Buffalo, New York, half Jewish, half Lutheran but generally secular and alienated in his sensibilities. Coming of age during the 1930s, Hofstadter joined the Young Communist League with his first wife, Felice Swados, and started graduate studies at Columbia University. He'd quit the party once he learned about the Moscow Trials. From then on, he was a liberal historian who had a penchant for irony and humor and sported the egghead uniform of a bow tie and glasses. While Nevins wrote biographies of great men, Hofstadter enjoyed taking great men down a peg or two. His breakthrough book had come the year that Truman beat Dewey for the presidency. *The American Political Tradition* had argued that few Americans—from Thomas Jefferson to Andrew Jackson to Abraham Lincoln to Teddy Roosevelt—could think beyond a one-dimensional genuflection to private property and markets. Though he wrote about celebrated figures from the past, he had "no desire to add to a literature of hero-worship and national self-congratulation."[26]

McCarthyism scared Hofstadter, who was worried that his past as a Communist might be discovered as he engaged political activism. A staunch defender of academic freedom, he was appalled by the loyalty oaths that the University of California made faculty members sign (he had considered a job there). And most of all, he didn't care much for Eisenhower, a man who loved football and crummy western pulp fiction. Should a man like that have been president of a prestigious university in the first place? wondered Hofstadter. And so he drafted the statement against Ike, while Nevins gathered signatures and raised financial support.[27]

Then the unexpected happened: A war opened within the ranks of the eggheads. One week after the advertisement for Stevenson appeared, another one was run under the title "Columbia University

Faculties and Staffs for Eisenhower." This one had 714 signatures to the measly 324 for Stevenson. Howell Ingraham, a professor of accounting at Columbia, said triumphantly, "The number of signers . . . provides rather striking evidence of the fact that Columbia's campus sentiment is much more in favor of the General than of his opponent." Their statement didn't make as full-fledged an argument as the Stevenson supporters had. They mostly bemoaned the fact that "Columbia University has been thrust into the national political situation" and wished the Stevensonites had "kept their university affiliations separate and distinct from their widely expressed political views."[28]

Hofstadter thought something amiss. He contacted his friend and fellow historian Peter Gay, and they started to scrutinize names on the list of their opponents. They hadn't heard of many before, and that was odd, since Hofstadter had then been at Columbia for six years. Poking around a bit, Gay wondered why the opposition group included "dietitians, building superintendents, stenographers and students, including non-matriculated students at the School of General Studies" in a list that purported to be faculty and staff? There was even a rumor that one signee was an apartment doorman who had been lobotomized. Hofstadter and Gay went to the *New York Times* and rejoined: Look at *our* list; it includes preeminent scholars of high repute, not stenographers. That sounded like the sort of endorsement that even Adlai Stevenson could blanch at. Where Hofstadter suggested foul play, his critics leveled the charge of elitism. Some in the press pointed out that the egghead liberals had contradicted themselves: They complained about the use of Columbia's resources by Ike and yet seemed to use their standing as Columbia professors to promote their own political intervention. They had entered politics on their own terms, considering it a purely rational and scholarly pursuit, only to face blowback as derisive snobs.[29]

The controversy was followed closely by the press, in part because it fit a narrative that Stevenson's campaign garnered energy from eggheads—highly educated intellectuals out of contact with ordinary citizens, like those janitors who cleaned the buildings on Columbia's campus. The pundit Stewart Alsop had taken note of this at the end of September, pointing out that the "young political amateurs" Stevenson surrounded himself with were predominantly "intellectuals." Alsop wondered: "Is intellect good politics?" In the case of Columbia, the answer was no. The professors had entered the rough-and-tumble world of campaigning and got blasted for doing so, for losing sight of their vocation's principles of objectivity and nonpartisanship. (Why, the *Washington Post* asked in an editorial, did they criticize only Nixon's fund and not Stevenson's?) The professors mimicked their hero, Adlai, who believed that the campaign of 1952 would be modeled on rational debate and high-minded speeches setting out the future of the republic. That's not what it was turning out to be at all.[30]

On Sunday, October 19, Norman Vincent Peale gave a sermon entitled "How to Have Good Personal Relations" at his Marble Collegiate Church with its "comfortable" setting and "overflow congregations" located in midtown Manhattan. The sermon wound down a flurry of activity in Peale's life. He had been campaigning for Ike and Nixon, all the while attacking Democrats for feasting "on power" and nurturing "big statism" (at one Daughters of the American Revolution event, Whittaker Chambers joined him). On October 12, while celebrating his twentieth anniversary at his chapel, Peale helped out as the vice-presidential candidate campaigned in New York City, having flown down from the upstate city of Binghamton. Amidst all of this activity, Peale still managed to find time to prep for a publicity blitz that would follow the October 13 release of his *The Power of*

Positive Thinking, a book whose publication and immediate popularity constituted one of the biggest cultural events of the year.[31]

Peale was born to be a man of the cloth and an intellectual antidote to the Columbia doubters uptown from him. He grew up the son of a Methodist minister in Ohio but struck out on his own to give journalism a try as a young man, writing for the *Morning Republican* in Findlay, Ohio, and then the *Detroit Journal*. But like his father, Peale decided on the ministry and attended the school of theology at Boston University. He didn't like it there, finding the city hostile and his fellow students priggish. Nor did he care for the "social gospel" his professors tried to cram down his throat, with their vision of Christ as a do-gooder who worried about the poor more than his own spiritual well-being. Too much guilt for Peale. He was more attracted to the upbeat writings of William James and Ralph Waldo Emerson, the latter being, in Peale's words, "the wisest man who ever lived in America." He imbibed their faith in individualism and their rejection of hardened theology for a looser spirituality that celebrated the energy derived from belief. After Boston University, he moved into ministering, starting in Walpole, Massachusetts, moving to Rhode Island, and ending up in upstate New York and then eventually at Marble Collegiate Church in New York City at the height of the Great Depression in 1932. He built his church to overflowing size over the next twenty years by emphasizing an "intimate relationship with Jesus" that could bring "emotional energy" and "enthusiasm" to an individual's life. He toned down sin and moralism. Wanting more men to attend his services, he often argued that religion need not be a "sissy" affair. One young man looking for a religion that was neither sissy nor demanding was Richard Nixon, who attended Marble Collegiate during the early 1940s when stationed in New York during his stint in the navy. Nixon returned to this church every chance he got when in Manhattan.[32]

Peale had always sought out a connection between his religious faith and politics and found his inspiration during the postwar years in an organization called Spiritual Mobilization, a group of religious and business leaders. Its founder was James Fifield, who had served as minister at the First Congregational Church in Los Angeles, a huge compound that included a gymnasium, fifty-plus classrooms, and three auditoriums. Fifield showed talent for recruiting wealthier businessmen to his pews, even holding a special golfers' service at 8:00 A.M. so that men could hit the courses at a reasonable hour. Schooled in the social gospel, much like Peale, Fifield rejected such liberal fluff by concluding that wealth was God's blessing and the markets divine. He explained in 1949: "It is a great spiritual tonic for me to read the New Testament formula, which culminates in the dignity, the supreme worth, and the effectual power of free and responsible individuals." This provided the basis for his attack against "pagan statism." Fifield had attracted numerous right-leaning laity, including Peale, especially during the years following World War II.[33]

As the election of 1952 approached, both Peale and Fifield became MacArthur acolytes. Fifield called the general a "symbol" of the "spiritual revival needed to save this country," and Peale talked with the general one-on-one to try to get him to run for the presidency. As MacArthur's prospects fizzled, Peale found transferring his loyalties to the Eisenhower-Nixon "crusade" easier than Fifield and other hard-line conservatives did. Peale never possessed an angry heart the way some MacArthurites and Taftites did.[34]

Peale's own popularity by 1952—what elevated his political voice above others—stemmed from his knack as an inspirational speaker and writer but also from the period in which he operated, a time of religious fervor. A postwar religious boom produced rising church attendance numbers (in 1952, 75 percent of Americans told pollsters that religion was "very important" in their lives). And numerous celebrities catered to this rise in devoutness, including Fulton Sheen, with his *Life Is Worth Living* television show, and Billy Graham, who by 1951 had brought his old tent-revivalist style to television as *Hour of Decision*. Graham had a special appeal in predominantly Protestant America, with his fiery and staccato talk of hellfire and sin— condemning adultery, divorce, crime, and Communism, the latter linked directly to Satan. He could pack in the crowds and was even successful in March 1952 in holding the "first-ever formal religious service on the Capitol steps." Graham, like Peale, saw connections between America's religious boom and political rebirth. He prayed for a crusade to return America to moral virtue, condemning the Truman administration's failure in Korea, a war that was "being fought because the nation's leaders blundered on foreign policy in the Far East." And he peppered his rhetoric with phrases like "time for a change," barely concealed endorsements of Ike and Nixon. He believed religious and political revival went hand in hand.[35]

There was just one problem with Graham, or rather a few problems that stemmed from one: He was a fundamentalist who believed the Bible was the direct word of God (a belief that Richard Nixon, for instance, had already rejected as an undergraduate at Whittier College, much to his mother's dismay). From his fundamentalism sprang Graham's heated-up sermons, his tent meetings full of emotion and vivid energy, becoming too fiery for some living in the era of air-conditioning, refrigerators, and television entertainment. Strident denunciations of satanic forces didn't always fit a white-collar world looking for pep and more upbeat lessons divined from God.[36]

Enter Peale. His sermons were more staid and soothing ("How to Have Good Personal Relations," for instance), and his book, *The Power of Positive Thinking*, built upon this comforting message, finding huge audiences and ratcheting up the bestseller lists soon after its release, staying at the top for two years straight (and still on the lists four years later). Peale started the book not with the principle of sin but with the therapeutic benefit of a "dynamic faith." The tribulations and challenges of the real world needn't trip believers up or lead to the morbid self-hatred the idea of sin promoted, Peale argued, because the mind-frame one brought to life's crises mattered most. Any fact of reality "facing us, however difficult, even seemingly hopeless, is not so important as our attitude toward that fact." God, for Peale, was not a spiteful or punishing being but a loving father, even a companion who empowered people by providing them with divine "energy." Peale then offered his readers a formula for getting out of problems and crises in life: "Prayerize—Pictureize—Actualize." He went to the Bible, more specifically to Mark 9:23—"Everything is possible to one who has faith." Faith didn't teach despair about the human condition—the way it had at times for Whittaker Chambers—but rather benefit, material and otherwise, including the curing of illness and the accumulation of wealth (Peale had joined religion and psychotherapy at Marble Collegiate Church by working with a psychologist who was appropriately named Smiley Blanton). Like Fifield, Peale enjoyed listening to and learning from stories provided by businessmen. He used their fables about religious faith buttressing their success throughout *The Power of Positive Thinking*. He often mimicked Dale Carnegie, whose classic self-help book *How to Win Friends and Influence People* (1936) stood as a foundation for Peale's own work. Peale littered his book with advice for business success that echoed Carnegie's: "Learn to remember names . . . Be a comfortable person so there is no strain in being with you. Be homey." *The Power of Positive Thinking* offered an ethic of salesmanship wedded to confidence and divine energy.[37]

The book provided a theology of sorts for the Checkers speech and its aftermath. It charted the path Nixon took from crisis to confidence man. *The Power of Positive Thinking* asked readers to embrace their internal salesmanship and overcome doubts. As Nixon explained, the fund crisis taught him that "it isn't what the facts are but what they appear to be that counts when you are under fire." A glow of positive attitude was much better than the doom and gloom that Nixon's earlier intellectual mentor, Whittaker Chambers, offered in the anxiety-ridden days of spring. Confidence offered the necessary state of mind for a crusade on the path toward victory. It was the same sort of attitude that Eisenhower spoke about in wartime. A reviewer in the *New York Times* might criticize Peale's teachings for being "too automatic and immediate, the answers a little too pat, and the underlying theology a shade too utilitarian." Such an egghead warning ignored the demands of the now: to project the confidence of victory before winning. As a chief campaign manual for Republicans in 1952 put it, long before Peale's book hit the stands, a political candidate should "think of himself as similar to the manager of a crew of house-to-house salesmen. His function is to give them confidence in their product." That statement along with attack politics and Peale's advice served up what could be called Nixon's philosophy of life as he moved on from the Checkers speech toward the end of the campaign.[38]

What projected more confidence than a presidential candidate saying he would solve the biggest problem the country faced by making a trip abroad? That's what Eisenhower did on October 24 to a crowd of five thousand at Detroit's Masonic Auditorium. He said it in five simple words: *I shall go to Korea.* The crowds rose to its feet when the words were uttered. It was the sort of statement that cut through the din of the campaign and laid things out in the starkest terms. Ike was going to end the war; he'd go over to Korea, sit down with other world leaders, and just get it done. He was that sort of guy—a man with military victories notching his belt, and a man who felt self-assured speaking about his own abilities to settle matters. Hadn't Truman begged him to take over NATO forces; hadn't Ike begun his presidential campaign by returning from Europe, where he had served as the liberator of that continent from Fascism and the threat of Communism? Some in the crowd at the Masonic Auditorium when hearing his words might have envisioned loved ones abroad returning home to a warm fire in the living room. Some might have remembered the iconic *V-J Day in Times Square*, the photograph shot by Alfred Eisenstaedt and published in *Life* at the end of World War II that showed a sailor kissing a nurse in front of happy men and women walking by. Whatever the crowd in the Masonic Auditorium was thinking, it likely missed that Ike refused to issue an "imminent exact date" of war's end during the speech. The whooping audience simply registered the five words about going to Korea and the vague promise implicit in them that war was over because Ike wanted it.[39]

Ike had been hinting at such talk throughout October. He had been reminded of a poll his research team had done in the Midwestern farm states that showed that the unpopularity of the Korean War had skyrocketed to the top concern in the heartland. So when he went through states like Illinois or Wisconsin, he'd often use the following line: "Farm boys should stay on the farm and college students in college. The South Koreans should stay in Korea and Americans should stay in America." That sounded good, but it wasn't sharp enough. Ike's men knew he needed something juicier to roll out, especially as the campaign wound to its end.[40]

It took a man who had been schooled in the hotbed of American optimism—*Life* magazine—to come up with the sharp line about going to Korea. Henry Luce had personally dispatched Emmet John Hughes, an editor at *Life*, to work on Ike's team as a speechwriter. Hughes had a sense that Ike needed a confident statement about Korea that could still hold to evasion. Promising a trip to Korea was just the thing. It would state that Ike would do something, but it didn't set out a clear-cut plan. As Hughes remembered writing up the five-word line, it "rose from the need to say something affirmative on the sharpest issue of the day—without engaging in frivolous assurances and without binding a future administration to policies or actions fashioned in mid-campaign by any distorting temptations of domestic policies." It became a "prudent avoidance of commitment on future Asian policy." In other words, a perfect declaration for a campaign. In trying the line out with colleagues, Hughes got the attention of C. D. Jackson, another speechwriter who had an inside line to Sherm Adams. Adams worried about the statement's vagueness (what plan did Ike really have and how would it work?) but gave permission to try it out on the general, who sat on a hotel bed one night and nodded at the speech as it was rehearsed for him. When the speech rolled out in mimeographed copies on the train barreling toward Detroit, journalists ran their fingers over the lines and fixated on the one about a visit to Korea. Most blurted out: "That does it—Ike is in."[41]

Ike knew that the line nailed it. He kept pressing it further as the days clicked down to the election. In Pittsburgh, three days after Detroit, he fancied it up a bit: "If a journey to Korea and a close study of our military and political problems there can save the life of a single American soldier and bring peace of mind to a single American family—I must make that journey. My good friends, I shall make that journey." Hearing this at home on the radio, Jacob Arvey, a man who had recruited Stevenson into electoral politics to run for governor and then remained as an adviser, exclaimed, "That's the speech that will beat us." Jack Bell, an Associated Press reporter who knew the presidential campaign inside and out, heard the speech and blurted out that "for all practical purposes, the contest ended that night" in Detroit. Confidence mixed with vagueness had done the trick. The declaration to go to Korea allowed Ike to remount his white horse.[42]

No one could stop Joseph McCarthy from making his own case why good Americans should reject Adlai Stevenson. On October 27, he would go in front of national television cameras and present the "Stevenson Story," clinching the case that the "debonair Democrat" candidate for high office was a Communist stooge. This was a personal fight. Two weeks ago, Joe was telling the Wisconsin Buttermakers and Managers Convention that he wanted to get on board Stevenson's train with a "slippery elm stick . . . to make a good American" [out of] Adlie." (When the Associated Press reported this out, the words changed: "If somebody would only smuggle me aboard the Democratic campaign special with a baseball bat in my hand, I'd teach patriotism to little Ad-lie.") Though some still remembered Joe thrashing his journalist foe, Drew Pearson, two years ago, the senator wasn't going to make it onto Adlai's train. So he planned to do the next best thing: Put on his lawyer's cap and play the sleuth who would present the case—piecing together what he'd call a "jigsaw puzzle"—that tied Stevenson to the wider communist conspiracy.[43]

It was to be his own presentation, for sure, but he was also riding the energy he felt from that friendly meeting with Ike earlier that month. A picture of the two men grinning and shaking hands still got play in the magazines and newspapers. Joe could remember making that "OK" sign at everything Ike said at the Milwaukee Arena. Holing himself up in a Wisconsin farmhouse, McCarthy had been penning a grand finale for the "Stevenson Story," in which he would call for citizens to "vote on November 4" for Ike and Nixon (he figured his own reelection was a cinch, which it would be). "Up until now I have been fighting tremendous odds," Joe had scrawled out on his pad of paper, but if Ike won, he could help him "scrub and wash" Communism from Washington, D.C. Hearing about this, Sherm Adams asked Arthur Summerfield to approach McCarthy, to see if they could get the speech in its entirety and figure out how to respond. McCarthy balked: "I am not going to be censored by anyone, and that is all there is to it." So the Eisenhower team figured the best thing to do was let Joe go on the airwaves and do his thing. The senator had popularity Eisenhower didn't want to squander. After all, a man didn't get a keynote slot at the Republican Convention or requests to endorse presidential candidates (Taft) or demands to campaign on behalf of candidates across the country for nothing.[44]

Joe wasn't going to find help from the Republican National Committee or from Eisenhower's team to fund his televised address. But he quickly raised enough money—much more than the seventy-eight thousand dollars he needed—to buy a half hour of national television time. Much of the bill was paid by General Robert Wood of Sears, Roebuck, a man with gobs of money and right-wing sentiments (he was a founder of America First, the isolationist organization that opposed U.S. entry into World War II). Wood primed the pump with money from Texas oilmen. In addition, the speech would be held at a $50-a-plate dinner at the tony Palmer House in downtown Chicago, garnering more funds. McCarthy knew it had to be big. Drawing on his enormous reserves of self-dramatizing skills, he announced his speech would serve as an "exposé."[45]

On October 27, McCarthy mounted the dais and waved papers in his hand. He began with how many members of Americans for Democratic Action—an organization that didn't like HUAC or loyalty oaths, he reminded his listeners—surrounded "Alger—I mean Adlai." Consider Arthur Schlesinger Jr., who wrote for "the *New York Post*, whose editor" was once a member of the "Young Communist League." McCarthy dribbled out to associations and then walked them back without taking the shot. Joe quoted Schlesinger's review of *Witness* in the *Saturday Review* (the same issue where Nixon had celebrated the book). Seems Schlesinger disputed Chambers's view that religious fervor was necessary to fight the Cold War when he wrote that "a belief in God has created human vanity as overweening and human arrogance as intolerable as the vanity and arrogance of the Communists." McCarthy zipped by this implied reference to the Crusades and religious wars from the past to suggest this Harvard man questioned the principle that a "belief in God was the hope of the free world." He had just painted a picture of an unprincipled atheist writing speeches for the Democratic candidate for president. He then turned to "Richard DeVoto," a name he butchered (it was Bernard), the "Easy Chair" columnist at *Harper's* magazine who was an adviser to Stevenson. DeVoto had criticized the FBI, McCarthy complained. At this point, Joe seemed to have started rambling.[46]

Finally, he zeroed in on "the debonair Democrat candidate," accusing Stevenson of membership in a World's Citizen Association and having vague connections to Italian Communists. But he really heated the drama by holding up a picture of a dilapidated barn. What was *that*, the audience must have asked. Well, McCarthy had sent his men to this barn to find documents from the Institute of Pacific Relations, an organization tagged a Communist front group. One document reported that Alger Hiss had "recommended Adlai Stevenson to the Mont Tremblant conference which was called for the purpose of establishing foreign police"—another mis-pronouncement, corrected quickly with "post-war foreign policy in Asia." The connection seemed rather tenuous, and someone in the room shouted out, "That's not so." But the point being made wasn't the point. It was that "jigsaw puzzle" that captured both Adlai Stevenson and Alger Hiss within it. It all went back to the character deposition Stevenson had given for Hiss when Richard Nixon was nailing him. Now it was spun out and provided drama with a picture of broken-down barn.[47]

McCarthy's next thought was likely *Damn*. The cameraman was waving his arms around and telling him he had no time left. He hadn't come to the best part: the photostats of the *Daily Worker* urging its Communist readers to vote for Stevenson. Well, the paper hadn't said exactly that; it said, as Joe had written down, that the Communist Party expressed "'their hatred of Eisenhowerism' and then" said that "they do not like Stevenson too well either, but that if Communists want to vote for Stevenson—okay, vote for him—but

vote for no one else on the Democrat ticket—elect local Progressive
Party candidates and pile up a big vote for those Communist-
candidates who are in the field." Joe told those gathered at the
Palmer House about this, though not his television audience. He
consoled himself by figuring that he had gotten enough of the jigsaw
puzzle out there and that the press would report, as the *Washington
Post* did the next morning on page one, that he had shown how the
"Governor Backs 'Kremlin-Shaped' U.S. Policies."[48]

McCarthy had made his stance, and Eisenhower's team made clear
it was his own. Still, Joe's attacks seemed awfully close to Richard
Nixon's throughout the course of October, a time when the liberal
op-ed writer Marquis Childs pointed to a "final blitz on communism . . .
by virtually every Republican candidate" running for office. As the
vice-presidential candidate's aggressiveness dial was turned up a
few notches, his rhetoric about Stevenson kept getting harsher, zero-
ing in on his supposed softness on Communism. By mid-October,
Dick reached new heights by absorbing McCarthy's speaking techniques, especially alliteration and hard-boiled repetition. He developed rhetoric that made it into history books: "Let me speak of Adlai
the Appeaser—the man whose slavish devotion to the dubious foreign policy of Truman and Acheson could bring on World War III."
Nixon went on to conflate "containment" and "appeasement" and
then derided "Adlai—who carries a Ph.D. from Dean Acheson's
Cowardly College of Communist Containment." That alliteration
was perfect. Containment no longer appeared just appeasement but
Communist in nature. Of course, containment was a doctrine that
wanted to *halt* the spread of Communism. But Nixon was implying it
was somehow Communist inspired itself—and that Stevenson would
continue Acheson's weakling performance. Nixon never let down
with this insinuation during October. Two days before McCarthy's
"Stevenson Story" show, Nixon spoke in the heartland (Indianapolis) and railed: "Mr. Stevenson has lined up consistently with those

who minimize and cover up the Communist threat. Their part in the Hiss case is typical of a defining pattern, which shows up Mr. Stevenson as a body-and-soul captive of his environment. He is color-blind on the Red issue." McCarthy had heard this language, and his televised appearance on October 27 became his own personal "OK" sign to Nixon, if not Ike. They would sprint together to the finish line.[49]

On October 30, the leading pollsters of the time—George Gallup of the American Institute of Public Opinion and Elmo Roper—appeared at a meeting of the American Marketing Association in Manhattan. They spoke about "Why the 1952 Polls Won't Go Wrong." Both predicted an Eisenhower victory, although they admitted that the number of undecideds was still high and that Stevenson seemed to be showing some movement upward. And then they admitted they both had gotten the last election dreadfully wrong, predicting that Dewey would defeat Truman soundly. So there was still some uncertainty, even though it was just five days before the election.[50]

Some pundits were more certain than these pollsters, especially as the close of the campaign dawned. Walter Lippmann, for one, had grown profoundly dismayed. He had pleaded with the general in print to "consider the anguish of his friends" about how he had run his campaign. The columnist, after all, had hoped Ike could unify the country. As the month of October drew to a close, he didn't even think Ike could unify his own political party, let alone the nation (as the editors of the Washington Post explained, they had "hoped that Ike would appeal to the people as a national leader" but now witnessed "an unedifying campaign"). For Lippmann, Ike had allowed the yahoos in his ranks to run the show. He noted McCarthy's televised speech and the "slippery elm stick" comment and laid the blame for such heated rhetoric and confusion, at least in part, at Ike's door.

The general hadn't done anything to calm the hounds on his side. Lippmann asked with exasperation, "What, in heaven's name, has happened to us?"[51]

Lippmann's question grew out of observations he'd already made by mid-October, that Ike "was not in control of his candidacy." He had "adjusted his position" to the "demands of the local political machines." He was "not, as we hoped last winter . . . the effective leader of his party." He had allowed his vice-presidential candidate to get out in front and call the shots, ever since the Checkers speech. He had become too chummy with Taft and McCarthy, letting them define his crusade. Ike had ceded authority; but even so, unlike Senator Wayne Morse of Oregon, a Republican who had earlier said he wouldn't campaign for Ike but now bolted his party altogether on October 24 due to disappointment in the general, Lippmann would still vote for Ike. He believed that if the general didn't win, the Republicans would become "wholly and irreconcilably Old Guard." As an endorsement, this one was rendered unenthusiastically. It was all head, no heart.[52]

Lippmann had been writing about politics for years, which gave him perspective. Although election night hadn't arrived yet, he was ready to make a pronouncement, not so much on outcome but quality. "This has been an ugly campaign," Lippmann wrote, "not quite so foul it seems to me as 1928 [when the Democratic candidate Al Smith was attacked viciously on anti-Catholic grounds] but in the perspective of the times we live in much too ugly." His friends the Alsops had predicted McCarthy's televised speech would become "the low-water mark of this not very high level campaign." Lippmann agreed with this prediction, growing particularly apoplectic about the comments McCarthy had made earlier about beating up Stevenson with a baseball bat. What did such sentiment say, Lippmann asked in his editorial printed on October 30, "that that most authentic, that original and classic American, who is Governor of Illinois, needs to be clubbed by Joe McCarthy in order to make a good American out of him"? Such a statement—and the fact that Ike had done nothing to condemn it—said "that our public life [had been] defiled [and] debased." And so, the campaign of 1952 had driven Walter Lippmann mad. He would hold his nose and pull the lever in the election booth with little more than an anguished sigh.[53]

And where was the man Lippmann called an "authentic" and "classic" American? The day those words appeared in print, Adlai Stevenson was heading to prison, the Menard State Prison in Chester, Illinois, to be precise. Just five days earlier, a prison riot had erupted there. Prisoners had seized seven guards hostage and had barricaded themselves inside a cellhouse, using chains to keep entranceways to the outside locked. They holed up, eating a stash of potato chips and candy bars, and started issuing demands, including those for fairer parole conditions and better medical care. They said they'd kill the guards if demands weren't met. Hearing that talks had broken down Thursday, Stevenson decided to fly out of Pittsburgh, where he was campaigning, and head home to help solve the problem. He still felt a "duty" to his state.[54]

His campaign staff went berserk. The governor was heading into the last weekend before the election, and the polls were suggesting he was bouncing upwards, even if still behind. Stay on the trail, they argued, instead of canceling big events or sending surrogates to speak for you. What if you go to Illinois and the prison riot grows worse, and you're left with that on your hands in the last few days before the big vote? They tried to reason with him: Lieutenant Governor Sherwood Dixon was handling the situation. Stevenson said he knew going to Chester was a "gamble" but that he still had obligations as governor. Lives were on the line; he had to govern, not campaign, at a time like this. "Illinois affairs are still my responsibility," he told his campaign team and the press as he boarded a flight out of Pittsburgh.[55]

Operating on two hours of sleep the morning of October 31, Stevenson wrote out an ultimatum to be read over the loudspeaker system of the prison. "We are going to enter this cell house with state police armed with guns immediately." It promised the prisoners food once they handed the guards over unharmed. Then Stevenson marched alongside 321 state troopers, most touting machine guns. The troopers fired three shots into the air to provide warning of their approach. And then they proceeded to seize back the cellhouse, using an acetylene torch to burn through the barricaded doors. Inside, some guards had broken out into fistfights with the prisoners, one of them using a shoe to smash a rioter's head in. After a half-hour skirmish, the guards had been freed, and the prisoners gathered together and marched back to their cells. Stevenson stuck around to talk with the guards, who appeared shell-shocked, and their wives and family members, who remained unhinged. He made no speech about the matter and just rushed back onto the campaign trail.[56]

Ironically, this mini-crisis might have served as relief to the governor. Just two days before departing, Adlai was calling the campaign a "ghastly ordeal." This wasn't the ordinary exhaustion that came from nonstop talking and shaking hands and answering press queries; over the course of the last two weeks, all he had been doing was defending himself against Nixon's and McCarthy's attacks or explaining to a hungry public why Ike's talk of ending the Korean War was just that—talk. A day before Ike made his "go to Korea" statement, October 23, Stevenson felt compelled to make a long speech at the Cleveland Arena explaining his role in the Hiss case, after Nixon and McCarthy had been hammering him on the subject for days. He explained that he "testified" regarding Hiss's character "only as to his reputation at the time I knew him." He elaborated: "I said his reputation was 'good'—and it was. I didn't say it was 'very good'; I didn't say he was a 'great patriot'; I didn't say any of the things the Wisconsin senator, whose best weapon is carelessness with facts, says I said." Besides, it was his duty to testify in court. But having to roll out the speech made him sound like a man on the defense. He admitted so much: "The Republican candidate for vice president has himself set the pace" of the campaign. He had helped instigate an "ugly" situation that Eisenhower seemed to wink at. And Stevenson saw no way to get out of that dynamic without spending his time and energy defending against the barrage it induced. In ending the speech, he returned to the biblical tones that had surrounded his original acceptance of his nomination back in July. This time, Stevenson quoted Mark 8:36: "In the final accounting, 'What shall it profit a man, if he shall gain the whole world, and lose his own soul?'" In these words, Richard Nixon could smell the blood of Adlai Stevenson, slumped exhausted against the ropes.[57]

And then when Eisenhower quipped about his trip to Korea, Stevenson just rolled his eyes. To the governor from Illinois, this was a gimmick concocted by a ghostwriter. He called it a "quick and . . . slick" quip, implying that the statement was like Ike's "spots" littering the television airwaves. "A speech writer from a slick magazine cooked up an idea to catch votes by playing upon our hopes, our desperate hopes for a quick end to the Korean War," Stevenson complained. He even got a joke out of it, playing upon the "if I get elected" nature of the "go to Korea" statement: "If elected," Stevenson quipped back, "I shall go to the White House." But a joke and angry retorts weren't enough, and so after dealing with the prison crisis, Stevenson decided he had to give another long speech about why Ike's one-liner about Korea was so troubling.[58]

Returning to his campaigning in the Midwest, Stevenson went home to Springfield, Illinois, where he gave on November 2 what would be one of his final speeches before election day. It condemned the sweep of Ike's ideas on the campaign trail—from his talk of liberating "Eastern Europe" in the early days of the campaign to the recent statements about Korea. Irresponsibility ran throughout, Stevenson argued. In making his case, though, the governor wound up driving himself into a corner, defending Truman's policy in Korea and suggesting that the long and hard-fought war wasn't going to end just because the general said he wanted it to. "We are in Korea," he explained, "because we must be there; and our purposes cannot be fully achieved by training South Korean troops to deal with the enemy alone." Pulling out now would mean that South Korea could fall to Communist forces. A visit to the area by the general wouldn't change that situation, nor would it solve the POW crisis that dragged on and that Stevenson went into detail about during his speech. And so Eisenhower was making nice-sounding promises to win votes, whereas Stevenson was making a long speech as to why the Korean War couldn't be ended overnight.[59]

The speech acted out the plotline Nixon wanted: Stevenson was too detail-oriented, too ineffective, too wordy and smart to offer citizens the confidence they expected. The man who started his campaign with the idea of a high-minded, civilized debate knew that the game had changed. The governor from Illinois had learned that the other side set the rules and had pressed him into a corner.

The day Stevenson rushed to his state to quell a prison riot, Richard Nixon was in his own home state of California. But he was doing nothing *but* campaigning. It was his job to sew up his state's thirty-two electoral votes, and he was doing just that by barnstorming. He juiced up his campaigning with more rhetoric stolen from the master of politics, FDR. He rang out his speeches with talk of the "forgotten men" whom FDR had anguished over back in 1932, except that Nixon's forgotten men weren't destitute farmers but overtaxed citizens faced with inflation and the "500,000 boys fighting in Korea." He even took time out from his stump speeches to zing Stevenson's visit to the prison. Stevenson "apparently thinks first hand information about a problem concerning a local prison is important—but that a first hand inspection and study of the battlefields of Korea, where 123,000 Americans are casualties is not important." Meaning: Forging campaign rhetoric about ending a war was more important than quelling a prison riot. This just went to show that Nixon understood the world of Campaign '52 much better than his Democratic opponent. He was writing the story line.[60]

Still, the stress of this last furious bout of campaigning was getting to him. He had been in California four days now, hopping onto planes or into auto parades or going on the radio nonstop. At one speaking event, a heckler showed up and started ripping into Nixon. The vice-presidential candidate, his nerves shattered, pointed to the man in the crowd and shouted: "When we're elected, we'll take care of people like you. Okay, boys, throw him out!" That command turned to action. During a speech in Long Beach, California, it was learned that "a gang of roughnecks in" Nixon's "entourage beat up several people in his crowds carrying anti-Nixon signs."[61]

The journalist and columnist Drew Pearson, who recounted this story in his journal, was also the last man ready to try to take Nixon down. He saw a coarse ugliness entering Nixon's campaign in its last leg. So he gathered his staff in his Georgetown house and renewed their efforts to dig up dirt about the vice-presidential candidate. He was a nationally syndicated op-ed writer who reached millions of readers and was something of a celebrity (he made a cameo appearance in the 1951 film *The Day the Earth Stood Still*). And he was one of the few writers on whom Nixon's campaign team kept an alert eye, clipping and cataloguing all of his columns.[62]

Pearson had spent the month of October trying to link Nixon's financial ties with his policy practices. He and his staff established some connections, some possible impropriety, but nothing substantial. Earlier in October, he had pointed out that the law firm that pronounced Nixon had not broken any law (and that produced the papers he had read from during the Checkers speech) had also represented "some of Nixon's biggest and most active donors." Pearson went on to speculate, out loud in his newspaper columns and on the radio, that maybe Nixon got help from wealthy donors to acquire his property in "exclusive Spring Valley." He emphasized that "Dana Smith, the lawyer who collected the $18,000 for Nixon, had used Nixon's influence through his administrative assistant to try to get a $500,000 tax refund from the Government." There were some names on Nixon's list of funders who had secured defense contracts: "K. T. Norris, president of the Norris Stamping Co., has a contract with the Defense Department for making shells and cartridges estimated at around 25 million dollars. Earl Adams is attorney for Guy Atkinson, a builder with large Government contracts." Maybe donors got what they wanted from Dick, even if there was no smoking gun. Realizing that Nixon was trying to do an end run around the press, Pearson just kept throwing out these accusations, one after the other, during the month of October. He seemed to stand alone in his self-proclaimed pursuit of justice. He wondered: Had the Checkers speech really worked to diminish all suspicions that men who gave money wanted something for their money?[63]

That was a legitimate question, but it never sullied Nixon's reputation or the following he had gained since the Checkers speech. Crowds at Nixon's rallies continued to grow; it looked like there was little that could stop the Ike-Nixon ticket. Pearson, however, wouldn't back down; he just became more incensed as election day approached. Jack Anderson, who had joined Pearson's staff five years earlier and worked hard on the Nixon investigation, feared that Drew too often mixed "reporting with political activism" and used "deduction to carry on from where investigative fact left off." Close to the election, Pearson and Anderson went public with the allegation that

Dick and Pat Nixon had tried to save fifty dollars on property taxes by claiming a veterans' benefit and by undervaluing their assets (it sounded small, but the point was they had lied, Pearson and Anderson suggested). Pearson had been handed the information by someone inside the Bureau of Internal Revenue. He didn't check the story out or call Nixon. It turned out that it was another Richard and Pat Nixon who owned property who had made the claim. But Pearson put the story out there anyway to linger in the days approaching the election, as something of a counter to McCarthy's exposé of Stevenson. Nixon's lawyer demanded a retraction (it would come after the election).[64]

None of Pearson's pushback would slow down or distract Nixon, who, by Friday, October 31—the day Stevenson was quashing the prison riot—was sprinting toward the electoral finish line. He moved from Inglewood to Santa Monica to Beverly Hills to Pasadena to Alhambra, and then finally to a big blowout at Hollywood Legion Stadium, which for Nixon was a perfect location, not just because it was connected to the American Legion but also because it was normally used to stage boxing matches. Just right for a final performance of a rocking and socking campaign. Nixon was joined by some big Hollywood names, and Bob Crosby, the big-band leader on Jack Benny's radio show and the younger brother of the crooner Bing, served as the master of ceremonies. The gala show went out over state radio and television. No small-time accusations from Pearson's columns could have an impact on Nixon's popularity. Hearing about Stevenson's trip to the prison, Nixon figured this was the last punch that would bounce his opponent off the ropes and onto the floor.[65]

On Sunday, November 2, after a short stint of campaigning in Wyoming, Montana, and Washington, Dick was on a plane to Boston, arriving late in the evening for another reunion with Ike. The next day was surprisingly slow for Dick, with none of the hustle and bustle of his California tour. But he'd have to remain fresh late into Monday evening. For around eleven o'clock television cameras would roll live on a set staged to look like an average American living room for an "at home" show. Ike would be there with Dick, joined by their wives, Mamie and Pat. They would be filmed watching a television set, just like average Americans wanting to keep up on the election before the fateful day.[66]

Anyone paying attention might have noticed that this looked an awful lot like an episode of Ike and Mamie's favorite television show, *I Love Lucy*. Ike and Mamie resembled Fred (balding) and Ethel (nicely dressed), the older couple, while Dick and Pat resembled Ricky (dark hair) and Lucy (redheaded). And they were being filmed by a television camera while watching television. They looked like the actors in the show for another reason: They were certain that they had risen to the number one rank.

It could have been written as a joke: *Two eggheads walk into an airport and get depressed.* On November 2, Max Lerner, a professional sociologist who was now an editorialist at the *New York Post*, was taking a plane out of New York City. Arthur Schlesinger Jr., the Harvard historian turned Stevenson speechwriter whom McCarthy attacked during his nationally televised speech, was changing planes in New York City on his way back from Springfield to Cambridge. The two ran into each other. Schlesinger had been pleased by a series of editorials Lerner had been writing about the excitement of Adlai Stevenson's campaign. In mid-October, Lerner had been quite optimistic about the governor's chances, believing, as many other journalists did, that "Eisenhower's collapse as a symbol of crusading moral fervor" had fallen with his "surrender to the Taft-Jenner-McCarthy forces." So it surprised Schlesinger to find the man completely down on Stevenson's prospects now. Schlesinger had occupied the bubble of the campaign office in Springfield and "was still completely sure that we would win." He didn't like how sad Lerner sounded, how certain of Stevenson's impending defeat he was, as they both ran for their planes.[67]

It wasn't as if Lerner had thrown in the towel. As opposed to the hold-your-nose vote that a pundit like Walter Lippmann would give Eisenhower, Lerner was still going to vote for Stevenson with a great deal of conviction—but now mixed with a sense of existential absurdity. Just a little over a week ago, Lerner had explained his convictions to his readers in a list of "becauses" for his upcoming vote. "Because . . . Stevenson is for the English sentence. Because he doesn't act as if he were taking a course on how to make friends and project his personality . . . Because he doesn't insult my intelligence." Most knew those last two lines were aimed at no one else but Nixon. And then there was perhaps the most evocative reason of all: "Because he doesn't have a dog named Checkers, or a wife with a Republican cloth coat." Those lines channeled a generalized egghead lament as election day approached.[68]

It ended as a slaughter. On November 4, Eisenhower seized 442 electoral votes to Stevenson's 89. A staggering 63.3 percent of the eligible population voted—a huge turnout—and gave Ike 55.2 to Stevenson's 44.3 percent. This made Eisenhower the highest vote getter so far in presidential history. Eisenhower even won Stevenson's home state of Illinois 55 to 45 percent (four years ago, Truman had won the state by a very slim margin). The general made a significant dent in the "Solid South" by winning the state of Virginia 56 to 44 percent (it had gone 48 to 41 percent in favor of Democrats four years earlier); Florida 55 to 45 percent (49 to 34 percent four years ago, with significant showing from the States' Rights Party); and Texas—where his campaigning on tidelands oil and civil rights paid off—by 53 to 47 percent (1928 was the last year the state went Republican, and in 1948 Truman won it 65 to 25 percent, with a 10 percent showing for the States' Rights Party). Ike won a whopping 61 to 39 percent in the state of Wisconsin (another state that went Democratic in 1948) and a big 58 to 41 percent in Indiana. And that meant his straight ticket strategy did well for the two McCarthyite senators, Joseph McCarthy himself and William Jenner of Indiana. Even Robert Taft, who didn't face reelection that year, could be pleased that Ohio went for Ike 57 to 43 percent (since Truman won the state in 1948).[69]

On election day, Richard Nixon was back in Los Angeles. He had flown out Monday night from Massachusetts and voted in the morning in Whittier. There was nothing more to do on election day. A day earlier, his manic work schedule had been duly recognized by the *New York Times*. It was reported that Richard Nixon was the leading campaigner in numerical terms. He had clocked 375 speeches and traversed 42,000 miles. Those numbers trounced Adlai Stevenson's 203 speeches and 32,000 miles. So Dick, feeling his work was done, called his friend Bill Rogers and suggested a drive to Laguna Beach. To his delight, they came across some Marines who were stationed at Camp Pendleton and were playing catch football on the beach. He was able to join their pickup game, returning momentarily to the joys of his favorite sport. And then he went to the Ambassador Hotel around 4:00 P.M., straight into his pajamas for a much-deserved nap. Two hours later, a gaggle of friends broke into his room, telling him it was going to be a landslide. Rare as it was, Nixon was all smiles. He learned soon thereafter that California had gone 57 to 43 percent in favor of Ike. His job was done, and he went back to sleep. If he cried that night, they were tears of joy.[70]

CONCLUSION

THE DOG THAT BIT

*And for a salesman, there is no rock bottom to the life . . . He's
a man way out there in the blue, riding on a smile and
a shoeshine . . . A salesman is got to dream, boy. It comes
with the territory.*

—ARTHUR MILLER, *DEATH OF A SALESMAN*

Landslide elections are easy to understand. One side pummels the other. That much was clear by November 5, 1952. But then the dust settled, and political scientists and pollsters assembled charts and statistics, searching for the bigger picture. They confirmed that Ike had driven fissures into the Democratic and New Deal coalition by moving some southern states onto the Republican side of the ledger and by stealing a sizable number of votes from the white ethnic working class in northern cities (a strategy that came to fuller fruition after the 1960s). But one of the biggest discoveries was how well Ike did among white-collar and suburban voters—a constituency whose numbers boomed in 1952 as America grew more prosperous. The pollster Louis Harris, two years after the election, explained that white-collar suburbanites "provided Eisenhower with a vote so large that it outweighed the traditional big-city majorities the Democrats always needed to win." This was a national phenomenon, not concentrated in one state or region, as the historian John Greene made clear: "In every part of the country, the suburbs went from 75 to 90 percent for Eisenhower." Harris quoted one Stevenson aide saying "The suburbs beat us." In other words, the "organization men" in gray flannel suits—those constituting America's "lonely crowd"—played a large role in pushing Eisenhower to victory.[1]

Like the rest of the nation, they voted for a charismatic war hero. But they also voted for a man who resembled them, who looked and talked like them, a man who served his country during World War II not as a hero but as a midlevel bureaucrat and who then scrimped and saved during the postwar years to buy a suburban-style home, a 1950 Olds, and a respectable cloth coat for his wife. Those biographical details resonated when Dick Nixon presented them to his audience on September 23. "The white collar man is all for Senator Nixon" rang out one of the many letters sent his way after the Checkers speech. The "common people" of the 1950s saw themselves in the man they watched that night on television. The speech provided the greatest drama of the entire campaign of 1952 and drew the largest audience; it confirmed Richard Nixon as "Just Plain Dick" and served as a "turning point" that drove up the size of Nixon's rallies—often larger than Ike's—on the sprint toward the November 4 victory. A reporter observing the rowdiness and fanfare of one of his rallies after Checkers wrote, "It looks like they think Nixon is running for President." For some, that might have been the case. But many probably just saw something in him they wanted to confirm, to cheer for at the rallies, to cry for when they watched his television performance. A man they could "take to their heart" as a "sincere" American.

It's hard to look back and understand this, to watch the speech today and comprehend its drama and significance. If we have any historical memory at all about Nixon that we might bring to watching the speech, it's what transpired *after* Checkers: the Watergate scandal that destroyed his second-term presidency in 1974. We remember the man who lied and covered up, which makes it easy to wince at the opening words of the Checkers speech when Nixon talks about "the usual political thing" being to "deny" details about wrongdoing. But even if we clear Watergate out of our receptors and go back to the original context in which the speech was given, it's still difficult to access. The speech appears to be another relic from the bland 1950s—a decade we associate with conformity and naïveté. We laugh at its sentimentalism and schmaltzy qualities. Nixon's emotional pleading, his throwing his arms out toward the national television audience, his maudlin references to a cloth coat and a puppy dog, look and sound silly to us. Its black-and-white tones—both literally and metaphorically—grate on our postmodern nerves. It plays like other television shows from the time, the sappy and overacted soap opera *The Guiding Light* (with its melodramatic organ music) or the bland domestic happiness of *The Adventures of Ozzie and Harriet* (both shows that moved from radio to television in 1952). When the radical film director Emile de Antonio dug up Checkers footage for his documentary *Millhouse* (1971), it had been almost twenty years since anyone had seen the speech in its entirety (it took de Antonio quite a lot of work to get the tape). As a man on the left who hated Richard Nixon, he simply dropped huge chunks of the Checkers speech, with little editing or commentary, into his movie, expecting his pre-Watergate audiences to roll their eyes and think of the whole thing as comedy.[2]

It's an easy reaction. But it denies the speech's political genius, its transformative power not just during the election of 1952 but in American political culture writ large. First and foremost, the speech pushed the theme of populist authenticity to the center of political appeal. Nixon consciously connected to people on television screens by projecting indicators of averageness—the dingy "GI bedroom den" set and the accounting of his and his wife's two-bit possessions.

This was a man who had just been discovered taking money from donors with interests in real estate, oil, and banking—not exactly businesses that would have played well to the populist persuasion from the past (the original populists attacked landowners and bankers who ripped off small farmers during the 1880s and 1890s, and FDR warred against the banks and Wall Street during the early New Deal of the 1930s). It was certainly not Nixon's policies that made him a man of the people (no domestic policies were even alluded to during the speech); it was his performance as "Just Plain Dick." The speech personalized populism and turned it into a style of sincerity that battled the phonies and elitists—the prep school and Ivy League set who populated the State Department. Nixon's style ripped into those who were "too suave" and "too smooth" (words he had used to describe Alger Hiss) or too pompous (Dean Acheson) or too "wisecracking" and "fey" (Adlai Stevenson). The speech saved Nixon's career by making him into a man of the people, a "real" American—a term that rang throughout the letters and telegrams that poured in for him. That style became a brand Nixon wore on the sleeve of his wife's cloth coat. We can laugh at it now—as the *New York Post* and *Variety* did at the time—or we can see what Stewart Alsop saw back then: that Nixon had tapped something deep in the American unconscious that wrote his success story.[3]

Nixon's was a white-collar populism that fit 1952, when the American "people"—or at least large swaths of them—discovered the pleasures and comforts of a burgeoning consumer culture. Nixon's "people," it goes without saying, were not the farmers mired in crop price depression during the late nineteenth century or the forgotten men and women suffering the Dust Bowl and bread lines of the 1930s; they were the white-collar employees hungering for the goods promised by postwar prosperity. This was a theme of Nixon's political career that surfaced explicitly in the Checkers speech. When he first ran for office in 1946, Nixon described the "new forgotten

man" as the "white-collar worker" looking for a "new car, a refrigerator," and a house, who chafed at the overregulatory state and
just wanted more stuff. Now, in the Checkers speech, he detailed
his own averageness by citing his nonhero status during World War
II, his mortgage, and, most important, the commodities he had
collected as his own. The speech was populist in tone but white-
collar in its imagery.

And he performed it all on television, which in this context takes
on deeper meaning. Obviously, television provided him with the
large audience he needed. But it was also a medium conducive to
Nixon's message. Television was fast becoming the place where
American salesmanship (huckstering, if you prefer the more cynical
expression) moved in the coming years; this was already apparent
when Betty Furness stroked refrigerators and Mobilair fans for millions of Americans. In going directly to the people, Nixon confirmed
just how much television was changing the nature of American politics, with its emphasis on selling and stage-managed image. (The
spontaneity of the conventions earlier that summer showed how dangerous a lack of staging could become—with faintings and failed
speeches aired for all to see.) One of Nixon's greatest allies, Robert
Humphreys, charted the future of American politics when he emphasized Dick's "salesmanship" qualities that worked best through
"informal, intimate television productions" aired directly to the "individual American and his family." Murray Chotiner was bolder:
Nixon needed to go directly to the people via television because the
press—reporters and op-ed writers—hated him. Walter Lippmann
identified the Checkers speech as an act of electronic "mob rule," for
him a source of danger but for Nixon and his inner circle a necessity
and a virtue. (Lippmann, after all, was one of those pesky elite journalists the vice-presidential candidate wanted to run around.) Nixon
employed telepopulism to cut through Eisenhower's original desire to
move ploddingly through a judicious fact-collecting process. He used

television to carve out his audience—to get to "the people" who would support him—and then invite those people to identify with him and provide him their vote of confidence.

Nixon wanted to go direct to their hearts—not their heads. The expressions "hearts" as well as "tears" were repeated ad nauseam in the letters and telegrams the speech garnered. To read through them today is mind-numbing. But they tell us how the speech worked in context. What the people wanted was an authentic, sincere, truthful man. What the critics of the speech recognized was just how much Nixon *staged* his authenticity, giving off cues in his performance art by using props (including his wife), mentioning his dog, and providing humble biographical details. Authenticity mixed with stage-managed appearance to such an extent that authenticity itself became staged. When *Life* reported on Nixon weeping in Wheeling, West Virginia, the night after the speech, the magazine admitted that "Hollywood might have hesitated to accept" Nixon's recent story as a "script." Where did reality—authentic tears—and stage performance—the scripted image—diverge now? That was becoming harder to discern. Nixon had the advantage that television was new to Americans, some of its shows (including his) still performed live. Americans hadn't become quite so jaded about "pseudo-events" and politicians considering themselves performers, incessantly spinning news to their own advantage. There actually was something real about the stage at that point, and certainly something real about the "crisis" that proceeded it. And it can't be denied that citizens claimed Nixon spoke to their "hearts" and registered as "sincere"— leaving behind a quality that many Americans still search for today (the "likability" or "would you want to have a beer with this person" tests we apply to candidates, for instance). Nixon's personalized populism and his talk about his own feelings ("Why do I feel so deeply?") throughout the speech pushed American politics where it has so often gone: into the realm of sentiment and emotion and away from where Adlai Stevenson had naïvely hoped it would travel, the realm of ideas and intellect.[4]

Which wraps around to another key theme the speech articulated: anti-intellectualism. That theme coursed throughout the context of the story told here, with the pejorative term "egghead" applied to Stevenson and his advisers and the attacks Ike and Nixon made against their opponent's "Harvard words." The Checkers speech hammered home a populist distrust of intellect in both explicit and subtle ways. Not just in the speech's maudlin and "soap opera" sections, but when Nixon waved his fists and spoke in his baritone about how "Stevenson pooh-poohed and ridiculed the Communist threat." The style here became more macho, employing the swaggering, he-man tones that Joseph McCarthy had pioneered in his "fighting" speeches. It suggested something wrong in the softer foreign policy of "containment" versus Nixon's feistier vision of "liberation." Nixon wanted his speech to be not just an emotional and sentimental self-defense based upon his love of wife and family, but a projection of himself as a red-blooded male on the warpath. That became more explicit after the speech, of course, as September turned to October and Nixon charged his rhetoric up with McCarthy's pugilistic alliterations. The reason that that style worked was because it resonated with the country's Cold War culture. Its appeal could be read in the angry face of the father depicted in *My Son John* who had pride in his two "halfback" sons marching off to war and who hit his Communist son over the head with a Bible; or in John Wayne's duking it out with Communists in the late-summer hit *Big Jim McLain*; or in the consistent celebration of college football by Eisenhower on the campaign trail; or in the subtle questions raised about Adlai Stevenson's unmarried status (and the stories that Pat Nixon told about her husband's he-man qualities). During the Checkers speech, Nixon offered a tough, hard-boiled attack on Stevenson for not having what it took to fight Communists at home or abroad. These were the "real

man" attributes he spoke to days after the speech. The toughness
Nixon projected—the love of a good fight and a "rocking and socking" campaign—confirmed his sincerity as much as his play for the
heartstrings did.[5]

To suggest that Nixon disparaged the intellectual element of
Stevenson's persona, characterizing it as indecisive and effeminate,
doesn't mean he was not a man of ideas himself. After all, during the
earlier part of this story, Nixon engaged in debates surrounding a
book that constituted a masterwork in the burgeoning American
conservative intellectual movement: Whittaker Chambers's *Witness*.
Although Nixon's commentary was fairly thin and focused on the
book's political points (and why Chambers wouldn't get a fair hearing from snobs and elitists), Nixon had thought about some of the
darker ideas Chambers explored. Ever since the Hiss case, Nixon
had worried, in his own words, about how America "could . . . instill
in brilliant young Americans the same dedication to the philosophy
of freedom that the Communists seemed to be able to instill in people
like Hiss." That was a central theme explored in *Witness*. Nixon
would stay loyal to Chambers's flair for melodrama and his populist
hatred of wealthy men like Hiss selling the country out to Communism. But the vice-presidential candidate toned down the pessimism
and gloom coursing through Chambers's conservatism by livening
up his mix of ideas with the faith and confidence that Eisenhower
projected and that would find full intellectual expression in Norman
Vincent Peale's *The Power of Positive Thinking*. Nixon's story here goes
from a man of anxiety and doubt to a man of confidence, a man who
moves from darkness into the spotlight as a salesman for himself.
Dour moralism and a tragic worldview, Nixon knew, did not fit America in 1952. Nor would Chambers's sense of sin or militant hatred of
materialism. The speech had to project Nixon's own confidence—
including faith in the culture of consumerism and abundance growing up at the time—and a man who would never be a quitter, a man

who realized that "it isn't what the facts are but what they appear to be that counts." A man who could never understand or accept tragedy and whose conservatism was profoundly optimistic, like the conservatism of *Life* magazine.[6]

Nixon pulled together many different qualities to make his speech the "smash hit" it became. The success of the speech in its own time—and the glimmerings of recognition it prompts today (many political dictionaries have entries under "Checkers Speech")—suggest that instead of rolling our eyes as we watch it on YouTube, we should recognize its brilliance. The story told here accentuates the amazing nature of Nixon's accomplishment. For it allows us to get inside the man who made the speech. By the evening of September 23, Richard Nixon had become what J. D. Salinger called in *The Catcher in the Rye* a "madman." His mind had exploded into a mania, as he approached (or had?) a nervous breakdown. He whipsawed between anger toward his enemies ("the bastards") and even toward his boss, Ike, to tears about his mother's prayers for him. From rage to sentimentalism in a pulsing heartbeat. When first getting the news about the fund story, Nixon thought in conspiratorial terms, suspecting that the sinister forces of Communism were out to get him. "When I received the nomination for the vice presidency I was warned," he intoned darkly, "that if I continued to attack the Communists in this government, they would continue to smear me." Behind the back of a young liberal college kid holding up a sign against Nixon at a rally stood the massing world forces of Communism. It's easy to imagine how Nixon must have neared internal meltdown when Tom Dewey made that berserk phone call just two hours before the speech, telling Dick he should quit as both vice-presidential candidate and senator. It's hard not to imagine Pat Nixon panicking as her steely man broke into tears and dark doubts just minutes before the speech. It's amazing to consider here that despite all of this, Nixon still wanted to face the cameras not with a rigid script but with a few written passages in addition to notes and documents. He wanted to get up and walk around and improvise like Fulton Sheen. He was willing to risk it, to go in front of sixty million Americans with their eyes glued to screens across the nation.[7]

That's what made the speech the most dramatic moment and turning point of the 1952 election. Nixon helped define that election, in a way that vice-presidential candidates aren't expected to. His self-salesmanship that night made clear that the election wasn't what the two chief opponents had professed it to be. It was not what Eisenhower wanted—a moral crusade based around the purity of outsiders charging the corrupted temples of power. Politics would never be that crystalline, of course, and when Eisenhower compromised his own ethical sensibilities by shaking hands with McCarthy and Jenner, he made that explicit. (When he handed the reins to Nixon for the Checkers speech, he took another step in that direction, or so Walter Lippmann argued.) Nor was the election what Adlai Stevenson so naïvely hoped—a quadrennial discussion of the important issues facing the nation. No, the election of 1952 was much more about its "rocking and socking" qualities and even more about selling personalities to the American people, using television's newfangled power. It could be seen in the "spots" Ike did and his employment of what today would be called sound bites ("I shall go to Korea"). It could be heard in the confirmations of thronging crowds at Ike's and Nixon's rallies that often clashed with the critical commentary offered by op-ed writers. But the spirit of the 1952 election came most explicitly on September 23 when a "salesman against socialization" went in front of millions to sell not policies, but himself. That's not to say that all Americans rushed to him with open arms—obviously not all did. There were the eggheads at Columbia, the editors (and likely many of the readers) of the *New York Post*, Drew Pearson, and, of course, Adlai Stevenson and those who voted for him. The voters that the political analyst Samuel Lubell interviewed after the election seemed wildly divided about Nixon, either loving or hating him. Still, "Just Plain Dick" became an everyman for 1950s America, a man of the people for millions of Americans, if not all.[8]

On the fateful evening of September 23, 1952, Richard Nixon became a regular guy who talked less about money given to his campaign by businessmen and more about his home, mortgage, life insurance plan, wife, two kids, and the eponymous dog. A man out to save his career by appearing authentic and sincere on television screens across America. An actor who staged his performance on a GI bedroom den set with proplike books on the shelves but who managed to connect to his audience, drawing tears and praise for his sincerity. A confidence man who hid from the cameras his neck pain, fear, and anxiety and projected instead his hard-boiled toughness mixed with an emotional appeal to the heartstrings. A "madman" who shifted from rage to sentimentalism with seeming ease. And a man who projected a political style that remains with us to this day.[9]

ACKNOWLEDGMENTS

Special thanks to my agent, Heather Schroder, for her help on this book but also for coming to my rescue when the chips were down. She went above and beyond the call of duty, and she'll know what I mean by that. Kathy Belden is one of the best editors an author could imagine. She knows what you want to say and helps you say it better. Thanks also to Emily DeHuff, an excellent copy editor, and Nathaniel Knaebel, for his help when the book moved to production. Patricia Connor Study has remained devoted to endowing a chair in her own name at Ohio University, which provided research funding for this project. She has also defended my university's commitment to the liberal arts at a time when that defense has become more difficult and thus more crucial. Thanks also to the staff of the Nixon and Eisenhower libraries, who made my research trips a pleasure. My colleagues at Ohio University's history department have put up with my craziness while working on this project. I apologize for my distraction. I thank Kevin Uhalde and Jackie Maxwell for being more than just colleagues (the well-read drafts at Jackie O's helped immensely). My friend Jeff Boxer not only drove me to and from the Nixon Library but helped me out through tough times as well, becoming my one real über-friend. George Cotkin, also a friend, read this book at the last minute and gave some very helpful and needed advice. Finally, to Vicky and Jay: Your love through the years has meant more to me than you know.

BIBLIOGRAPHIC NOTES

The research for this book is documented in the endnotes. To avoid redundancy I list here just a few key sources without which I could not have written this book.

Richard Nixon has generated, as expected, a rich literature about his life. There's an abundance of biographies of him, and I highlight only those that examine the earlier part of his career in detail. The finest, because it is both thoroughly researched and beautifully written, is Roger Morris, *Richard Milhous Nixon: The Rise of an American Politician* (New York: Holt, 1990). There is also Stephen Ambrose, *Nixon: The Education of a Politician, 1913–1962* (New York: Simon & Schuster, 1987). Two full-fledged biographies that focus a great deal on the earlier parts of Nixon's career and that I found particularly useful are Herbert Parmet, *Richard Nixon and His America* (Boston: Little, Brown, 1990) and Conrad Black, *Richard M. Nixon: A Life in Full* (New York: Public Affairs, 2007). Two earlier works on Nixon are also quite useful: Earl Mazo and Stephen Hess, *Nixon: A Political Portrait* (New York: Harper & Row, 1968) and William Costello, *The Facts About Nixon: An Authorized Biography* (New York: Viking, 1960). For its beautiful writing and marvelous speculations—as well as for placing Checkers at the center of Nixon's biography—there is the classic: Garry Wills, *Nixon Agonistes: The Crisis of the Self-Made Man* (New York: New American Library, 1979).

Books specifically about the election of 1952 and about the speech itself are surprisingly few. A nice overview can be found in John Robert Greene, *The Crusade: The Presidential Election of 1952* (Lanham, MD: University Press of America, 1985). There's also a nifty little book about the speech, the authors of which went through just about every telegram and letter that Nixon received after the speech (no small feat, that!): Robert O'Brien and

Elizabeth Jones, *The Night Nixon Spoke: A Study of Political Effectiveness* (Los Alamitos: Hwong Publishing, 1976).

There are many memoirs and biographies written by or about the secondary figures this book focuses on, too many to list here. There's one, though, that deserves mention, since it's about a man who has gotten very little attention even though he deserves more: Robert Humphreys. It's a poorly titled book but one chock-full of important information: Harold Lavine, *Smoke-Filled Rooms* (Englewood Cliffs, NJ: Prentice-Hall, 1970).

On the broad issue of television's history, I have relied upon Erik Barnouw, *Tube of Plenty: The Evolution of American Television* (New York: Oxford University Press, 1990) and the very insightful book by Thomas Doherty, *Cold War, Cool Medium* (New York: Columbia University Press, 1993).

There are numerous overviews of the 1950s. Let me cite just two: David Halberstam's classic and expansive *The Fifties* (New York: Fawcett, 1993) was especially helpful in understanding the cultural and political context of the times. There's also J. Ronald Oakley, *God's Country: America in the Fifties* (New York: Dembner Books, 1990).

If there's anything of an intellectual history behind the worldview that Nixon sold America in 1952, I'd say it can be traced to three books: Bruce Barton, *The Man Nobody Knows* (Indianapolis: Bobbs-Merrill, 1925); Dale Carnegie, *How to Win Friends and Influence People* (1936; reprint, New York: Pocket Books, 1961); and of course Norman Vincent Peale, *The Power of Positive Thinking* (New York: Prentice-Hall, 1952).

The archives at the Richard Nixon Library (Yorba Linda, California) and the Dwight Eisenhower Library (Abilene, Kansas) contain extensive materials about the 1952 campaign. I have cited those throughout. Especially important were drafts of speeches, itineraries, and some correspondence regarding the campaign.

Much of my research was done in the popular press of the time. I read through the following magazines for the spring into the winter of 1952 (cited in the notes simply by title of magazine, date, and page number):

America
American Legion Magazine

The Atlantic
Commonweal
Faith and Freedom
Freeman
Harper's
Human Events
Life
Look
The Nation
New Republic
Newsweek
Reader's Digest
The Reporter
Saturday Evening Post
Saturday Review
Time
U.S. News & World Report
Variety

I also consulted the following newspapers, again from spring into winter of 1952:

New York Post
The New York Times
The Washington Post

NOTES

INTRODUCTION: PORTRAIT OF THE YOUNG POLITICAL ARTIST AS MADMAN

1. *New York Post*, September 18, 1952, 3.
2. *The Reporter*, October 14, 1952, 30.
3. Earl Mazo and Stephen Hess, *Nixon: A Political Portrait* (New York: Harper & Row, 1967), 106–7.
4. Richard Nixon, *Six Crises* (Garden City, NY: Doubleday, 1962), 83.
5. Roger Morris, *Richard Milhous Nixon: The Rise of an American Politician* (New York: Henry Holt, 1990), 778.
6. Richard Nixon, *Six Crises*, 110; Roger Morris, *Richard Milhous Nixon*, 795; Richard Nixon, *The Memoirs of Richard Nixon* (New York: Simon & Schuster, 1990), 88.
7. Stephen Ambrose, *Eisenhower: Soldier and President* (New York: Touchstone, 1990); Nixon speech on September 24, 1952, in Richard Nixon Papers, Box PPS (208), Folder: Resolution of Fund Crisis; *New York Post*, September 25, 1952, 3; *Washington Post*, June 1, 1952, 1; *Washington Post*, September 20, 1952, 1. The sources for this phone conversation are conflicted. In Nixon's own recounting of them, they change form: There is a difference between his account in *Six Crises* and the account in his *Memoirs of Richard Nixon*. In the first, he quotes himself as saying "fish or cut bait." In the memoirs, that becomes "shit or get off the pot." It was likely that Nixon didn't feel comfortable letting on that the potty mouth he had as president (which became abundantly clear when the infamous Watergate tapes were released) had been with him from the beginning. There is also a "Memorandum" of the phone conversation in the Nixon Papers that was clearly closer to the time

of the actual speech but that is dated, curiously enough, September 20, a day before the conversation took place (it has "shit or get off"). That memorandum is found in the Richard Nixon Papers, Campaign 52, Box 174, Folder: September 20–21. In view of all of these conflicting accounts, I have relied on a variety of sources to reconstruct this conversation, not just Nixon's but also Conrad Black, *Richard M. Nixon: A Life in Full* (New York: Public Affairs, 2007), 241, and Roger Morris, *Richard Milhous Nixon*, 806–7.

8.   "Madman" as in the usage found in J. D. Salinger, *The Catcher in the Rye* (1951; reprint, New York: Bantam, 1986). This word appears first on page one ("this madman stuff") and throughout. I take it to mean the central character, Holden Caulfield, and his conception of living a life that moves maniacally from anger and hatred about the "phony" and insincere adult world and the "bastards" who populate it to a sentimentalism about his own ideals and love for his kid sister, Phoebe. The term also became something of a "keyword" in American culture during the 1950s, along with the novel's most popular term, "phony." Nixon too moves from extreme anger to sentimentalism as he moves towards his Checkers speech. In later life, Nixon developed the idea of being a "madman" in foreign policy toward the Soviets and Vietnamese—to intimidate his enemies. I am not using the term in that fashion here.

9.   *The Reporter*, August 19, 1952, 16; Stephen Ambrose, *Nixon: The Education of a Politician, 1913–1962* (New York: Simon & Schuster, 1987), 204.

10.   Patricia Ryan Nixon, "I Say He's a Wonderful Guy," *Saturday Evening Post*, September 6, 1952, 93; Sam Tanenhaus, *Whittaker Chambers* (New York: Random House, 1997), 309; Stephen Ambrose, *Nixon*, 193; Roger Morris, *Richard Milhous Nixon*, 475, 802; on Nixon taking over the Hiss case for HUAC, see Allen Weinstein, *Perjury: The Hiss-Chambers Case* (New York: Vintage, 1979), 16.

11.   Lester David, *The Lonely Lady of San Clemente* (New York: Thomas Y. Crowell, 1978), 93; see also Roger Morris, *Richard Milhous Nixon*, 781.

12.   Mickey Spillane, *Kiss Me Deadly* (1952; reprint, New York: E. P. Dutton, 1953), 177; see also the portrait of Spillane in *Life*, June 23, 1952; on *Dragnet*, see Daniel Moyer and Eugene Alvarez, *Just the Facts, Ma'am* (Santa Ana: Seven Locks, 2001), and *Dragnet—A Mark VII Production* (VHS; Burbank: Hollywood's Attic, 1996). On the interesting politics behind *High Noon*—a complicated story that can't be done justice here—see Jeremy Byman, *Showdown at High Noon: Witchhunts, Critics, and the End of the Western* (Lanham, MD: Scarecrow, 2004), and J. Hoberman, *An Army of Phantoms:*

American Movies and the Making of the Cold War (New York: New Press, 2011). Of course, the type of masculinity traced out here is just one variety. For more on the issue, see James Gilbert, *Men in the Middle: Searching for Masculinity in the 1950s* (Chicago: University of Chicago Press, 2005).

13. Richard Nixon, *Six Crises*, xv, 93.

14. Checkers speech, found in Richard Nixon Papers, PPS 208 (1952), Folder: Fund Speech Text, 7; James Jones, *From Here to Eternity* (1951; reprint, New York: Delta, 1991), 79.

15. For the truth on the Lincoln quote, see Paul Boller and John George, *They Never Said It* (New York: Oxford University Press, 1989), 84.

CHAPTER ONE: ANXIETIES . . . OF A COLD WAR SPRING AND AN "INSIDE DOPESTER"

Chapter epigraph: *Reader's Digest*, May 1952, 114.

1. Ridgway quoted in David Halberstam, *The Fifties* (New York: Fawcett, 1993), 111; Samuel Lubell, *The Future of American Politics* (New York: Harper & Brothers, 1952), 157; Bill Mauldin, *Bill Mauldin in Korea* (New York: Norton, 1952), 10; speech outline, Richard Nixon Papers, Box PPS 208 (1952), Folder: Opening of Campaign.

2. Richard Whelan, *Drawing the Line* (Boston: Little, Brown, 1990), 335 (see also p. 269 for Truman's mention of using the atomic bomb in Korea); Clay Blair, *The Forgotten War: America in Korea, 1950–1953* (New York: Anchor, 1989), 963–67; James Patterson, *Grand Expectations* (New York: Oxford University Press, 1996), 214; David Halberstam, *Fifties*, 70; Clay Blair, *Forgotten War*, 904.

3. *Washington Post*, May 1, 1952, 1; *Faith and Freedom*, April 1952, 12; see also *Human Events*, April 9, 1952, 1; see Alonzo Hamby, *Man of the People: A Life of Harry S. Truman* (New York: Oxford University Press, 1995), 593–95.

4. Alonzo Hamby, *Man of the People*, 595; David Halberstam, *Fifties*, 10, 56; Sam Tanenhaus, *Whittaker Chambers* (New York: Random House, 1997), 437; David Halberstam, *Fifties*, 17. See also Robert Beisner, *Dean Acheson: A Life in the Cold War* (New York: Oxford University Press, 2006).

5. Roger Morris, *Richard Milhous Nixon: The Rise of an American Politician* (New York: Henry Holt, 1990), 667.

6. *New York Times*, May 5, 1952, 21.

7. *Washington Post*, May 6, 1952, 19; Helen Hayes, *My Life in Three Acts*

(San Diego: Harcourt Brace Jovanovich, 1990), 216–17; Stephen Ambrose, *Nixon: The Education of a Politician, 1913–1962* (New York: Simon & Schuster, 1987), 159; Stephen Whitfield, *The Culture of the Cold War* (Baltimore: Johns Hopkins University Press, 1991), 136.

   8.   Robert Warshow, *The Immediate Experience* (Cambridge: Harvard University Press, 2001), 134 (this is a reprint of his essay about the film, published originally in 1952).

   9.   Robert Warshow, *Immediate Experience*, 136; see also Wes Gehring, *Leo McCarey: From Marx to McCarthy* (Lanham, MD: Scarecrow Press, 2005), 44.

   10.   Joseph McCarthy, *The Fight for America* (Hamilton: Poor Richard's Bookshop, 1952), 201–2; for the biographical details about Robert Walker, see http://www.imdb.com/name/nm0908153/bio and J. Hoberman, *An Army of Phantoms: American Movies and the Making of the Cold War* (New York: New Press, 2011), 194.

   11.   Robert Warshow, *Immediate Experience*, 133; *New York Times*, April 9, 1952, 27; Frank Eugene Beaver, *Bosley Crowther: Social Critic of the Film, 1940–1967* (New York: Arno Press, 1964), 77; *America*, April 19, 1952, 90–91.

   12.   *American Legion*, April 1952, 33; Warshow, *Immediate Experience*, 135.

   13.   Richard Nixon, *The Memoirs of Richard Nixon* (New York: Simon & Schuster, 1990), 84; see also the photo in Phillip Andrews, *This Man Nixon* (Philadelphia: Winston, 1952), 24.

   14.   Quoted in Stephen Ambrose, *Nixon*, 251–52; Herbert Parmet, *Richard Nixon and His America* (Boston: Little, Brown, 1990), 234.

   15.   James Patterson, *Mr. Republican: A Biography of Robert A. Taft* (Boston: Houghton Mifflin, 1972), 378, 425; Erik Barnouw, *Tube of Plenty* (New York: Oxford University Press, 1990), 112; Zachary Karabell, *The Last Campaign: How Harry Truman Won the 1948 Election* (New York: Knopf, 2000), 77.

   16.   Quoted in Richard Norton Smith, *Thomas E. Dewey and His Times* (New York: Simon & Schuster, 1982), 547, 589; Richard Rovere, *Senator Joe McCarthy* (New York: Meridian, 1967), 48; Herbert Parmet, *Richard Nixon and His America*, 235.

   17.   Richard Nixon, *Memoirs*, 84; Richard Norton Smith, *Thomas E. Dewey and His Times*, 487; Stephen Ambrose, *Nixon*, 238; John Patrick Diggins, *The Proud Decades* (New York: Norton, 1988), 93; Fred Cook, *The Nightmare Decade* (New York: Random House, 1971), 329.

   18.   Quoted in William Costello, *The Facts About Nixon* (New York: Viking, 1960), 77; Stephen Ambrose, *Nixon*, 226; draft of speech in Richard Nixon Papers, Box PPS 208 (1951), Folder: Campaign 52.

19. Conrad Black, *Richard M. Nixon: A Life in Full* (New York: Public Affairs, 2008), 162; Greg Mitchell, *Tricky Dick and the Pink Lady* (New York: Random House, 1998), 157.

20. Garry Wills, *Nixon Agonistes* (New York: New American, 1979), 126, 89; Julie Nixon Eisenhower, *Pat Nixon: The Untold Story* (New York: Simon & Schuster, 1986), 110.

21. Conrad Black, *Richard M. Nixon*, 81–82; Stephen Ambrose, *Nixon*, 136.

22. Roger Morris, *Richard Milhous Nixon*, 331; Stephen Ambrose, *Nixon*, 119; Conrad Black, *Richard M. Nixon*, 73, 12; Stephen Ambrose, *Nixon*, 120–21; Richard Nixon, *Memoirs*, 37; John Patrick Diggins, *Proud Decades*, 102; Richard Nixon, *Memoirs*, 42.

23. Roger Morris, *Richard Milhous Nixon*, 91; Mark Feeney, *Nixon at the Movies* (Chicago: University of Chicago Press, 2004), 34.

24. Sam Tanenhaus, *Whittaker Chambers*, 461, 463; *Washington Post*, May 25, 1952, 7B.

25. The biographical details given here can be found in both Sam Tanenhaus, *Whittaker Chambers*, and Chambers's own *Witness* (1952; reprint, Washington, DC: Regnery, 1980).

26. Sam Tanenhaus, *Whittaker Chambers*, 166.

27. Whittaker Chambers, "I Was the Witness," *Reader's Digest*, May 1952, 115–16; *Nation*, October 4, 1952, 291; *Nation*, May 10, 1952, 502, 503; Arthur Schlesinger Jr., "Whittaker Chambers and His Witness" (1952), reprinted in *The Politics of Hope* and *The Bitter Heritage* (Princeton: Princeton University Press, 2008), 233; Kempton quoted in David Halberstam, *Fifties*, 13.

28. Whittaker Chambers, *Witness*, 472, 473, 12, 449, 616.

29. Sam Tanenhaus, *Whittaker Chambers*, 453; Whittaker Chambers, *Witness*, 626; Stephen Ambrose, *Nixon*, 14.

30. Richard Nixon, *Memoirs*, 52–53, 55; Richard Nixon, *Six Crises* (Garden City, NY: Doubleday, 1962), 2; Susan Jacoby, *Alger Hiss and the Battle for History* (New Haven: Yale University Press, 2009), 96; Roger Morris, *Richard Milhous Nixon*, 110.

31. *Saturday Review*, May 24, 1952, 12; *Life*, June 9, 1952, 36.

32. *Washington Post*, June 1, 1952, 5B; *Life*, June 9, 1952, 41, 43; James Patterson, *Mr. Republican*, 541; *New York Times*, May 28, 1952, 24; Richard Rovere, *Affairs of State: The Eisenhower Years* (New York: Farrar, Straus and Cudahy, 1956), 24.

33. James Patterson, *Mr. Republican*, 523, 529; Stephen Ambrose,

Eisenhower: Soldier and President (New York: Simon & Schuster, 1990), 265; *New York Times*, May 25, 1952, 32.

34. James Patterson, *Mr. Republican*, 245; David Halberstam, *Fifties*, 207; Stephen Ambrose, *Eisenhower*, 232; Greg Behrman, *The Most Noble Adventure: The Marshall Plan and the Time When America Helped Save Europe* (New York: Free Press, 2007), 149; Stephen Ambrose, *Nixon*, 155; Richard Nixon, *Memoirs*, 51; *Harper's*, April 1952, 42, 39; *Atlantic*, May 1952, 34.

35. James Patterson, *Mr. Republican*, 176, 337; *Washington Post*, June 20, 1952, 1; *Human Events*, April 16, 1952, 1, April 9, 1952, 3; for more on Ike's friendships with businessmen, see Stephen Ambrose, *Eisenhower*, 221, 238–39.

36. *Harper's*, April 1952, 42; James Patterson, *Mr. Republican*, 166; David Halberstam, *Fifties*, 208; James Patterson, *Mr. Republican*, 100; *New York Times*, June 1, 1952, 32.

37. *New York Times*, May 25, 1952, 32, and May 26, 1952, 15; John Robert Greene, *The Crusade: The Presidential Election of 1952* (Lanham, MD: University Press of America, 1985), 92.

38. *New York Times*, May 25, 1952, 32, and May 26, 1952, 15; *Human Events*, June 4, 1952, 1, and July 9, 1952, 1; *New York Times*, May 28, 1952, 24; *Washington Post*, June 1, 1952, 5B; Richard Norton Smith, *Thomas E. Dewey and His Times*, 586.

39. Zweifel quoted in John Robert Greene, *Crusade*, 93; Robert Merry, *Taking On the World: Joseph and Stewart Alsop—Guardians of the American Century* (New York: Viking, 1996), 231; *Time*, July 14, 1952, 21; *Life*, June 9, 1952, 41–44; *Washington Post*, May 26, 1952, 9.

40. *New York Times*, June 1, 1952, 48, 47.

41. Stephen Ambrose, *Eisenhower*, 34, 62, 258.

42. Stephen Ambrose, *Eisenhower*, 240–41, 241, 249; Eisenhower to Truman, January 1, 1952, in Eisenhower Papers, Diaries, Box 1, Folder: DDE Diary, January 1, 1950–February 28, 1952 (3); Stephen Ambrose, *Eisenhower*, 252.

43. Robert Merry, *Taking On the World*, xx, 215–16; Joseph and Stewart Alsop, *The Reporter's Trade* (New York: Reynal, 1959), 185.

44. Ronald Steel, *Walter Lippmann and the American Century* (New York: Vintage, 1980), 474. The biographical details about Lippmann in this paragraph also come from Steel's biography.

45. *Washington Post*, June 2, 1952, 9; Ronald Steel, *Walter Lippmann and the American Century*, 481.

46. *Washington Post*, June 1, 1952, 1; David Halberstam, *The Powers That Be* (New York: Knopf, 1979), 231; *Washington Post*, June 5, 1952, 1, 7, and June 6, 1952, 24.

47. *Washington Post*, June 9, 1952, 9; June 17, 1952, 15; July 10, 1952, 13.

48. *Washington Post*, June 9, 1952, 2.

49. John Weaver, *Warren: The Man, the Court, the Era* (Boston: Little, Brown, 1967), 179.

50. William Costello, *The Facts About Nixon: An Unauthorized Biography* (New York: Viking, 1969), 85; Roger Morris, *Richard Milhous Nixon*, 691–92; Conrad Black, *Richard M. Nixon*, 181, 198; Jim Newton, *Justice for All: Earl Warren and the Nation He Made* (New York: Riverhead, 2006), 245; Nixon to Goodspeed, June 21, 1952, found in Richard Nixon Papers, Campaign 52, Box 1, Folder 4.

51. David Riesman with Nathan Glazer and Reuel Denney, *The Lonely Crowd* (1950; reprint, New Haven: Yale University Press, 1961), 184, 181; *New York Times*, September 28, 1952, SM48; C. Wright Mills, *White Collar* (1951; reprint, New York: Oxford University Press, 1956), xvii.

52. Roger Morris, *Richard Milhous Nixon*, 739, 676; see also the report of Earl Behrens, a journalist and editor who followed the campaign of Warren for president: Oral History (OH 17), Eisenhower Library, 14.

CHAPTER TWO: A SUMMER OF "THE GREAT SALESROOM"

Chapter title: The term "great salesroom" comes from C. Wright Mills, *White Collar* (1951; reprint, New York: Oxford University Press, 1956), chapter 8.

Chapter epigraph: *Washington Post: Parade Magazine*, September 7, 1952, 17.

1. *Time*, July 21, 1952, 60.

2. Jim Newton, *Justice for All: Earl Warren and the Nation He Made* (New York: Riverhead, 2006), 239; for good treatments of this, see John Weaver, *Warren: The Man, the Court, the Era* (Boston: Little, Brown, 1967), 181–82 and following pages, and Roger Morris, *Richard Milhous Nixon: The Rise of an American Politician* (New York: Henry Holt, 1990), 708, 712.

3. Conrad Black, *Richard M. Nixon: A Life in Full* (New York: Public Affairs, 2008), 199.

4. *Time*, July 14, 1952, 7; Margaret Ingels, *Willis Haviland Carrier: Father*

of Air Conditioning (Garden City, NY: Country Life Press, 1952), 105–6; *Reader's Digest*, April 1952, 67; *New York Times*, July 9, 1952, 22.

5.   *Harper's*, November 1952, 27; *Newsweek*, July 14, 1952, 84; Harold Lavine, *Smoke-Filled Rooms* (Englewood Cliffs, NJ: Prentice-Hall, 1970), 61–62. It's odd that Lavine's book has no subtitle indicating that it is a book about Robert Humphreys and his political advice.

6.   Thomas Hine, *Populuxe* (New York: MJF Books, 1999), 10; advertisement in the *New York Post*, September 25, 1952, 49; Karal Ann Marling, *As Seen on TV: The Visual Culture of Everyday Life in the 1950s* (Cambridge, MA: Harvard University Press, 1994), 232; see also the advertisements for televisions reprinted in Jim Heimann, ed., *50s: All-American Ads* (New York: Taschen, 2001), 414–31.

7.   *Newsweek*, July 14, 1952, 84; *Time*, July 14, 1952, 21; David Halberstam, *The Powers That Be* (New York: Knopf, 1979), 226; *Time*, July 14, 1952, 22.

8.   *Reporter*, August 5, 1952, 11; *Time*, July 21, 1952, 58; *Reporter*, August 5, 1952, 11; Robert Merry, *Taking On the World: Joseph and Stewart Alsop—Guardians of the American Century* (New York: Viking, 1996), 234; *Washington Post*, July 20, 1952, 7C; see also Walter Cronkite, *A Reporter's Life* (New York: Knopf, 1996), 179–80.

9.   Rick Shenkman, "Television, Democracy, and Presidential Politics," in *The Columbia History of Post–World War II America*, edited by Mark Carnes (New York: Columbia University Press, 2007), 260; *Life*, June 9, 1952, 139; *Washington Post*, May 25, 1952, 1L.

10.   *Washington Post*, June 27, 1952, 1.

11.   *Time*, July 14, 1952, 17–18; James Patterson, *Mr. Republican: A Biography of Robert A. Taft* (Boston: Houghton Mifflin, 1972), 552; *New York Times*, July 8, 1952, 1.

12.   *Newsweek*, July 14, 1952, 84; Rick Shenkman, "Television, Democracy, and Presidential Politics," 267; *Time*, July 14, 1952, 21.

13.   When Truman fired MacArthur, Ike said, "When you put on a uniform there are certain inhibitions you accept." See William Manchester, *American Caesar: Douglas MacArthur, 1880–1964* (Boston: Little, Brown, 1978), 648; on rumors that Mac was interested in the presidency for himself, see *New York Times*, July 11, 1952, 7; see also William Manchester, *American Caesar*, 564, 630.

14.   MacArthur quoted in John Patrick Diggins, *The Proud Decades: America in War and in Peace, 1941–1960* (New York: Norton, 1988), 92; *Wash-

ington Post, July 8, 1952, 1, 8, 10; *Time*, July 14, 1952, 23; *Newsweek*, July 14, 1952, 21.

15. *Newsweek*, July 14, 1952, 21.

16. William Manchester, *American Caesar*, 686.

17. Richard Rovere, *Senator Joe McCarthy* (Cleveland: World Publishing Company, 1960), 180.

18. Richard Rovere, *Senator Joe McCarthy*, 79; Ted Morgan, *Reds: McCarthyism in Twentieth-Century America* (New York: Random House, 2003), 350, 326; Jack Anderson and Ronald May, *McCarthy: The Man, the Senator, the "Ism"* (Boston: Beacon Press, 1952), 207; Eric Goldman describing McCarthy's physical appearance, quoted in Richard Rovere, *Senator Joe McCarthy*, 80; Stephen Ambrose, *Nixon: The Education of a Politician, 1913–1962* (New York: Simon & Schuster, 1987), 88; Ted Morgan, *Reds*, 353; Fred Cook, *The Nightmare Decade* (New York: Random House, 1971), 109; Robert Merry, *Taking On the World*, 212.

19. Fred Cook, *Nightmare Decade*, 264; *New York Times*, June 5, 1952, 4; *Washington Post*, June 10, 1952, 4, July 4, 1952, 1, June 10, 1952, 4, and August 21, 1952, 9; Stephen Ambrose, *Nixon*, 238.

20. Jack Anderson and Ronald May, *McCarthy*, 221 (they declare the book was released June 22); on the writing of the book by others, see Arthur Herman, *Joseph McCarthy* (New York: Free Press, 2000), 200; Richard Rovere, *Senator Joe McCarthy* (New York: Meridian, 1967), 7; see also Herb Block, *The Herblock Book* (Boston: Beacon Press, 1952).

21. *New Republic*, August 18, 1952, 14; Joseph McCarthy, *The Fight for America* (Hamilton, MT: Poor Richard's Bookshop, 1952), 144, 159; David Oshinsky, *A Conspiracy So Immense: The World of Joe McCarthy* (New York: Free Press, 1983), 233.

22. David Oshinsky, *A Conspiracy So Immense*, 229; *Official Report of the Proceedings of the Twenty-fifth Republican National Convention* (Washington, DC: Republican National Committee, 1952), 143; *Washington Post*, July 10, 1952, 7; *New York Times*, July 10, 1952, 21.

23. *New York Times*, July 10, 1952, 21.

24. *Washington Post*, July 11, 1952, 1; David Halberstam, *The Fifties* (New York: Fawcett, 1993), 212; *New York Times*, July 10, 1952, 18; Byron Hulsey, *Everett Dirksen and His Presidents* (Lawrence: University Press of Kansas, 2000), 32, 40.

25. *New York Times*, July 11, 1952, 9; *Washington Post*, July 11, 1952, 2; *New York Times*, July 11, 1952, 11; *Official Report of the Proceedings of the Twenty-fifth*

Republican National Convention, 347–85; *New York Times*, July 11, 1952, 11, 7; *Time*, July 21, 1952, 18; *Washington Post*, July 12, 1952, 2.

26.   *Time*, July 21, 1952, 19; *Washington Post*, July 12, 1952, 1.

27.   Erik Barnouw, *Tube of Plenty: The Evolution of American Television* (New York: Oxford University Press, 1990), 135.

28.   All information on Furness comes from David Halberstam, *Fifties*, 497–500. On Brownie Wise, see Bob Kealing, *Tupperware Unsealed: Brownie Wise, Earl Tupper, and the Home Party Pioneers* (Gainesville: University of Florida Press, 2008).

29.   *Washington Post*, July 13, 1952, 3M.

30.   *Washington Post*, July 13, 1952, 3M; Fawn Brodie, *Richard Nixon: The Shaping of His Character* (Cambridge, MA: Harvard University Press, 1983), 151.

31.   Stephen Ambrose, *Nixon*, 245; *Washington Post*, July 14, 1952, 15.

32.   Sherman Adams, *Firsthand Report* (New York: Harper, 1961), 35; Frank Carlson, Oral History Interview, Eisenhower Library: 54; *Washington Post*, July 12, 1952, 2; Roger Morris, *Richard Milhous Nixon*, 732.

33.   Richard Nixon, *Six Crises* (Garden City: Doubleday, 1962), 75; Richard Nixon, *The Memoirs of Richard Nixon* (New York: Simon & Schuster, 1990), 87.

34.   David Halberstam, *Fifties*, 313; Herbert Parmet, *Richard Nixon and His America* (Boston: Little, Brown, 1990), 232; speech found in Richard Nixon Papers, Box PPS 208 (1952), Folder: Acceptance Speech Republican Convention; Fawn Brodie, *Richard Nixon*, 144; a picture of this very thing can be seen in the puff piece by Phillip Andrews, *This Man Nixon* (Philadelphia: Winston, 1952), 34.

35.   *Washington Post*, July 15, 1952, 3; McCarthy quoted in Richard Rovere, *Senator Joe McCarthy*, 181.

36.   Jeff Broadwater, *Adlai Stevenson and American Politics* (New York: Twayne, 1994), 1 (this book, along with Porter McKeever, *Adlai Stevenson* (New York: William Morrow, 1989), provided biographical details here); *New Republic*, August 25, 1952, 11; *Washington Post*, July 14, 1952, 9, and July 25, 1952, 10; *Newsweek*, July 7, 1952, 47.

37.   *Time*, July 21, 1952, 21; *Washington Post*, July 29, 1952, 10, and July 21, 1952, 1.

38.   *New Republic*, September 8, 1952, 3, and September 15, 1942, 3; *Washington Post*, September 1, 1952, 1; Phillip Andrews, *This Man Nixon*, 10;

Washington Post, September 16, 1952, 13, and August 16, 1952, 1; Conrad Black, *Richard M. Nixon,* 37; Roger Morris, *Richard Milhous Nixon,* 550.

39.   Stevenson on "rats" quoted in Steven Gillon, *Politics and Vision: The ADA and American Liberalism, 1947–1985* (New York: Oxford University Press, 1987), 84; on Wilson Wyatt, see *Washington Post,* August 2, 1952, 1; *Saturday Evening Post,* September 20, 1952, 31.

40.   *Washington Post,* July 27, 1952, 1; Porter McKeever, *Adlai Stevenson,* 200–201.

41.   Dwight Eisenhower, *Mandate for Change* (Garden City, NY: Doubleday, 1963), 50; Richard Nixon, *Six Crises,* 96.

42.   *Time,* July 28, 1952, 13.

43.   Roger Morris, *Richard Milhous Nixon,* 743; pictures of the events here are available in Phillip Andrews, *This Man Nixon,* 42–43. Footage of the fishing trip can also be seen in Emile de Antonio's documentary, *Millhouse* (1971).

44.   *Time,* July 21, 1952, 13; *Look,* October 21, 1952, 59.

45.   *Washington Post,* August 22, 1952, 1; Stephen Ambrose, *Eisenhower: Soldier and President* (New York: Simon & Schuster, 1990), 273; on Dulles's article, see John Robert Greene, *The Crusade: The Presidential Election of 1952* (Lanham, MD: University Press of America, 1985), 186–87; Conrad Black, *Richard M. Nixon,* 207.

46.   From July press release found in Richard Nixon Papers, Campaign 52, Box 2, Folder: July 12–31.

47.   Conrad Black, *Richard M. Nixon,* 202; Roger Morris, *Richard Milhous Nixon,* 292; Conrad Black, *Richard M. Nixon,* 79; William Costello, *The Facts About Nixon: An Unauthorized Biography* (New York: Viking, 1960), 45.

48.   Biographical details here come from Nixon's schedule found in Richard Nixon Papers, Campaign 52, Box 5, Folders: 1952 July and August; *U.S. News & World Report,* August 29, 1952, 32; William Costello, *Facts About Nixon,* 96–97; document found in Richard Nixon Papers, Campaign 52, Box 184, Folder: Stevenson, Adlai.

49.   *Washington Post,* August 3, 1952, 1; *Human Events,* August 6, 1952, 1.

50.   Drafted speech, Richard Nixon Papers, Box PPS 208 (1952), Folder: Campaign Speech, Bangor, Maine.

51.   Memo found in Richard Nixon Papers, Campaign 52, Box 184, Folder: Stevenson, Adlai; *Washington Post,* August 7, 1952, 8.

52.   Drafted speech, Richard Nixon Papers, Box PPS 208 (1952),

Folder: Campaign Speech, Bangor, Maine; another strongly worded speech dated August 29 can be found in Richard Nixon Papers, Campaign 52, Box 173, Folder: August 29–31.

53.   Richard Nixon to George MacKinnon, September 1, 1952, found in Richard Nixon Papers, Campaign 52, Box 173, Folder: August 29–31; press release found in Richard Nixon Papers, Campaign 52, Box 173, Folder: August 22–25.

54.   Richard Nixon to Bernard Brennan, August 26, 1952, found in Richard Nixon Papers, Campaign 52, Box 173, Folder: August 22–25; drafted speech found in Richard Nixon Papers, Campaign 52, Box 173, Folder: August 29–31; Nixon to George Creel, August 30, 1952, found in Richard Nixon Papers, Campaign 52, Box 173, Folder: August 29–31.

55.   *Washington Post*, August 12, 1952, 1; *New York Times*, August 5, 1952, 22, and August 23, 1952, 4.

56.   *New York Times*, August 27, 1952, 1, 17; *Newsweek*, September 8, 1952, 23; Judy Kutulas, *The American Civil Liberties Union and the Making of Modern Liberalism, 1930–1960* (Chapel Hill: University of North Carolina Press, 2006), 192.

57.   *New York Times*, August 26, 1952, 12.

58.   "Liberation" is mentioned in a story about Ike's speech: *New York Times*, August 27, 1952, 15; *New York Times*, August 26, 1952, 12.

59.   *New York Times*, August 26, 1962, 12.

60.   *Washington Post*, August 28, 1952, 8.

61.   Ibid.

62.   *New York Times*, August 25, 1952, 1; Dwight Eisenhower, *Mandate for Change*, 54; Nixon to Loyal Phillips, August 23, 1952, Richard Nixon Papers, Campaign 52, Box 173, Folder: August 22–25.

63.   *Newsweek*, September 8, 1952, 24.

64.   *Time*, March 3, 1952: http://www.time.com/time/magazine/article/0,9171,890271,00.html; Garry Wills, *John Wayne's America* (New York: Simon & Schuster, 1997), 12, 109.

65.   Roger Morris, *Richard Milhous Nixon*, 646; Greg Mitchell, *Tricky Dick and the Pink Lady* (New York: Random House, 1998), 101.

66.   Randy Roberts and James Olson, *John Wayne: American* (New York: Free Press, 1995), 371; David Halberstam, *Fifties*, 212; David Oshinsky, *Conspiracy So Immense*, 243.

67.   Russell Shain, "Hollywood's Cold War," *Journal of Popular Film* 3 (1974): 347.

68. *New York Times*, September 18, 1952, 35; some parts of the review are quoted in Randy Roberts and James Olson, *John Wayne*, 378.

69. Quoted in Frank Eugene Beaver, *Bosley Crowther: Social Critic of the Film, 1940–1967* (New York: Arno Press, 1964), 77; Randy Roberts and James Olson, *John Wayne*, 378.

CHAPTER THREE: "A WONDERFUL GUY"?

Chapter epigraph: Patricia Nixon, "I Say He's a Wonderful Guy," *Saturday Evening Post*, September 6, 1952, 96.

1. *Washington Post*, September 14, 1952, Section II, 1; *New York Times*, September 3, 1952, 16; *Washington Post*, September 3, 1952, 1.

2. *New Republic*, September 15, 1952, 4.

3. Patricia Nixon, "I Say He's a Wonderful Guy," 17–19, 93–96.

4. *Washington Post*, September 8, 1952, 2; Nixon's itinerary found in Richard Nixon Library, Campaign 52, Box 5, Folder: September 1–9.

5. *Washington Post*, September 10, 1952, 1, 2.

6. *Washington Post*, September 10, 1952, 13; *New Republic*, September 1, 1952, 5–6.

7. Bernard Shanley Diaries, Box 1, Folder: The Eisenhower Campaign (1), Eisenhower Library, pp. 494, 503; Murray Kempton, *America Comes of Middle Age* (Boston: Little, Brown, 1963), 243.

8. *Washington Post*, September 10, 1952, 13.

9. *Washington Post*, September 7, 1952, 5B, and September 14, 1952, Section II, 1.

10. John Hollitz, "Eisenhower and the Admen: The Television 'Spot' Campaign of 1952," *Wisconsin Magazine of History*, Autumn 1982, 31; see also Noel Griese, "Rosser Reeves and the 1952 Eisenhower TV Spot Blitz," *Journal of Advertising* 4 (1975): 34; Stephen Fox, *The Mirror Makers: A History of American Advertising and Its Creators* (New York: William Morrow, 1984), 188–89.

11. Noel Griese, "Rosser Reeves and the 1952 Eisenhower TV Spot Blitz," 35.

12. Noel Griese, "Rosser Reeves and the 1952 Eisenhower TV Spot Blitz," 36; Edwin Diamond and Stephen Bates, *The Spot* (Cambridge, MA: MIT, 1988), 54.

13. Thomas Reeves, *America's Bishop: The Life and Times of Fulton J. Sheen*

(San Francisco: Encounter, 2001), 2; John Hollitz, "Eisenhower and the Admen: The Television 'Spot' Campaign of 1952," 28.

14. Noel Griese, "Rosser Reeves and the 1952 Eisenhower TV Spot Blitz," 36.

15. Edwin Diamond and Stephen Bates, *Spot*, 56–57.

16. Dwight Eisenhower, *Mandate for Change* (Garden City, NY: Doubleday, 1963), 64; James Patterson, *Mr. Republican: A Biography of Robert A. Taft* (Boston: Houghton Mifflin, 1972), 571.

17. James Patterson, *Mr. Republican*, 577–78.

18. *New York Times*, September 14, 1952, 1, 74; Ronald Steel, *Walter Lippmann and the American Century* (New York: Vintage, 1980), 481; *Washington Post*, September 9, 1952, 11, and September 16, 1952, 13.

19. Press release found in Richard Nixon Papers, Campaign 52, Box 6, Folder: California/Western Tour September 16–27; press release dated September 15, 1952, Richard Nixon Papers, Prepresidential, Box 173, Folder: September 5–11; Roger Morris, *Richard Milhous Nixon: The Rise of an American Politician* (New York: Henry Holt, 1990), 755; Robert O'Brien and Elizabeth Jones, *The Night Nixon Spoke: A Study of Political Effectiveness* (Los Alamitos: Hwong Publishing, 1976), 8.

20. Erik Barnouw, *Tube of Plenty: The Evolution of American Television* (New York: Oxford University Press, 1990), 102; remarks transcribed in Richard Nixon Papers, Box PPS 208 (1952), Folder: Meet the Press.

21. Stephen Ambrose, *Nixon: The Education of a Politician, 1913–1962* (New York: Simon & Schuster, 1987), 275.

22. Richard Nixon to George MacKinnon, September 15, 1952, found in Richard Nixon Papers, Campaign 52, Box 173, Folder: September 12–15; *New York Times*, September 16, 1952, 22; Nixon's schedule is found in Richard Nixon Papers, Prepresidential, Box 5, Folder: September 15–23.

23. *New York Times*, September 15, 1952, 1; see the document "Labor for Eisenhower" found in Eisenhower Papers, Ann Whitman File, Box 2, Folder: Appointments and Trips—DDE, October 16–November 22.

24. *New York Times*, September 15, 1952, 1, and September 15, 1952, 1, 16.

25. *New York Times*, September 16, 1952, 28; *Washington Post*, September 16, 1952, 1, 2.

26. *New York Times*, September 17, 1952, 1, 24.

27. *New York Times*, September 17, 1952, 24.

28. *New York Times*, September 17, 1952, 25, 1.

29. David Robinson, *Chaplin: His Life and Art* (New York: Da Capo, 1994), 571, 573; *Washington Post*, September 21, 1952, 13M.

30. Stephen Ambrose, *Nixon*, 233–34; Charles Maland, *Chaplin and American Culture* (Princeton: Princeton University Press, 1989), 193–94, on Chaplin's pro-Soviet views; David Robinson, *Chaplin*, 576; Jennifer Frost, *Hedda Hopper's Hollywood: Celebrity Gossip and American Conservatism* (New York: New York University Press, 2011), 87. Frost's book also provides much background on Hopper's ideological leanings.

31. Stephen Whitfield, *The Culture of the Cold War* (Baltimore: Johns Hopkins University Press, 1991), 189; see also *Limelight* (Burbank: Warner Home Video, 2003).

32. *New York Times*, September 28, 1952, X1, and October 24, 1952, 27; on the American Legion, see Nora Sayre, *Running Time: Films of the Cold War* (New York: Dial, 1982), 22–23.

33. Murray Chotiner memo, September 23, found in Richard Nixon Papers, Campaign 52, Box 174, Folder: 1952 September 22–23.

34. Roger Morris, *Richard Milhous Nixon*, 633; "Facts Concerning Dana Smith Trustee Fund," in Richard Nixon Papers, Campaign 52, Box 174, Folder: Trust Fund Statistics; *New Republic*, September 29, 1952, 10.

35. *New York Post*, September 18, 1952, 3; Peter Edson to Richard Nixon, plus attached story, September 17, 1952, in Richard Nixon Papers, Campaign 52, Box 173, Folder: 1952, September 16–19; Roger Morris, *Richard Milhous Nixon*, 750; *Newsweek*, September 29, 1952, 25, and September 18, 1952, 26; letter from Gibson, Dunn and Crutcher lawyers to Sherman Adams, September 23, 1952, regarding the fund: Richard Nixon Papers, Campaign 52, Box 174, Folder: September 23 Broadcast.

36. *Reporter*, October 14, 1952, 30.

37. Peter Edson to Richard Nixon, plus attached story, September 17, 1952, in Richard Nixon Papers, Campaign 52, Box 173, Folder: 1952, September 16–19; *Washington Post*, September 21, 1952, 2M; notes found in Richard Nixon Papers, Campaign 52, Box 174, File: Trust Fund Contributors; letter from Gibson, Dunn and Crutcher lawyers to Sherman Adams, September 23, 1952, regarding the fund: Richard Nixon Papers, Campaign 52, Box 174, Folder: September 23 Broadcast.

38. Roger Morris, *Richard Milhous Nixon*, 650; *New York Post*, September 30, 1952, 12; press wire 9/19, found in Robert Humphreys Papers, Box 6, Nixon Folder (6).

39. The quotes surrounding campaign finance reform legislation come

from Michael Kazin, ed., *The Princeton Encyclopedia of American Political History*, vol. 1 (Princeton: Princeton University Press, 2010), 97, 98; *New York Times*, November 2, 1952, SM13. For the flurry of action during the Progressive Era, see Richard McCormick, "The Discovery That Business Corrupts Politics: A Reappraisal of the Origins of Progressivism," *American Historical Review* 86 (1981): 247–74.

40.   *Atlantic*, August 1952, 43–44; *Washington Post*, September 20, 1952, 9.

41.   *Reporter*, October 14, 1952, 33.

42.   *New York Post*, September 18, 1952, 3, 26.

43.   *New York Post*, September 22, 1951, 4; telephone conversation with Alfred Kohlberg, reported 9/21/52, and "Check Editorials from January 1, 1948" memo, found in Richard Nixon Papers, Campaign 52, Box 174, Folder: New York Post; *New York Post*, September 7, 1952, M9; Arthur Edward Rowse, *Slanted News: A Case Study of the Nixon and Stevenson Fund Stories* (Boston: Beacon Press, 1957), 2. For how Wechsler was largely right about the press and its attitude toward Ike and Nixon, see Douglas Danie, "They Like Ike: Pro-Eisenhower Publishers and His Decision to Run for President," *Journalism and Mass Communication Quarterly* 77 (2000): 393–404.

44.   Press wire 9/18, found in Robert Humphreys, Box 6, Folder: Nixon, Richard (6); schedule found in Richard Nixon Papers, Campaign 52, Box 5, Folder: September 15–23.

45.   Richard Nixon, *Six Crises* (Garden City, NY: Doubleday, 1962), 83.

46.   Schedule found in Richard Nixon Papers, Campaign 52, Box 5, Folder: September 15–23; those lines from Redding, California, speech found in Richard Nixon Papers, PPS 208: September 19–October 5, Folder: Redding, California; Richard Nixon, *Six Crises*, 86.

47.   Dwight Eisenhower, *Mandate for Change*, 66; *Washington Post*, September 20, 1952, 1; press wire 9/19, found in Robert Humphreys Papers: Box 6, Nixon Folder (6).

48.   Press wire, 9/19, found in Robert Humphreys Papers: Box 6, Nixon Folder (6); *Washington Post*, September 20, 1952, 2; Herbert Parmet, *Richard Nixon and His America* (Boston: Little, Brown, 1990), 241.

49.   Lester David, *The Lonely Lady of San Clemente* (New York: Thomas Y. Crowell, 1978), 93; see also Roger Morris, *Richard Milhous Nixon*, 781.

50.   *Washington Post*, September 20, 1952, 8.

51.   Telegram, September 20, 1952, found in Eisenhower Papers, Staff File, Records of Sherman Adams as Assistant to President, 1952–1959, Research, General, Box 37, Folder: Nixon.

52. Earl Mazo and Stephen Hess, *Nixon: A Political Portrait* (New York: Harper & Row, 1967), 107; *Washington Post*, September 21, 1952, 2M; Richard Nixon, *Six Crises*, 88; press wire, "Nixon Riot," 9/20, found in Robert Humphreys Papers: Box 6, Nixon Folder (7).

53. Harold Lavine, *Smoke-Filled Rooms* (Englewood Cliffs, NJ: Prentice-Hall, 1970), 10; Roger Morris, *Richard Milhous Nixon*, 782; curriculum vitae of Humphreys in Robert Humphreys Papers, Box 8, Folder: Robert Humphreys—Biographical Information (1).

54. Harold Lavine, *Smoke-Filled Rooms*, 71, 37, 47–48 (this book contains the actual document that Humphreys wrote).

55. Richard Nixon, *Six Crises*, 95.

56. Richard Nixon, *The Memoirs of Richard Nixon* (New York: Simon & Schuster, 1990), 96; *Washington Post*, September 22, 1952, 2; Richard Nixon, *Six Crises*, 92.

57. Richard Nixon, *Memoirs*, 96; Richard Nixon, *Six Crises*, 93.

58. "Remarks by Senator Richard Nixon at Portland, Ore.," in Richard Nixon Papers, Box PPS 208 (1952), Folder: Portland, Ore.—RE Campaign "Crusade."

59. Press wire 9/21, found in Robert Humphreys Papers, Box 6, Nixon Folder (6).

60. Richard Nixon, *Memoirs*, 95–96; Robert Humphreys Papers, Box 6, Nixon Folder (4), Eisenhower Library.

61. Roger Morris, *Richard Milhous Nixon*, 800–802.

62. Press wire report 9/19, Robert Humphreys Papers, Box 6: Nixon Folder (7); *Newsweek*, September 29, 1952, 25; Press wire 9/21 in Robert Humphreys Papers, Box 6: Nixon Folder (7).

63. Harold Lavine, *Smoke-Filled Rooms*, 79–80; Burroughs to Eisenhower and Adams, September 22, 1952, found in Eisenhower Papers, Staff File, Records of Sherman Adams as Assistant to President, 1952–1959, Research, General, Box 37, Folder: Nixon.

64. The office and desk description are found in the portrait: Ben Cole, "He Runs the Show," *Indianapolis Star Magazine*, September 7, 1952, 12; Harold Lavine, *Smoke-Filled Rooms*, 82–83.

65. Harold Lavine, *Smoke-Filled Rooms*, 83, 84.

66. Harold Lavine, *Smoke-Filled Rooms*, 85; Roger Morris, *Richard Milhous Nixon*, 808.

67. Memorandum on Telephone Conversation, Richard Nixon Papers, Campaign 52, Box 174, Folder: 1952, September 20–21.

68.   The sources on this phone conversation are conflicted, as noted in the citations to the Introduction. I rely here upon *Six Crises* and *Memoirs*, plus the memorandum found in the Richard Nixon Papers, Campaign 52, Box 174, Folder: September 20–21, and Conrad Black, *Richard M. Nixon: A Life in Full* (New York: Public Affairs, 2008), 241, and Roger Morris, *Richard Milhous Nixon*, 806–7.

69.   Quoted in Roger Morris, *Richard Milhous Nixon*, 808.

70.   Phillip Andrews, *This Man Nixon* (Philadelphia: Winston, 1952), 45–47; Roger Morris, *Richard Milhous Nixon*, 819.

CHAPTER FOUR: "CHIN UP"

Chapter epigraph: Found in Richard Nixon Papers, PPS 208 (1952), Folder: Fund Speech and Corrected Drafts.

1.   Harold Lavine, *Smoke-Filled Rooms* (Englewood Cliffs, NJ: Prentice-Hall, 1970), 86; Richard Nixon, *Six Crises* (Garden City, NY: Doubleday, 1962), 103.

2.   Elaine Tyler May, *Homeward Bound: American Families in the Cold War Era* (New York: Basic Books, 1988), 172–73; Julie Nixon Eisenhower, *Pat Nixon: The Untold Story* (New York: Simon & Schuster, 1986), 111; list of possessions and incomes in Richard Nixon Papers, Campaign 52, Box 174, Folder: Trust Fund Statistics.

3.   On the change in American cars throughout the 1950s, see Thomas Hine, *Populuxe* (New York: MJF Books, 1999).

4.   See the obituary of Lou Carrol, the man who gave Checkers to Nixon, in the *New York Times*, May 17, 2006, http://www.nytimes.com /2006/05/17/us/17carrol.html; David Halberstam, *The Fifties* (New York: Fawcett, 1993), 315; Frederick Reiter, *You Train Your Dog* (New York: Macmillan, 1952), 17; see the Diamond Alkali Chemicals ad about the importance of having good leather slippers to let your feet breathe, showing a dog called "Man's Best Friend," a campaign in numerous publications including *Newsweek*, September 8, 1952, 51; Katherine Grier, *Pets in America: A History* (Chapel Hill: University of North Carolina Press, 2006), 71, 288, 85; see also Mary Elizabeth Thurston, *The Lost History of the Canine Race* (Kansas City: Andrews and McMeel, 1996), 237.

5.   Quoted in Doris Kearns Goodwin, *No Ordinary Time: Franklin and Eleanor Roosevelt, the Home Front in World War II* (New York: Simon & Schuster,

1994), 548; Richard Nixon, *Six Crises* (Garden City, NY: Doubleday, 1962) 103; there was an interesting fear of dognapping in 1952: George Burton, "How to Protect Your Dog," *American Legion*, April 1952.

6.   *Washington Post*, September 23, 1952, 1; Lester David, *The Lonely Lady of San Clemente* (New York: Thomas Y. Crowell, 1978), 93.

7.   *New York Post*, September 23, 1952, 30; *Newsweek*, October 6, 1952, 27.

8.   Karal Ann Marling, *As Seen on TV: The Visual Culture of Everyday Life in the 1950s* (Cambridge, MA: Harvard University Press, 1994), 38; *Variety*, April 2, 1952, 1; *Washington Post*, August 3, 1952, 3L.

9.   Stefan Kanfer, *Ball of Fire: The Tumultuous Life and Comic Art of Lucille Ball* (New York: Knopf, 2003), 150; Thomas Doherty, *Cold War, Cool Medium* (New York: Columbia University Press, 1993), 49; David Halberstam, *Fifties*, 197–201; Stefan Kanfer, *Ball of Fire*, 152–53.

10.   The show is "Lucy Gets Ricky on the Radio," aired May 19, 1952.

11.   Milton Berle, *Milton Berle: An Autobiography* (New York: Applause, 2002), 293; *Reader's Digest*, July 1952, 58, 60, 61; Christopher Owen Lynch, *Selling Catholicism: Bishop Sheen and the Power of Television* (Lexington: University Press of Kentucky, 1998), 7; *Newsweek*, September 29, 1952, 60.

12.   David Halberstam, *Fifties*, 239; *Newsweek*, October 6, 1952, 24.

13.   This story is told well by Porter McKeever, *Adlai Stevenson* (New York: William Morrow, 1989), 228–29.

14.   *Washington Post*, September 24, 1952, 10, 1.

15.   Itineraries found in Eisenhower Papers, Ann Whitman File, Box 1, Folder: Appointments and Trips—DDE, September 16–30 (2).

16.   Harold Lavine, *Smoke-Filled Rooms*, 87–88.

17.   Ibid., 91.

18.   William Costello, *The Facts About Nixon* (New York: Viking, 1960), 107.

19.   Richard Nixon, *Six Crises*, 108, 109, 102.

20.   Ibid., 110.

21.   Richard Nixon, *The Memoirs of Richard Nixon* (New York: Simon & Schuster, 1990), 102–3; Richard Nixon, *Six Crises*, 112; *Newsweek*, October 6, 1952, 23–24; David Halberstam, *Fifties*, 326.

22.   Roger Morris, *Richard Milhous Nixon: The Rise of an American Politician* (New York: Henry Holt, 1990), 826; Richard Nixon, *Six Crises*, 112, 107; Pat Nixon in Helen Erskine, "Dick and Pat Nixon," *Collier's*, July 9, 1954, 36.

23.   Richard Nixon, *Six Crises*, 113; letter on exhibit at Nixon Library and Museum in section on Fund Speech.

24.   I have used the version of the speech found in PPS Box 208 (1952), 9/19–10/5; Folder: Found Speech Text. I also viewed the version of the speech at the Nixon Library to catch mispronounced words and errors captured herein.

25.   On Nixon getting Pat's birthday wrong (also, her original name wasn't Patricia, but Thelma Catherine), see Fawn Brodie, *Richard Nixon: The Shaping of His Character* (Cambridge, MA: Harvard University Press, 1983), 149–50.

26.   *Newsweek*, October 6, 1952, 25; Richard Nixon, *Memoirs*, 105; *Life*, October 6, 1952, 29; Earl Mazo and Stephen Hess, *Nixon: A Political Portrait* (New York: Harper & Row, 1967), 122; Herbert Parmet, *Richard Nixon and His America* (Boston: Little, Brown, 1990), 238 (on viewership).

27.   *New York Post*, September 24, 1952, 3; Harold Lavine, *Smoke-Filled Rooms*, 92–93; an exemplary photograph can be found in *Newsweek*, October 6, 1952, 25.

28.   F. Witcher, September 24, 1952, found in Richard Nixon Papers, Campaign 52, Box 35, Folder: California Redding and Redlands; Anderson to RNC, 9/24, in Richard Nixon Papers, Campaign 52, Box 53, Folder: Letters Illinois Chicago Alli-Beez; Carl Schmitt, Milwaukee, September 24, 1952, in Richard Nixon Papers, Campaign 52, Box 142, Folder: Milwaukee S; Henry Traub and Walter Traub of Traub Bros Manufacturers in Yakima, Washington, 9/23, Richard Nixon Papers, Campaign 52, Box 142, Folder: Washington Yakima—West Virginia, Charleston; *Washington Post*, September 25, 1952, 2; see, for instance, May Van Tassel to Nixon, September 23, in Richard Nixon Papers, Campaign 52, Box 35, Folder: Connecticut Darien Glenbrook; Helen Shoults, Jackson, Missouri, to Nixon, September 24, Richard Nixon Papers, Campaign 52, Box 82, Folder: Letters Missouri, Independence—Jefferson City; Donald Howard from Minnesota, no date on letter, Richard Nixon Papers, Campaign 52, Box 82, Folder: Letters Minneapolis Minn H; Richard Nixon Papers, Campaign 52, Box 20, Folder: Los Angeles Dal–De; E. L. Earnhart, Mawry (?) to Nixon, no date, found in Richard Nixon Papers, Box 116, Folder: Ohio Massillon Miamisburg; *New York Post*, September 25, 1952, 22.

29.   Julie Nixon Eisenhower, *Pat Nixon*, 124; Richard Nixon, *Six Crises*, 125; multiple letters in Richard Nixon Papers, Campaign 52, Box 186, Folder: Insurance Company Letters; Stephen Ambrose, *Nixon: The Education of a Politician, 1913–1962* (New York: Simon & Schuster, 1987), 290.

30.   Richard Nixon, *Six Crises*, 95.

31.   Bernard Shanley Diaries, Box 1, Folder: The Eisenhower Campaign (1), 516, in Eisenhower Library; *New York Post*, September 24, 1952, 45; the *St. Louis Post-Dispatch* also called the speech "soap opera": see *Washington Post*, September 25, 1952, 4; *New York Post*, September 26, 1952, 41, and September 29, 1952, 18.

32.   Jim Cox, *Frank and Anne Hummert's Radio Factory* (Jefferson: McFarland and Company, 2003) (on p. 101 Cox discusses the show *Just Plain Bill*); *Variety*, October 1, 1952, 101; *New York Post*, September 24, 1952, 45; *Newsweek*, July 14, 1952, 85; this last point comes from a memo from Idella Grindlay to Mr. Ted Rogers, September 27, 1952, quoting what *Billboard*'s Joe Csida had written: Richard Nixon Papers, Campaign 52, Box 174, Folder: 1952, September 25–27.

33.   Ronald Steel, *Walter Lippmann and the American Century* (New York: Vintage, 1980), 483.

34.   *Washington Post*, September 25, 1952, 10.

35.   *Washington Post*, September 24, 1952, 11.

36.   Jim Gleason, memo to Nixon (no date), Richard Nixon Prepresidential Papers, Box 172, Folder: Correspondence, 1952, August 1–9; *Washington Post*, September 26, 1952, 25.

37.   David Halberstam, *The Powers That Be* (New York: Knopf, 1979), 228; Porter McKeever, *Adlai Stevenson*, 185.

38.   Warren Sussman, *Culture as History* (New York: Pantheon, 1984), 127; David Halberstam, *Fifties*, 241.

39.   *Newsweek*, October 6, 1952, 25.

40.   Ike to Nixon, September 23, in Richard Nixon Papers, Campaign 52, Box 174, Folder: September 23–24.

41.   Roger Morris, *Richard Milhous Nixon*, 839; *Newsweek*, October 6, 1952, 25; Earl Behrens, Oral History (OH 17), Eisenhower Library: "Nixon made a very caustic and profane remark which I will not repeat about the General" (28).

42.   "Making a President Posthumously," found in Robert Humphreys Papers, Box 6, Folder: Nixon, Richard M.—1952 (1).

43.   Harold Lavine, *Smoke-Filled Rooms*, 96.

44.   *Washington Post*, September 25, 1952, 1.

CHAPTER FIVE:"AMERICA HAS TAKEN
DICK NIXON TO ITS HEART"

Chapter epigraph: Richard Nixon, *Six Crises* (Garden City, NY: Double-day, 1962), 38.

1.   John Welch to Eisenhower campaign leaders, September 24, 1952, in Eisenhower Papers, Central Files, President's Personal File PPF, Box 874, Folder: Republican Presidential Campaign (5).

2.   Richard Nixon, *The Memoirs of Richard Nixon* (New York: Simon & Schuster, 1990), 106.

3.   Sherman Adams Oral History (OH 162), Eisenhower Library, 104; *Washington Post*, September 25, 1952, 1.

4.   Speech at Wheeling found in Richard Nixon Papers, Box PPS 208, Folder: Resolution of Fund Crisis; *New York Post*, September 25, 1952, 3.

5.   *Life*, October 6, 1952, 25.

6.   Bernard Shanley Diaries, Box 1, Folder: The Eisenhower Campaign (1), found at Eisenhower Library; Richard Nixon, *Memoirs*, 107.

7.   Itinerary found in Richard Nixon Papers, Box 5, Folder: September 15–23.

8.   Speech found in Richard Nixon Papers, PPS 208 (1952), Folder: Campaign Speech—Corruption Salt Lake City.

9.   Handwritten note, September 23, by "Falta" (?), found in Richard Nixon Papers, Box 46, Folder: Colorado Englewood Grand Junction; letter of September 24 found in Richard Nixon Papers, Box 51, Folder: Florida, Tampa–Verde Beach; Leota Reinking, Columbus, Wisconsin, to Nixon campaign, 9/24, letter found in Richard Nixon Papers, Box 142, Folder: Wisconsin: Cable-Elroy; response quoted in Robert O'Brien and Elizabeth Jones, *The Night Nixon Spoke: A Study of Political Effectiveness* (Los Alamitos, CA: Hwang, 1976), 50.

10.   *Radio Reports*, September 19, 20, 21, 1952, found in Richard Nixon Papers, Campaign 52, Box 174, Folder: September 28–30; *Radio Reports*, September 24, 1952, found in Richard Nixon Papers, Campaign 52, Box 174, Folder: September 28–30; Booton Herndon, *Praised and Damned: The Story of Fulton Lewis, Jr.* (New York: Duell, Sloan and Pearce, 1954), 100, 102; *Radio Reports*, September 23, 1952, found in Richard Nixon Papers, Campaign 52, Box 174, Folder: September 28–30. Many correspondents referred to the way that Lewis called Richard Nixon "Dick." See, for example, a letter from Jack Mitchell, September 27, 1952, to Nixon: "Due to the fact that

Fulton Lewis always refers to you as 'Dick,' I think it is 'O.K.' for a private in the ranks to do so too." Numerous letters in Nixon's papers cite Lewis. Richard Nixon Papers, Box 51, Folder: Florida, Tampa-Verde Beach.

11. Jim Murray quoted in Julie Nixon Eisenhower, *Pat Nixon: The Untold Story* (New York: Simon & Schuster, 1986), 128; Wheeler Mayo's comment was relayed by Drew Pearson. The comment is found in an October 2, 1952, column in the Richard Nixon Papers, Box 184, Folder: Collection of Drew Pearson Columns.

12. *Washington Post*, September 30, 1952, 1, and October 1, 1952, 1; speech dated October 3, 1952, in Richard Nixon Papers, PPS 208 (1952), Folder: Campaign Speech Criticism of Truman and Stevenson; speech dated October 3, 1952, in Richard Nixon Papers, PPS 208 (1952), Folder: Campaign speech re Truman's attack on Eisenhower.

13. Cut words recounted in Fred Cook, *The Nightmare Decade* (New York: Random House, 1971), 384; Sherman Adams, Oral History, OH 162, Eisenhower Library: 69.

14. J. Ronald Oakley, *God's Country: America in the Fifties* (New York: Dembner, 1990), 135; *Time*, September 1, 1952, 10; *New York Post*, October 6, 1952, 2.

15. Itinerary found in Eisenhower Papers, Ann Whitman File, Box 2, Folder: Appointments and Trips—DDE October 1–15 (1); *New York Times*, October 4, 1952, 8; *New York Post*, October 6, 1952, 2; *New York Times*, October 4, 1952, 8; *New York Post*, October 6, 1952, 2.

16. *New York Times*, October 4, 1952, 8.

17. *New York Times*, October 4, 1952, 8; *New York Post*, October 6, 1952, 2, 23; *New York Times*, October 4, 1952, 8; *New York Post*, October 6, 1952, 2, 23.

18. *Washington Post*, October 6, 1952, 6.

19. *New York Times*, October 9, 1952, 3; *Washington Post*, October 9, 1952, 15.

20. *New York Times*, October 10, 1952, 19.

21. Schedule and itinerary found in Richard Nixon Papers, Box 5, Folder: October 1–24; speech drafted with edits found in Richard Nixon Papers, PPS 208 (1952), Folder: Foreign Policy Disasters of HST.

22. John Hollitz, "Eisenhower and the Admen: The Television 'Spot' Campaign of 1952," *Wisconsin Magazine of History*, Autumn 1982, 37.

23. *Variety*, October 1, 1952, 1; Adlai Stevenson quoted in Rick Shenkman, "Television, Democracy, and Presidential Politics," in *The Columbia*

History of Post–World War II America, edited by Mark Carnes (New York: Columbia University Press, 2007), 269; *Time*, October 27, 1952, 31; David Halberstam, *The Fifties* (New York: Fawcett, 1993), 232.

24. *New York Times*, October 16, 1952, 21.

25. Neil Jumonville, *Henry Steele Commager: Midcentury Liberalism and the History of the Present* (Chapel Hill: University of North Carolina Press, 1999), 22; Travis Beal Jacobs, *Eisenhower at Columbia* (New Brunswick: Transaction, 2001), 285, 300, 287; Neil Jumonville, *Henry Steele Commager*, 140; Gerald Fetner, *Immersed in Great Affairs: Allan Nevins and the Heroic Age of American History* (Albany: State University of New York Press, 2004), 148; Travis Beal Jacobs, *Eisenhower at Columbia*, 286.

26. Richard Hofstadter, *The American Political Tradition* (New York: Knopf, 1948), xi.

27. David S. Brown, *Richard Hofstadter: An Intellectual Biography* (Chicago: University of Chicago Press, 2006), 131–32.

28. *New York Times*, October 23, 1952, 1.

29. *New York Times*, October 23, 1952, 1; Travis Beal Jacobs, *Eisenhower at Columbia*, 297; quoted in David Brown, *Richard Hofstadter*, 84; see also *New York Post*, October 23, 1952, 3.

30. Joseph and Stewart Alsop, *The Reporter's Trade* (New York: Reynal, 1958), 188; Robert Merry, *Taking On the World: Joseph and Stewart Alsop— Guardians of the American Century* (New York: Viking, 1996), 236; Travis Beal Jacobs, *Eisenhower at Columbia*, 298.

31. *New York Times*, October 18, 1952, 14, and October 9, 1952, 26; Roger Morris, *Richard Milhous Nixon: The Rise of an American Politician* (New York: Henry Holt, 1990), 857; the twentieth anniversary is listed in his sermon advertised in the *New York Times*, October 11, 1952, 15; *New York Times*, October 13, 1952, 19.

32. Norman Vincent Peale, *The Power of Positive Thinking* (New York: Prentice-Hall, 1952), 175; Carol George, *God's Salesman: Norman Vincent Peale and the Power of Positive Thinking* (New York: Oxford University Press, 1993), 62, 94, 199. All biographical details about Peale come from George's fine book.

33. Kim Phillips Fein, *Invisible Hands: The Making of the Conservative Movement from the New Deal to Reagan* (New York: Norton, 2009), 72–74; *Faith and Freedom*, December 1949, 4; Carol George, *God's Salesman*, 171; *Faith and Freedom*, January 1951, 12.

34. Fifield quoted in *Washington Post*, May 18, 1952, 7; Carol George, *God's Salesman*, 182.

35.   On rising church attendance in the early to mid-1950s, see the figures in Stephen Whitfield, *The Culture of the Cold War* (Baltimore: Johns Hopkins University Press, 1991), 83; for the polling that showed 75 percent, see Thomas Reeves, *America's Bishop: The Life and Times of Fulton J. Sheen* (San Francisco: Encounter, 2001), 229; William Martin, *A Prophet with Honor* (New York: William Morrow, 1991), 137, 143, 147.

36.   Stephen Ambrose, *Nixon: The Education of a Politician, 1913–1962* (New York: Simon & Schuster, 1987), 58.

37.   Arthur Gordon, *One Man's Way: The Story and Message of Norman Vincent Peale* (Englewood Cliffs, NJ: Prentice Hall, 1972), 229; Stephen Whitfield, *The Culture of the Cold War*, 84; Donald Meyer, *The Positive Thinkers: Religion as Pop Psychology from Mary Baker Eddy to Oral Roberts* (New York: Pantheon, 1980), 262; Norman Vincent Peale, *The Power of Positive Thinking*, 6, 11, 33, 48, 210; Stephen Ambrose, *Nixon*, 39. It should be noted that Peale's book had a predecessor in the work of Bruce Barton, a man now giving advice to the Eisenhower campaign. His classic *The Man Nobody Knows* (1925) drew direct parallels between Jesus Christ's life and the culture of business and salesmanship. Barton wrote, "Nothing splendid has ever been achieved except by those who dared believe that something inside themselves was superior to circumstances." Jesus was a good salesman of faith because he had "personal magnetism" based upon his own positive sense of himself. And Jesus, like any good businessman, was a populist, for he showed "an affection for folks which so shone in his eyes and rang in his tones, that even the commonest man in a crowd felt instinctively that here was a friend." Bruce Barton, *The Man Nobody Knows* (Indianapolis: Bobbs-Merrill, 1925), 11, 18, 19, 100. The book was wildly popular in the 1920s in large part because it evaded the 1920s debate between fundamentalism and modernism (it was thoroughly modern but didn't attack any other doctrine). Some called the book an expression of "Rotarian pastors" who made religion too materialistic. New editions of the book appeared throughout the 1950s, to try to make as much as possible of the religious revival of the decade. See here Richard Fried, *The Man Everybody Knew* (Chicago: Ivan Dee, 2005), 100, 212. For more on Dale Carnegie, see his *How to Win Friends and Influence People* (1936; reprint, New York: Pocket Books, 1961). There he wrote (p. 107): "Remember that a man's name is to him the sweetest and most important sound in any language" and that you should "become genuinely interested in other people." This sort of language and advice crept into Peale's *The Power of Positive Thinking*.

38.   Stephen Ambrose, *Nixon*, 294; *New York Times*, October 26, 1952, BR36; James L. Wick, *How NOT to Run for President: A Handbook for Republicans* (New York: Vantage, 1952), 12.

39.   *New York Times*, October 25, 1952, 1.

40.   *Washington Post*, October 17, 1952, 24.

41.   Emmet John Hughes, *The Ordeal of Power: A Political Memoir of the Eisenhower Years* (New York: Atheneum, 1963), 33, 34; on Luce and Hughes, see Alan Brinkley, *The Publisher: Henry Luce and His American Century* (New York: Knopf, 2010), 370–71; Sherman Adams, *Firsthand Report* (New York: Harper, 1961), 42–44.

42.   Speech in Eisenhower Papers, Staff File, Records of Sherman Adams as Assistant to the President, Box 37, Folder: Eisenhower Speeches (1); *Washington Post*, October 26, 1952, 1; *Washington Post*, October 30, 1952, 4; Stevenson quoted in John Robert Greene, *The Crusade: The Presidential Election of 1952* (Lanham, MD: University Press of America, 1985), 219; Arthur Schlesinger to Adlai Stevenson, August 5, 1953, found in Arthur Schlesinger Papers, JFK Library, Series 1; Arvey quoted in Porter McKeever, *Adlai Stevenson*, 244; Sherman Adams, *Firsthand Report*, 44.

43.   Quoted in Richard Rovere, *Senator Joe McCarthy* (Cleveland: World Publishing, 1967), 182; *New York Post*, October 23, 1952, 29; Fred Cook, *The Nightmare Decade*, 6: on page 581, Cook explains the source of this quote and backs it up.

44.   *New York Times*, October 27, 1952, 19; October 28, 1952, 27; *New York Post*, October 19, 1952, 7M.

45.   Donald Crosby, *God, Church, and Flag: Senator Joseph McCarthy and the Catholic Church, 1950–1957* (Chapel Hill: University of North Carolina Press, 1978), 88; *Washington Post*, October 24, 1952, 25; Fred Cook, *Nightmare Decade*, 385; *Nation*, November 15, 1952, 449; *Washington Post*, October 28, 1952, 1.

46.   *New York Post*, October 28, 1952, 28; speech reprinted in *New York Times*, October 28, 1952, 26.

47.   *New York Times*, October 28, 1952, 26, 27; Richard Rovere, *Senator Joe McCarthy* 182.

48.   *New York Times*, October 28, 1952, 26; *Washington Post*, October 28, 1952, 1. The speech also garnered an exceptional amount of push-back from the press, with journalists pointing out McCarthy's mischaracterization of the CP's line on the election. See, for instance, *New York Post*, October 28, 1952, 3, and October 28, 1952, 29; *New York Times*, October 28, 1952,

27; the liberal Catholic magazine *America* also spent a great deal of time tracking down McCarthy's assertions and printed a story about the senator's falsehoods but not until December 13, 1952, 303.

49. Marquis Childs in *Washington Post*, October 16, 1952, 13; Speech in Richard Nixon Papers, Box PPS 208 (1952), Speech File, October 14–December 31: Folder: Campaign Theme: Korea; *Washington Post*, October 26, 1952, 6M.

50. *New York Times*, October 31, 1952, 17.

51. *Washington Post*, October 27, 1952, 8; October 16, 1952, 13; October 30, 1952, 17.

52. *Washington Post*, October 16, 1952, 13; October 23, 1952, 11; quoted in Ronald Steel, *Walter Lippmann and the American Century* (New York: Vintage, 1980), 483; Senator Morse's resignation from the Republican Party is reported in *Washington Post*, October 25, 1952, 1.

53. *Washington Post*, October 24, 1952, 25; October 30, 1952, 17.

54. *New York Times*, November 1, 1952, 1, 16; October 31, 1952, 12.

55. *New York Times*, November 1, 1952, 15; October 31, 1952, 1.

56. *New York Times*, November 1, 1952, 1, 16.

57. *The Papers of Adlai E. Stevenson, Volume IV: "Let's Talk Sense to the American People," 1952–1955*, eds. Walter Johnson, Carol Evans, C. Eric Sears (Boston: Little, Brown, 1974), 180, 167, 166, 164, 169, 170.

58. *Washington Post*, October 25, 1952, 1; *New York Times*, October 30, 1952, 1; Stevenson's joke quoted in John Robert Greene, *The Crusade*, 219.

59. *New York Times*, November 3, 1952, 15.

60. *New York Times*, October 30, 1952, 20; November 1, 1952, 13.

61. *New York Post*, September 30, 1952, 12; itinerary found in Richard Nixon Papers, Box 5, Folder: October 26–November 4; reported both in William Costello, *The Facts About Nixon* (New York: Viking Press, 1960), 6, and Roger Morris, *Richard Milhous Nixon*, 863; Drew Pearson, *Diaries, 1949–1959* (New York: Holt, Rinehart and Winston, 1964), 227.

62. Jack Anderson, *Confessions of a Muckraker* (New York: Random House, 1979), 209.

63. Pearson in *Los Angeles Daily News*, October 6, 1952, found in Richard Nixon Papers, Box 184; Folder: Collection of Drew Pearson Columns; Drew Pearson, "How Did Nixon Get Two Houses," column dated October 8, 1952, found in Richard Nixon Papers, Campaign 52, Box 184, Folder: Collection of Drew Pearson Columns; also Western Union message sent from Murray Chotiner, September 21, 1952, to Eisenhower headquarters,

Richard Nixon Papers, Campaign 52, Box 174, Folder: 1952, September 20–21; *Washington Post*, October 10, 1952, 55, and September 24, 1952, B.

64. Jack Anderson, *Confessions of a Muckraker*, 338; see Mark Feldstein, *Poisoning the Press: Richard Nixon, Jack Anderson, and the Rise of Washington's Scandal Culture* (New York: Farrar, Straus and Giroux, 2010), 46–47; Richard Nixon, *Memoirs*, 109.

65. Itinerary found in Richard Nixon Papers, Box 5, Folder: October 26–November 4.

66. *Nation*, November 15, 1952, 449.

67. *New York Post*, October 13, 1952, 22; Arthur Schlesinger Jr., *Journals* (New York: Penguin, 2007), 20.

68. *New York Post*, October 22, 1952, 48.

69. John Robert Greene, *Crusade*, 223; Paul T. David et al., eds., *Presidential Nominating Politics in 1952: The South*, vol. 3 (Baltimore: Johns Hopkins University Press, 1954), 8, 116, 314; Paul T. David et al., eds., *Presidential Nominating Politics in 1952: The Middle West*, vol. 4 (Baltimore: Johns Hopkins University Press, 1954), 96, 126, 76, 8.

70. *New York Times*, November 3, 1952, 15; Richard Nixon, *Memoirs*, 112–113; Paul T. David et al., eds., *Presidential Nominating Politics in 1952*, for the California election results.

CONCLUSION: THE DOG THAT BIT

Chapter epigraph: Arthur Miller, *Death of a Salesman* (New York: Penguin, 1987), 138.

1. John Robert Greene, *The Crusade: The Presidential Election of 1952* (Lanham, MD: University Press of America, 1985), 225, 226; Louis Harris, *Is There a Republican Majority? Political Trends, 1952–1956* (New York: Harper & Brothers, 1954), 136, 124, 134.

2. For the difficulties de Antonio had in getting his hands on a copy of the Checkers speech film (he got the run-around from NBC, the Republican National Committee, and then finally Nixon's own office, who didn't want a copy released to a radical like de Antonio), see Randolph Lewis, *Emile de Antonio: Radical Filmmaker in Cold War America* (Madison: University of Wisconsin Press, 2000), 116–17. For the idea that de Antonio expected his audience to see Checkers as a form of comedy, see 134–35. For the best

biographical treatment of Nixon that places the Checkers speech as a central component, see Garry Wills, *Nixon Agonistes* (New York: New American, 1979), especially 93–145. At the time of this writing, the entirety of Nixon's Checkers speech was posted to YouTube: http://www.youtube.com/watch?v=S4Uev_ijPL0. The quality of the version that I have from the Nixon Library is much better, but the YouTube version is obviously more accessible.

3.   One can clearly see in the Checkers speech shades of Nixon's later language about a "silent majority" that he would use in 1969. For more on the populist thread in American history, see Michael Kazin, *The Populist Persuasion: An American History* (Ithaca: Cornell University Press, 1998). And for more on the contemporary politics of populism, see my own essay for the *American Prospect*: "Forget Populism," http://prospect.org/article/forget-populism-0.

4.   For more on "pseudo-events" and the increasingly staged nature of American politics on the heels of this event, see Daniel Boorstin's classic *The Image: A Guide to Pseudo-Events in America* (1961; reprint, New York: Atheneum, 1977). It should be noted here that conventions after 1952 became increasingly stage-managed, less spontaneous, and directed toward television audiences solely. See Alan Brinkley, "The Taming of the Political Convention," in *Liberalism and Its Discontents* (Cambridge, MA: Harvard University Press, 1998), 251.

5.   The whole idea of anti-intellectualism is tied directly to the election of 1952; it was that election that prompted Richard Hofstadter to write the classic statement on the topic: *Anti-Intellectualism in American Life* (New York: Vintage, 1963). To get a sense of how it grew from the 1952 election, see the introduction to the book, and also David Brown, *Richard Hofstadter: An Intellectual Biography* (Chicago: University of Chicago Press, 2005), 131–32. For further discussion about how the term "egghead"—already in circulation in the American language—was "applied . . . to the nation's intellectuals" in 1952, see Arthur Schlesinger Jr., "The Highbrow in American Politics" (1953), in *The Politics of Hope* and *The Bitter Heritage* (Princeton: Princeton University Press, 2008), 271.

6.   Richard Nixon, *The Memoirs of Richard Nixon* (New York: Touchstone, 1990), 71. Whittaker Chambers's spirituality made it difficult for him to square his beliefs with a consumer culture. That was evident earlier but became explicit in his *Cold Friday* (New York: Random House, 1964), 14.

On the importance of *Witness* to the conservative intellectual movement, see George Nash, *The Conservative Intellectual Movement in America* (Wilmington, DE: ISI, 1996), 92–93.

7.   Again, as explained in the preface, see J. D. Salinger, *The Catcher in the Rye* (1951; reprint New York: Bantam, 1986). For examples of entries for Checkers in political dictionaries, see William Safire, *The New Language of Politics* (New York: Random House, 1968), 73–74 (Safire became a speechwriter for Nixon during his presidency); Jay Shafritz, *The Dorsey Dictionary of American Government and Politics* (Chicago: Dorsey, 1988), 90; and political dictionary.com/words/checkers-speech.

8.   Samuel Lubell, *Revolt of the Moderates* (New York: Harper & Brothers, 1956), 84–85.

9.   It was just one week after the speech that Nixon founded "The Order of the Hound's Tooth," whose membership included everyone involved in the fund crisis and the speech. They were given cards bearing a drawing of Checkers. See Earl Mazo and Stephen Hess, *Nixon: A Political Portrait* (New York: Harper & Row, 1968), 123.

INDEX

A NOTE ON THE AUTHOR

Kevin Mattson is the Connor Study Professor of Contemporary History at Ohio University, and was named a Top Young Historian by History News Network. His books include *Intellectuals in Action*; *When America Was Great, Upton Sinclair and the Other American Century*; *Rebels All!*; named a *Choice* Outstanding Academic Title; and, most recently, *"What the Heck Are You Up To, Mr. President?"* He has written for the *American Prospect, Dissent*, the *Nation*, the *New York Times Book Review*, the *Washington Post Book World*, and many others.